Nancy's Wedding Feast and Other Tasty Tales

James O. St.Clair
Yvonne C. LeVert

Illustrated by Peter Rankin

CAPE BRETON UNIVERSITY
·P·R·E·S·S·

In Partnership with

cbcradio

Cape Breton University Press recognizes the support of the Province of Nova Scotia, through the Department of Tourism, Culture and Heritage. We are pleased to work in partnership with the Culture Division to develop and promote our cultural resources for Nova Scotians. We acknowledge the support of the Canada Council for the Arts for our publishing program.

NOVA SCOTIA
Tourism, Culture and Heritage

Canada Council   Conseil des Arts
for the Arts   du Canada

Cover design Cathy MacLean, Pleasant Bay, NS.
Cover illustration Peter Rankin, 2007.
Layout by Mike Hunter, Louisbourg, NS.
Printing by Kromar Printing Ltd., Winnipeg, Manitoba.

Library and Archives Canada Cataloguing in Publication

St. Clair, James O.
    Nancy's wedding feast : and other tasty tales / James O. St.Clair and Yvonne C. LeVert.

Includes bibliographical references and index.
ISBN 978-1-897009-24-6

    1. Cape Breton Island (N.S.)--History. 2. Cape Breton Island (N.S.)--Social life and customs. 3. Cookery--Nova Scotia--Cape Breton Island. I. LeVert, Yvonne II. Title.

FC2343.5.S24 2007   971.6'9   C2007-904570-7

Cape Breton University Press
PO Box 5300
Sydney, Nova Scotia
B1P 6L2 Canada

Nancy's Wedding Feast
and Other Tasty Tales

❧ MENU ❧

Dedicated with Affection

to

Jill Spellicsy
Program Manager, CBC, Sydney

Her enthusiasm, support, encouragement and organizational skills,
along with her love of Cape Breton culture, have been essential in the
bringing of a concept to publication.

We are grateful.
Yvonne LeVert/Jim St.Clair

Acknowledgements

For their encouragement, advice, patience, information and caring, we express our appreciation to the following:

Bernard LeVert, Mike Hunter and Gail Jones at CBU Press, Kathy Large and Staff at CBC Cape Breton, Dorothy Frank, Chiasson family, Nova Scotia Highland Village, Pauline MacLean, Kendra MacKenzie, Donald Stuart Dunbar, Bonnie Thornhill, Betty Powell and Waipu (New Zealand) House of Memories, Strathspey Place Board Members, Linda Rankin, Donna MacLean Tourneur, Eleanor Anderson, Laurie Stanley-Blackwell, Yvonne Fox, Gut of Canso Museum, MacFarlane and Marsh and St.Clair families, Theophilus Smith, Glace Bay Historical Society, Old Sydney Society, Glace Bay Miners Museum, Diane Chisholm at the Mi'kmaq Resource Centre and staff at the Beaton Institute at Cape Breton University, Staff of Nova Scotia Archives and Records Management, Chestico Historical Society, Susan Wright, Ian McNeil, Don Ward, Mack and Hansen families. Thank you to Kimberly Vallis for work on the illustrations with the recipes.

Foreword

East Lake Ainslie, May 2007:

During the years hosting *Information Morning*, on CBC Cape Breton, I was privileged daily to hold up a mirror on Cape Breton and to ask: Who are we? Then, because change is constant, I would ask why it happened that way. Some of the best answers emerged from Yvonne LeVert's and Jim St.Clair's regular segments, two people with such credibility that it was an honour to be associated with them – a pair perfectly suited to reflecting and explaining what we see in that mirror. We are a people who must tell our stories; we are a people who value breaking bread with each other in peace.

Each week, and each in their own way, Jim and Yvonne break bread with CBC listeners as they go about the business of readying for their day: Yvonne sharing a recipe or method appropriate to the season, the occasion and the budget of average Cape Bretoners; Jim sharing stories in a way that shed light on how even the smallest event or life has had an effect on who and what Cape Bretoners are today.

Yvonne and Jim have devoted their lives to harnessing the power unleashed when stories and food are shared. I have witnessed their sense of occasion and sense of our shared humanity when they fulfilled the two essential missions of *Information Morning*: reflecting who we are and explaining why we have changed.

Each has roots in my own home county of Inverness, Yvonne in Margaree Forks and Jim in Mull River. Each is well educated, steeped in the traditions and methods of their disciplines, Jim at Harvard and Yvonne at Le Cordon Bleu, in Paris. Each has a reputation for creativity and innovation during accomplished careers, Yvonne in the kitchen, Jim in the classroom. Leaders in their fields and experts in what is possible, they have earned credibility that permitted freedom to experiment. They remained current, but also took risks and made sacrifices, in order to advance our knowledge. This may be the first book they've made together, but together they have shared their thoughts and spirits with many people in many ways.

Jim and Yvonne have arrived at places in their lives where they could be forgiven for putting aside professional pursuits. They could rest comfortably upon their accomplishments, yet they continue to pursue excellence. These two are not mere performers or informers. They are teachers, who live by the highest ethical and professional standards.

I miss our regular encounters, for their impact remains with me. Yvonne is there when I steep, rather than boil, chicken stock or salvage the sweet parts of shrivelled garlic cloves. Her confidence in the universal ability to prepare for ourselves the food we enjoy has enabled me to share remarkable times with my loved ones. Jim's generosity with stories and his willingness to listen to them motivates me daily as I develop a business that helps to build people's confidence when dealing with media and the public.

Just as my medium was radio, theirs are history and food. These are fine things unto themselves, yet powerful when used to their potential. Ultimately, Jim St.Clair and Yvonne LeVert use their media to teach us to share our humanity. Their efforts remind us that it's not enough to merely survive, that to thrive, we must share.

They have shared the space between these covers so that we may unite over the food and stories of this incredible place with its many names: U'nama'kik, Île Royale, Cape Breton. The feast of thoughts and memories it inspires is arrayed on a table that spreads from East Lake Ainslie to Sydney, from Arichat to Cape North. May we meet at that table some day and give thanks to Yvonne and Jim for uniting us.

Ian McNeil, former host

CBC Cape Breton's *Information Morning*

❁

You Are Cordially Invited

to

Nancy's Wedding Feast

(and other tasty tales)

A Celebration of Food and Culture

Jim St.Clair and Yvonne LeVert

❁

Join us, as we partake of this feast of stories and recipes – as we visit places on Cape Breton Island where tales of individuals and their accomplishments have been told for generations around tables well set with carefully prepared meals.

Consider any of the grassy mounds in fields near where you live or the quiet rural crossroads found on your travels; look again at 19th-century houses standing on a hill in the afternoon sun or walk along a beach scoured by the waves. Hike across a hayfield green with growth, as bees move from blossom to blossom, or stand in an ancient cemetery and try to read a nearly obliterated name and date. Each of these places has a story of local or family lore, an association with a love story or a sad event of the past.

From the time I was very young, places came to be alive with the stories of people and events. From relatives and friends, I received the accounts of events humorous and sad as we travelled around the island. These were gifts of stories freely given. Each one had a connection with a particular location. When I was a child, I was encouraged to repeat a story I had heard about my aunt losing her handkerchief at a brook many years earlier. That location came to be known to us as Aunt Betty's Brook, though others might call it MacLellan's Brook. Another time, when standing on a hillside near the graves of my great-grandparents, I heard of a remarkable event in their lives. It took place on an autumn day in 1853, at an outdoor church service during which people felt a spirit of religious ecstasy moving through the crowd. I remembered the account and associated the place with the individuals mentioned to me. Perhaps that way of associating a place with people was just part of my nature; perhaps I wished to please my relatives by remembering and by telling the story again in my own words. In this way, from my early years I acquired a collection of narratives, storing them away for some future use.

For some years, I was unaware of the significance of these tales of people and places of Cape Breton Island so generously shared with me. I didn't place great value on this treasure, from which I could draw various anecdotes and bring back to life people of years past. But I did begin to investigate the circumstances surrounding the stories, to see if any of them had some historical basis. Slowly, I developed a new appreciation for them as I found a historical basis for many of them.

Through the encouragement of the staff of CBC Cape Breton radio, I found a medium to share these accounts and others I learned in adult years. For two decades, segments of Cape Breton local history and lore have travelled through the airwaves in a format known as "Up and Down the Island" on the *Information Morning* program. People in the listening audience expressed appreciation for the sense of place that these accounts brought to them.

During one of our many, but brief, conversations with Yvonne LeVert – who had been bringing her enthusiasm for recipes and the traditions of food to the same listening audience of *Information Morning* – she and I came to realize how often food was a part of our stories. We recognized how the narratives and the culinary ingredients together conjure the richness of oral tradition evoking the time and place where stories are told – the smells of kitchens, the sense of remembering what brings us together. Recipes can be seen as the result of popular culture – oral exchanges – baked, broiled, steeped into edible form. We are what we eat. In the act of cooking and consuming we fashion the past inside the kitchens of the present. Food and the stories evoked reveal the state of a place, the ethics of caring, the distribution of wealth, the sense of possibility, class distinctions, human ingenuity, diversity, nature, invention, celebration – among the elite and the everyday.

While speaking with Jill Spellicsy, CBC Cape Breton station manager, Yvonne began to develop a vision that has come to reality in these tasty tales, an amalgam of my stories of long ago with Yvonne's competent dedication to interesting menus, thorough research into culinary pursuits and enthusiasm for foods well prepared. Encouraged by the cooperative relationship developed between CBC and Cape Breton University Press, Yvonne and I developed the format of this publication.

In these stories of Cape Breton, historical facts have been interspersed with imagined details, and real names have been surrounded by others brought to life by the craft of storytelling. Thus stories are created that are full of memory, that are visual and also delight in the products of the kitchen and the fruits of the berry patch. Yvonne and I are both aware that the history of Cape Breton is a tapestry with deep hues reminiscent of grief, bright yellow recalling joys, a range of blues celebrating the gatherings of people. For the Mi'kmaq, as well as for Celts, Acadians and other ethnic groups, the landscape is alive with the lore of individuals and of groups.

In these tasty tales, each story is for today's enjoyment, though they recall events and people of days gone by. As well, each recipe is a contemporary, useful version of older descriptions of the preparation of food. Yvonne LeVert well notes that the recipes enjoyed in the past remain current, since we use the same basic ingredients, tried and true.

It is my hope and that of Yvonne, that this combination of the craft of storytelling and of the procedures for excellent cooking will take the reader on unexpected journeys. So, welcome to these tasty tales – tell them to others, partake of the food, whether it is a recipe or a manner of cooking that attracts you, and find nourishment for your heart and your body in this feast drawn from the life of Cape Breton Island.

Jim St.Clair, Mull River

"Dear Mosie"

Peter Rankin 2007

13

Come with us to look inside one of the large farm houses at Margaree Forks, In-verness County, Cape Breton – this particular house was at La Butte, on the Acadian Road near the Forks. There, in 1900, a recently widowed young woman was making a very difficult decision. She determined that the best thing for her father-less children was for her to leave them with their grandparents and to go to work in Boston, Massachusetts, "The Boston States," as many still refer to New England. For generations, young people went "down the road" to work as housemaids and cooks and gardeners or in factories. Most sent money home to help keep the farm going or to aid their younger brothers and sisters, perhaps paying for their education. Some went away to school, particularly to study for nursing and medicine. But very few young widows would have chosen to leave their families to find employment and to remain away for the rest of their lives. Marguerite Chiasson was a descendant of Acadian families expelled from the Annapolis Valley in the mid-1700s. She loved her children, cherished her heritage, did not marry a second time and left a legacy of courage and determination.

"Dear Mosie"

"My dear son, Mosie;" In her small room on the top floor of a large, fashion-able house in a suburb of Boston, Massachusetts, Marguerite Chiasson firmly steadied the writing paper with her left hand and took her fountain pen in her strong right hand.

"My dear son, Mosie;" It was the same greeting she used every week as she wrote to her son, the nearby envelope addressed to La Butte, Acadian Road, Margaree Forks, Inverness County, Nova Scotia. Her day's work as a housekeeper for a wealthy family here was finished. Though weary, she held herself to the task of writing to her son back on the farm, his well-being uppermost in her mind.

The words evoked a memory of her boy, left in the care of his grandparents so long ago when, as a young widow, she departed for The Boston States to earn money to provide for her young fatherless family. She would never free herself of the loneli-ness she had felt that day and every day since. The image of their large kitchen in the big flat-roofed house overlooking the valley, was as though in front of her eyes. The aroma of chicken *fricot* bubbling in a large pot on top of a kitchen range was fresh in her mind, and in her nostrils, for she had prepared it for her Boston employers just that evening.

"My dear son, Mosie;" How had she been able to remain away all these years? Should she have tried somehow to have stayed in Margaree Forks? Could she ever have foreseen the path of her life when she was a young bride?

No, nothing had prepared her for the decision she had had to make: just the courage of her ancestors held her to the task. Certainly, her life as a housekeeper for a prosperous family in Boston was very different from what she had imagined when she married Laurent Chiasson in 1891. As eighteen-year-old Marguerite Arsenault, she had left the happy home of her parents in a nearby community to live as Marguerite Chiasson, in the large house twelve miles away, with her young husband and his parents. Capt. Moise and Dentile (LeBlanc) Chiasson welcomed her warmly. They all spoke Acadian French and were of similar ancestry. Younger than most brides of her day, when young women generally married in their twenties, she expected a long life with Laurent and his kind parents, on the large farm near the Margaree River. But fate was not as kind.

"My dear son, Mosie;" Again the familiar words brought a welling-up of the grief she had experienced that dreadful day in 1900. All had gone well for the first nine years of their marriage. Five daughters and a son had all come into the world in good health and were growing and chattering in English and in French. Her husband's parents were kind to her and loving grandparents to her children. In earlier years, Capt. Moise Chiasson had sailed in his own trading vessels up and down the coast of Nova Scotia. In his retirement, he had income from those earlier ventures that helped with the expenses of running the farm and providing some extras like books for his grandchildren, including his namesake, whom everybody called Mosie.

Their big kitchen was always busy as meals were prepared for family and visitors at La Butte. Vegetables from their own fields, prepared fresh for the day's meals, were also processed so that some would be put away for the winter. In season, salmon from the river and beef, lamb and pork from their own pasture were cooked fresh or salted away for the winter months. Her dear mother-in-law, Dentile, shared in the household chores and they chatted in French as they worked. Dentile had so enjoyed her special *pate en croute Acadien* (Acadian meat pie), that she now sometimes made for her Boston family. Perhaps she should bake some *biscuits au sucre*, the sugar cookies equally devoured by her children at home and by the children here.

"My dear son, Mosie;" How his life and the lives of everyone in the household changed when an especially violent *suête* wind blew with hurricane force that day in early September, 1900. Windows had to be shuttered and children brought inside. Thirty-five-year-old Laurent went to ensure that the huge barn doors were tightly secured to protect the animals and the crops stored within the big structure. As he maneuvered a large wooden prop against the doors, he strained himself. The rupture was severe. Local doctors were unable to heal the wound and hospitals were far away. Within days, the young man was dead, leaving an inconsolable widow, six young children and his aged parents.

"My dear son, Mosie;" What was she to do? How could they manage the farm, feed and clothe the children and run a household on the income from her father-in-law? No insurance, no social benefits in those days, and no able-bodied man to do the work? A relative, recently returned from The Boston States, told her of an opportunity to cook and do housework for a well-to-do family with only two children. They were said to be very kind and offered as good a wage as any other employers. Perhaps, for a time, she should go; just to gain a bit of money to provide for winter clothing. With reluctance, she consulted Laurent's parents who agreed to look after the children and help out as much as they could. With the courage of her ancestors who had faced greater difficulties, she determined what she thought was the right thing to do – she would go.

"My dear son, Mosie;" Those had been her words to him as she announced her decision to leave them in order to provide for them. In the annals of Cape Breton, many stories are told of single young women and men leaving home to seek both adventure and new economic possibilities. But who had ever heard of a young widow with the courage and determination to go forth to work in unknown circumstances? How she missed the laughter of her children upstairs and down, their excursions picking berries in the field. How she missed the fresh vegetables, the game of the surrounding woods and the salmon from the river nearby. She could still feel the tears she cried as she packed her few good clothes and prepared to say goodbye to her children.

No more evening and weekend visits from relatives in the Acadian District of Cape Breton as they gathered at La Butte for card games and storytelling about their ancestors' desire for safe homes after the disruptions of the mid-1700s. No more delight in the comfort of her warm, large kitchen. No more daily delight in the growth of her children! Her dear husband lay in his grave at the East Margaree Cemetery – too young to die, surely; too full of life and hope. No longer could they together plan for the future.

"My dear son, Mosie;" How could she leave him and his sisters in the care of their grandparents? How to keep in touch with her children? How to ensure that they had enough to eat and to wear? She must plan to write as often as possible. How would she learn to cook new styles of food in a Yankee household? Oh, yes, the Parker House rolls were easy for she was used to making raised biscuits for her family. To be sure, the strawberry shortcakes would not be very different, though the fruit came from cultivated plants, not from the wild berries of the pasture at home. But the names of things would be all different, English, not French.

"My dear son, Mosie;" Almost every week she had addressed the letter the same way in her firm, bold hand. Almost always she enclosed an American ten or twenty dollar bill saved from her small wages. Mosie and the girls had grown up well, even though she rarely saw them – maybe once every three or four years. Now, several of the girls were here in the suburbs of Boston too, employed as housekeepers and governesses, though she hardly ever saw them. But Mosie was still at home, managing the farm, and he had married a capable young neighbour and was now a father himself. Dentile and Capt. Moise, having fulfilled their responsibilities for their grandchildren and the work of the farm, had passed away.

"My dear son, Mosie;" As she wrote those familiar words, she was hoping that he would read to his young children the passages in her letter in which she spoke of each of them and how she hoped to see them soon and wished them to do well in their school work. Did Mosie and his energetic and thoughtful wife remember to include her always in the evening prayers, so much a part of any Acadian household? Would he pay attention to the suggestions she made for improving the farm, for buying new equipment? Would he agree with her that he ought to purchase a new, rather than used, hay mower? She must remember to enclose the money she had saved for the last two weeks.

"My dear son, Mosie;" With a smile on her tired lips, she wrote: "Soon, I will have a month's vacation as the family will go on a trip to France. They thought I might like to go with them to see the home of my ancestors, but I wish to be with you all in my home on La Butte. I will send word by telegram about the day of my arrival at Orangedale Station. I hope you are all well and that you will buy new equipment."

Marguerite laughed to herself as she recalled a trip home to Cape Breton some years before, during the war years, as she came near the final part of her journey. At that time, on the last leg of the train's journey between the Strait of Canso and Orangedale Station, she sat near a man on his way home as well. He was returning from a period of training for the army. He looked familiar; and he spoke French to a fellow passenger. What a strange event to have been away so long that she didn't recognize her own son – Mosie, scarcely known to her! She hadn't even known he was preparing to go to war. Oh, how they talked that day and all the way home to Margaree! Would he be waiting for her at the Orangedale Station this time? Would she recognize him this time? Would she know which grandchild was which? Would her grandchildren be frightened of her? Her heart was full of joy at the prospect of being with them and participating in a family meal after so many months of eating alone. Her anxieties were needless, for all went well at the station and they then hastened across country to the old house on the hill.

What a feast they had the next day! Her daughter-in-law and grandchildren outdid themselves in picking fresh garden vegetables. Mosie had obtained a large salmon fresh from the Margaree River; his wife prepared it with onions and butter and spinach, just the way Marguerite loved it. The children said grace in French and even sang a short song in her honour. So much conversation in French and in English as her grandchildren learned to enjoy her company! So much good food in the Acadian tradition! Encouraged by her daughter-in law, Marguerite even prepared her famous Boston-style raised bread, the Parker House Rolls.

"My dear son, Mosie;" The letters continued after she went back to her work and even after she retired. For sixty-four years, she lived as a widow, alone: sixty-four years of separation from her children in their growing-up years; few opportunities to show her appreciation to her in-laws who had done so much for her children – they had even deeded the property to young Mosie when he was of age. The importance of the family home had been uppermost for them all, as it was for her in her difficult circumstances and the decision those long years ago, the only one she could have made, her own needs never considered. Indeed, rarely did she speak of herself, but always of her children and then her grandchildren and the improvement of the farm and the house. Almost always, a check or an American bill was included within the envelope, along with some strong suggestion.

"My dear brother, Mosie;" This letter, in 1964 was from his sister, Mae, telling him that Marguerite, now age 91, was very ill. Soon another message arrived telling him that Marguerite Arsenault Chiasson had died after a long life. Her body would be buried in a fine graveyard to the west of Boston, near where she had lived the most of her life, but far away from the final resting place of her young husband.

There were no more letters to her dear son, but her letters home are cherished by her descendants to this day. The mention of them brings forth the image of a courageous and determined woman who sacrificed her own happiness to keep the home fires burning. Unlike many widows of her age and generation, she never married again. She was absent from the good cooking in the old house on the hill on the Acadian Road in Margaree Forks. She had refused to subject her children to the struggle of increasing poverty at home and so learned to adapt to new surroundings and to manage her own affairs and to provide for them for many years.

Today, as her grandchildren and great-grandchildren gather to enjoy *fricot au poulet*, or Acadian *rôti de porc farci à la sariette*, or Grandmother's rolls in the Parker House style, they recall this brave woman who drew strength from the stories of her courageous ancestors who had endured hardships in their own times. They have kept alive their interest in the language and culture of their forebears. Indeed, Marguerite has left a good legacy. We can all enjoy some of the foods so cherished by her more than a century ago, before that dreadful day when she realized she would have to go out on an uncharted journey of life in order to support her dear son, Mosie.

Celebrating Marguerite's Visit Home

❈

❧ MENU ❧

Fricot au poulet
(Chicken Fricot)

Pâté en croûte acadien
(Acadian Pâté)

Rôti de porc farci à la sarriette
(Roast Pork with Savory Dressing)

Saumon de Magré étouffé à la sauce au beurre
(Margaree Smothered Salmon in Butter Sauce)

Mélange de légumes du jardin
(Medley of Garden Vegetables)

Tarte aux raisins
(Raisin Pie)

"Shortcake" aux fraises
(Strawberry Shortcake)

Biscuits au sucre
(Sugar Cookies)

Petits pains Parkerhouse
(Parkerhouse Rolls)

❈

Fricot au poulet
(Chicken Fricot)

1 5-lb chicken (2.5 kg)
¼ lb salt pork cubed (125 g)
2 large onion peeled and diced (2)
2 large carrots peeled and diced (2)
8-10 large potatoes peeled and diced (8-10)

3 tbsp flour (45 ml)
4 qts hot chicken stock (4 L)
1 tbsp salt (15 ml)
2 tsp black pepper (10 ml)
1 tbsp dried summer savory (15 ml)

- Cut the chicken in pieces. Melt the cubed pork in heated skillet until crisp.
- Fry chicken pieces in pork fat until golden, turning pieces frequently. Remove chicken pieces from skillet and set aside.
- Sauté onion and carrots for one (1) minute in remaining fat. Sprinkle flour over sautéed vegetables and cook, stirring for one (1) minute.
- Place chicken pieces in large pot. Add sautéed onion and carrots (deglaze skillet with stock).
- Add heated stock, potatoes, salt, pepper and savory.
- Bring to a boil. Reduce heat to simmer and cook for one (1) hour or until chicken is tender. Taste to adjust seasoning if necessary. Serves 8-10.

> **NOTE**
> This wonderful stew soup was a staple in Acadian homes and can be served as an appetizer or served in large bowls as a main course with crusty bread.

Pâté en croûte acadien
(Acadian Pâté)

<u>Meat Filling</u>

2 lbs pork shoulder or leg cubed (1 kg)
2 lbs rabbit or chicken cubed (1 kg)
3 large onion diced (3)
2 cloves garlic minced (2)

2 tbsp salt (30 ml)
1 tbsp black pepper (15 ml)
3-4 tbsp summer savory (45 ml)
Cold water to barely cover meat

- In a large heavy-bottomed pot combine pork, rabbit or chicken. Add onion, garlic, salt and pepper. Add just enough water to barely cover ingredients.
- Bring to a boil. Reduce heat to simmer and cook uncovered for one (1) hour. Add the savory and continue cooking until meat is tender and falls away from bones, and meat flakes easily.
- Remove from heat, spread out on a large shallow pan and cool completely.
- Remove bones and flake meat or cut in pieces.
- Taste meat and add additional seasoning if necessary.

Pâté enrichie pour pâté en croûte
(Pâté Pastry)

8 cups flour (2 L)

3 tbsp baking powder (45 ml)

4 tsp salt (20 ml)

3 cups lard (750 ml)

1 cup butter (250 ml)

3 cups milk (750 ml)

1 egg (for glaze) (1)

NOTE

Pâté en croûte was enjoyed by the Acadians for special occasions, and especially at the "réveillon," a Christmas Eve celebration after Midnight Mass.

It is a rich pâté with simple ingredients. The secret is to cook the meat uncovered, thus allowing the liquid to evaporate, leaving a rich soft meat filling.

- In a large bowl measure flour, baking powder and salt.
- Cut lard and butter in cubes and add to flour. Using a pastry blender or finger-tips work lard mixture into flour mixture.
- Make a well in centre and add the milk. Mix well to form a dough.
- Knead dough on floured surface for 1-2 minutes.

- Assembly: Divide the dough into 6-8 pieces. Roll each piece of dough to ¼-inch (6 mm) thickness. Line the bottom of three (3) 10-inch (25 cm) springform pans or pie plates.
- Spread filling in pastry shell, approximately one (1) inch (2½ cm) thickness.
- Cover with top crust and flute the edges. Trim away excess dough. Prick the top to allow steam to escape. Using a small wheel, cut pastry strips and form a lattice top on pastry. (Optional)
- Whisk egg and brush pastry with egg wash.
- Bake in 400⁰ F (200⁰ C) oven for 25-30 minutes or until crust is golden brown. 3-4 10-inch (25-cm) pâtés. Cut into wedges to serve.

Peter Rankin 2007

Rôti de porc farci à la sarriette
(Roast Pork with Savory Dressing)

1 4-lb pork loin (2 kg)
(or pork loin boned and tied)
2 tbsp soft butter (30 ml)
1 tbsp flour (15 ml)
2 tsp dried summer savory (10 ml)

1 tsp salt (5 ml)
1 tsp black pepper (5 ml)
2 large onion chopped (2)
1 large carrot chopped (1)
1½ cups water (375 ml)

- In a small bowl mix together soft butter, flour, summer savory, salt and pepper.
- Rub mixture over top and sides of roast to coat.
- Place roast on rack in roaster. Arrange onions and carrots around roast.
- Place uncovered roast in a 350^0 F (180^0 C) oven. Add water to pan after one (1) hour.
- Cook roast for approximately two (2) hours or until meat thermometer reads 170^0 F (78^0 C).
- Remove from oven and cover loosely with foil to hold.
- Use pan drippings to make a brown gravy. Serves 8-10

Farce à la sarriette
(Savory Dressing)

½ cup butter (125 ml)
2 cups chopped onion (500 ml)
1 cup chopped celery (250 ml)
1 tbsp dried summer savory (15 ml)
1 tsp dried thyme (5 ml)
2 tsp black pepper (10 ml)

1 tsp salt (5 ml)
1 cup stock (250 ml) {Use as needed}
1 cup chopped parsley (250 ml)
2 cups cranberries (500 ml)
12 cups bread cut in ½-inch (1 cm) cubes (3 L)

- In a large skillet melt butter. Cook onion, celery, savory, thyme, salt and pepper over a low heat, stirring frequently until vegetables are tender. Cool slightly.
- Place cubed bread in a large bowl. Toss in onion mixture, parsley and cranberries. Mix well.
- If mixture is too dry, add just enough stock to moisten.
- Taste and adjust seasoning if necessary.
- Pack dressing in a buttered pan. Cover with foil and heat slowly in a 275^0 F (150^0 C) oven for one (1) hour or until hot. Serve with pork.

Saumon de Magré étouffé à la sauce au beurre
(Margaree Salmon Smothered in Butter Sauce)

NOTE
The Acadians would have cooked this in a cast iron pan resting on the back of the stove, and would have allowed it to "mijoter" (simmer slowly) as they basted the sauce over the fish.

2-lb piece of salmon (1 kg)
5 oz spinach leaves (140 g)
1 medium onion sliced (1)
1 tsp salt (5 ml)

½ tsp black pepper (2 ml)
1 tsp summer savory (5 ml)
¼ cup melted butter (125 ml)
1 cup warm water (250 ml)

- In a medium casserole dish, arrange spinach leaves and onion.
- Place salmon in casserole. Season with salt, pepper and summer savory.
- Combine melted butter and water, and pour over salmon.
- Cover casserole with lid or aluminum foil. Place in a 325⁰ F (170⁰ C) oven and cook for 35-40 minutes, basting with butter mixture several times to keep fish moist and smother it.
- Remove from oven. Serve accompanied by the sauce and spinach mixture. Serves 6.

Mélange de légumes du jardin
(Medley of Garden Vegetables)

NOTE
This mélange would have been cooked at the back of the stove simmering slowly. During the season of Lent, this would have been served as a meatless meal.

1 bunch green onion chopped (1)
2 large onions sliced (2)
1 lb baby carrots (450 g)
2 cups peas (500 ml)
1 lb green beans (450 g)
1 lb yellow beans (450 g)

2 cups diced turnip partially cooked (500 ml)
1 tsp salt (5 ml)
1 tsp black pepper (5 ml)
2 tsp summer savory (10 ml)
4 tbsp melted butter (60 ml)
1 cup cream (250 ml)

- In a large casserole, combine onions, carrots, partially cooked turnip, green and yellow beans, and peas.
- Season with salt, pepper and summer savory.
- Combine melted butter and cream. Pour over vegetables. Toss well.
- Place lid or foil securely over casserole, and cook in a 325⁰ F (160⁰ C) oven until vegetables are tender, basting juices over vegetables twice during cooking, approximately 35 minutes. Serves 6.

Tarte aux raisins
(Raisin Pie)

Pastry

3 cups all-purpose flour (750 ml)
1 tsp salt (5 ml)
1 cup lard (250 ml)
¼ cup butter (60 ml)
½ cup iced water (125 ml)
1 egg for glaze (1)

Filling

1½ cups raisins (375 ml)
3 cups water (750 ml)
2 cups brown sugar (500 ml)
5 tbsp flour (75 ml)
3 tbsp lemon juice (45 ml)
2 tsp grated lemon zest (10 ml)
1 tsp vanilla (5 ml)
4 tbsp butter (60 ml)

- Combine flour and salt in a medium mixing bowl. Using a pastry blender or fingertips, cut lard and butter into flour until crumbly. Add water a little at a time, tossing with a fork.
- Gather dough in a ball and shape in a disk. Wrap in plastic wrap and refrigerate for 30 minutes.
- Meanwhile, combine raisins and water in a medium saucepan. Bring to a boil. Reduce heat and simmer for 20 minutes or until raisins are plump.
- In a bowl, combine sugar and flour; carefully add to hot raisin mixture, stirring to incorporate. Increase heat and cook for 15 minutes, stirring occasionally until thickened.
- Add lemon juice, zest, vanilla and butter. Cool.
- Divide pastry in half. Roll one piece out on floured surface, and line a 10-inch (25-cm) pie or tart pan.
- Spread cooled filling in pastry. Roll out remaining pastry and cut in strips. Arrange in a lattice design over filling. Trim and flute edges. Brush strips with egg glaze.
- Bake in a 375° F (190° C) oven for 30-35 minutes or until golden. Remove from oven and cool completely. Makes a 10-inch (25-cm) pie.

Peter Rankin 2007

"Shortcake" aux fraises
(Strawberry Shortcake)

Shortcake

2 cups all-purpose flour (500 ml)

4 tsp baking powder (60 ml)

4 tbsp granulated sugar (60 ml)

1 tsp salt (5 ml)

¾ cup butter or lard (175 ml)

¾ cup milk (175 ml)

1 egg for brushing (1)

Strawberry and Cream

1 qt strawberries hulled (1 L)

¾ cup granulated sugar (175 ml)

1 cup whipping cream (250 ml)

2 tbsp granulated sugar (30 ml)

½ tsp vanilla (2 ml)

- In a medium-size bowl, combine flour, baking powder, sugar and salt. Using pastry blender or fingertips, work butter or lard into flour until crumbly.
- Make a well in the centre and add milk. Stir into dry ingredients until blended.
- On a lightly floured surface, roll dough to ½-inch (1-cm) thickness. Cut in 3-inch (7.5-cm) circles. Place on baking sheet. Whisk egg, brush shortcakes with egg.
- Bake in a 415° F (210° C) oven for 12-15 minutes until golden. Cool.
- Crush strawberries and add sugar. Beat cream with sugar and vanilla until stiff.
- To Serve: Split shortcake and place half on plate. Spoon strawberries over shortcake. Top with other half. Garnish with whipped cream and small spoon of berries.

Biscuits au sucre
(Sugar Cookies)

1 cup butter (250 ml)

1 cup granulated sugar (250 ml)

2 eggs (2)

2½ cups all-purpose flour (625 ml)

3 tsp baking powder (15 ml)

½ tsp salt (2 ml)

1 tsp vanilla (5 ml)

Sugar for sprinkling

- Cream butter and sugar until light and fluffy. Add eggs, beating well after each addition.
- Combine flour, baking powder and salt. Add flour to creamed mixture in two additions, beating well after each addition. Add vanilla. Mix well.
- Wrap dough in plastic wrap and chill for 30 minutes.
- On a lightly floured surface, roll dough ¼ inch (5 mm) thick. Cut in desired circles or shapes. Place on greased baking sheet. Sprinkle with sugar.
- Bake in a 375° F (190° C) oven for 8-10 minutes until golden. Makes approximately 4 dozen cookies.

Petits pains Parkerhouse
(Parkerhouse Rolls)

2 cups hot milk (500 ml)
4 tbsp butter (60 ml)
4 tbsp granulated sugar (60 ml)
2 eggs well beaten (2)
2 tsp salt (10 ml)

2 tbsp regular yeast (30 ml)
½ cup warm water (125 ml)
1 tsp granulated sugar (5 ml)
7 cups, approximately, of flour (1750 ml)

• Heat milk. Remove from the stove. Add butter, sugar and salt. Cool to barely warm.

• In a small bowl place warm water, sugar and yeast. Allow to sit for 8-10 minutes until frothy.

• Pour milk mixture in a medium-size bowl. Add yeast and eggs. Beat in 3 cups (750 ml) of flour to make a sponge. Cover with towel and let rise for 30 minutes until light.

• Add remaining flour in two additions, creating a soft dough that can be kneaded. (Dough should be soft but not sticky.) Knead dough for 2 minutes until it is elastic.

• Place in lightly greased bowl. Let rise until double in bulk, and turn onto slightly floured surface.

• Roll dough to half-inch (1-cm) thickness and cut in circles with 3-inch (7.5-cm) cookie cutter. Dip the handle of a dinner knife in flour and with it make an indentation through the middle of each circle.

• Brush circle with melted butter and fold in half, pressing edges together.

• Place in greased baking pan one inch (2.5 cm) apart. Allow to rise for 30 minutes.

• Bake in a 425° F (220° C) oven for 15-20 minutes until golden. Makes approximately 2 dozen.

> **NOTE**
> The recipe for Parkerhouse Rolls was brought to Cape Breton by numerous relatives who worked in the Boston area. There were several versions of this delicate bread product that was made for special family gatherings, especially for visitors from away.

Peter Rankin 2007

Peter Rankin 2007

Fuarag at Edith's

Remember when houses had no electricity, let alone televisions or computers? Remember when, in rural areas, one house in each area seemed to be a "ceilidh house," a home where the neighbours gathered spontaneously to share stories and music – a gathering known in Scottish Gaelic as a "ceilidh"? Entertainment was homemade – hospitality the order of the day. Deep personal connections were maintained between people as they danced together, played cards or simply chatted over tea and sandwiches or a hot toddy. The custom of casual visiting seems long gone, its departure lamented, and newer social practices – calling ahead or waiting for an invitation – seem more appropriate. Or people just stay home in front of the television set. Even if you don't remember, come along with us to Edith Beaton's home, one such "ceilidh house," for a special evening, Halloween, when a traditional dish is prepared and shared around the room. Come with us for fuarag at Edith's.

Fuarag at Edith's

*I*n western Cape Breton, in a small community of just ten households lined up along the two banks of a small river, the people came and went from one side of the rural area to the other by means of a narrow gravel road that crossed the river on an aging iron bridge. At the junction of the crossroad and one of the community's two main roads, there stood a one-room schoolhouse, the only public building in our tiny settlement. Nearby, on the western side of the river, was the home of Edith Beaton, the schoolteacher for many years. Her aging house sat close to the road across from a small barn where her brother kept a few cows and an old horse. A buggy rested in a tiny shed attached to the barn. Edith and her brother Jim lived with their aged mother, Maggie, who was so crippled with arthritis that she rarely left her small bedroom located just off the kitchen.

In this community, people came often to Edith's house for she was also the postmistress. Those were the days before rural delivery to post boxes at the end of the lanes. In a corner of her front hall, a small desk served as the counter where business was transacted. Above it were cubby holes for each family's mail. Edith paid careful attention to the record keeping required for the sale of stamps and the issuing of money orders, in much the same way that she was meticulous about the progress of each child under her instruction.

After receiving their mail or perhaps purchasing a money order to send to Eaton's for something from the mail order catalogue, people would often linger for a time in Edith's warm kitchen, enjoying a cup of tea and maybe a game of cards before proceeding to their homes on one side of the river or the other. In those days before the arrival of electricity, illumination was supplied by kerosene lamps. Edith kept one burning in the front hall with the wick turned low so that she was always ready to respond to people's postal needs. In those days the postmistress was on duty any hour, day or night. Edith loved lots of light, and she had many lamps, some with fancy bases and others with ornate chimneys, in various locations around the house. She welcomed people to her door even after dark, lamp in hand and with a cheery greeting.

Edith and Jim and Maggie's house was by tradition the *ceilidh* house for their small community – hospitality the rule at any hour. People just dropped in for a friendly visit or to exchange some gossip or to play a game of cribbage with Jim, an enthusiastic card player. Sometimes a local musician, a fiddler or a piper might come just to play or sometimes a square set or two would take place, just for the fun of it. Nobody expected to be invited, nor did they expect anybody to call them on the party line telephone to say they were coming by. They just came, enjoyed one another's company and went home renewed by the easy camaraderie.

By long-established custom, however, some evenings at Edith's were special and did require a bit of pre-planning. In the late 1940s, more than half-a-century ago, everybody in the community looked forward to Halloween at Edith's house, for the festivities were quite traditional and featured lots of laughter and good food. Just after dark, everybody, old and young, came to this central location, many in homemade disguises. Children giggled as adults pretended not to know who they were and oohed and aahed at the masks or expressed fright at a scary appearance. Hilarity went through the house as people tried to guess who was under a wig or behind a made-up face. There were candies for all on the table in the big kitchen and a drink of rum for the adults as a special treat. Most people brought plates of sandwiches and cakes to share with one another after a time of card games or checkers and the telling of ghost stories for the entertainment of the children. All the while, the old-fashioned wood stove supplied abundant heat, for Jim kept it well filled with dry firewood.

After all had arrived and real identities were revealed, it was time for the major event of the evening – bringing out the big bowl of "fuarag." Even old Maggie Beaton came out of her room with a look of anticipation on her lined face. She was helped to a seat of honour at the head of the dining room table which was placed in the middle of the big kitchen. Edith asked two of her older students to go into the pantry and bring out the large crockery bowl, the same one used for mixing dough for bread and raised buns. This night, it was filled with heavy cream fresh from the milk separator. Having beaten the cream until it was almost stiff, Edith stirred in two cups of oatmeal; the adults nodded their approval that it was the "old-fashioned kind," ground very fine. Here and there throughout the cream could be seen flecks of fine, raw oatmeal. People wanted to stick their fingers into it as soon as they saw it, but Edith said they had to use spoons for there were objects placed deep in the thick cream.

Hidden in the mixture were a number of items: several buttons, a couple of thimbles, two or three rings, half a dozen coins and a tiny wooden doll. Each item had a special meaning and might even predict the future. In some houses, there was only one of each object hidden, but Edith wanted every child to find something so she added more buttons and coins and rings. All crowded around the bowl with much speculation about what each might find.

As Edith brought out a sufficient number of large spoons, her mother clapped her hands with glee, recalling how her mother and grandmother made the fuarag some eighty years earlier. She remembered that they had just one big spoon in her childhood, a wooden one made by her father, and everyone used the same spoon in turn. Tonight there was a spoon for each of them and lots of fuarag to go around. Everybody was chattering and waiting their turn to dip into the mixture.

Each item had a meaning for the coming year: a button meant that the recipient would be a bachelor or be kept busy at sewing on lost buttons; a coin meant new wealth; the thimble predicted the person would be an old maid; the ring foretold a wedding. When there was a tiny doll found, it meant a baby coming in the next year. It was a simple old custom, which Maggie said had been brought from Scotland, and was very much cherished at this season of the year. She added that she understood from her grandmother that in the old days Halloween marked the end of one year and the start of another.

So, Maggie Beaton dipped her spoon into the cream and, coming up with no surprise, tasted the traditional treat, pronouncing it just right; only then did the others take a spoon and begin to dig into the bowl and to come up with a spoonful of the rich concoction. With much laughter and teasing, people compared who got a button and who found a ring in their spoon, and who rejoiced to find a coin or groaned when they obtained a thimble. Grownups and children alike kept returning to the bowl and comparing their unexpected finds, all the while complimenting Edith on the quality of the fuarag.

As mothers wiped cream from the chins of small children and fathers toasted one another with a warm rum toddy, Edith and the older girls from the school set out cups for tea, the neighbours brought forth plates of sandwiches and cupcakes from the pantry and old Maggie Beaton wished everybody a "happy Halloween." She then asked if Johnny MacMaster had brought his fiddle, for she wanted to hear a good tune before she went back to her room. He assured her that he had and expressed the hope that she would favour them with a little dancing step.

Conversation was continuous as people helped themselves to tea from the big pot, kept warm on the cast-iron stove. They added cream and sugar to taste and helped small children to find the sandwiches and cakes most to their liking. Children enjoyed hot chocolate with marshmallows served in sturdy mugs. So much good feeling! So many recollections of who got the ring in the fuarag last year and who was destined to sew on their own buttons. Everyone had a memory to share, teasing the young unmarried people or the old bachelors who had found rings in their fuarag.

As small children looking sleepy cuddled up on the long kitchen bench and the table was removed from the middle of the room, Johnny MacMaster tuned his fiddle. He applied rosin to the bow. The men moved the parlour organ into the front hall so that Janie Ross could accompany him. Kerosene lamps were put firmly on side tables and on window sills. And then to the tune "The Reel of Tulloch," the melody most favoured by Maggie Beaton, a descendant of the MacDonalds of Tulloch, people started to dance. They stopped as one when the old lady, her legs finding a momentary youthful vigour, rose to her feet with a look of delight in her eyes and did a short step dance in the middle of the floor. Mrs. Beaton suggested that the fuarag had given her new strength and all applauded. After hugging and kissing all the children and many of the adults, she returned to her room, apparently well satisfied by the events of the evening, and wishing all a "happy Halloween" and "good fortune in the future."

After Johnny MacMaster played for several square sets and some individual demonstrations of fancy steps, people began to find their coats and to rouse snoozing children. All agreed it had been a fine Halloween and that Edith had indeed provided an excellent fuarag. With a smile of contentment on her face, Edith stood at the door with a lamp in her hand and waved farewell to all. People went along to their homes, their progress guided by light from outdoor kerosene lamps or flashlights. With his fiddle and bow back in their case, Johnny MacMaster too returned to his house just down the road, humming a tune or two to keep himself company. Edith and her brother turned down the lamps in the windows and on the table and sat for a time in the kitchen with just the light from the wood stove illuminating the room. There was a feeling of abundant contentment in their quiet review of the evening: all was well at Edith's as another evening with fuarag had come and gone. Then came a time of quiet prayer and "good nights."

That's how it was two generations ago one Halloween in a rural community where a traditional dish provided joy to people of all ages. The sandwiches of homemade bread and special fillings and the small cakes and squares from local ovens were enjoyed by all – women and men and children. Some of the prophecies may have come true, others did not, but everyone cherished the good wishes of old Maggie Beaton, her enjoyment in her own dancing and the presence of all their neighbours at a fuarag party at Edith's. Such were the joys of rural hospitality and sharing in simpler times: goodwill and friendliness were the glue that held communities in a close relationship.

Family and Neighbours Share
A Halloween Celebration

❧ MENU ❧

Traditional Fuarag

Sandwiches
Ham Sandwiches
Devilled Egg Sandwiches
Chicken Sandwiches

Sweet Treats & Breads
Fat Archies
Pecan Squares
Tweed Squares
Raspberry Bars
Cupcakes with Jam Filling
Baking Powder Biscuits
Whole Wheat Bread

Traditional Fuarag

1 quart chilled whipping cream (1 L)
1 cup finely ground oatmeal (250 ml)
A thimble, button, ring, small image of person

- Whip cream until it is almost thick. Stir oatmeal into cream. Add thimble, button, ring, small image. To serve, give everyone a spoon and let them find objects, taste the fuarag and enjoy the fun of sharing!

- Modern Version for Fuarag: Add 1 tbsp (15 ml) vanilla or fresh fruit and serve chilled as a dessert.

Ham Sandwiches

6 slices baked ham (6)
½ cup real mayonnaise (125 ml)
1 tbsp mustard (15 ml)
1 loaf bread (1)
Butter as needed

Peter Rankin 2007

- Combine mayonnaise and mustard. Set aside.
- Butter bread and spread with mayonnaise mustard. Place a slice of ham between 2 slices of bread.
- Using a sharp knife, remove crusts and cut in triangles. Arrange on serving tray.

Devilled Egg Sandwich

6 eggs hard cooked (6)
3 green onion chopped (3)
1 rib celery chopped (1)
½ tsp salt (2 ml)
1 tsp pepper (5 ml)

½ cup real mayonnaise (125 ml)
2 tsp Dijon mustard (10 ml)
1 loaf sandwich bread (1)
Butter for bread

- Peel and coarsely chop eggs. In a bowl place chopped eggs, onion, celery, salt and pepper. Add mayonnaise and mustard. Combine well.
- Butter slices of bread. Put 2-3 oz (55-85 g) of filling on one slice. Spread filling. Top with buttered slice.
- Using a sharp knife, remove crusts. Cut in 4 triangles. Arrange on serving tray.

Chicken Sandwiches

3 cups cooked, diced chicken (750 ml)
2 tbsp minced onion (30 ml)
¼ cup diced celery (60 ml)
½ tsp salt (2 ml)
½ tsp pepper (2 ml)

½ cup mayonnaise (125 ml)
1 tbsp lemon juice (15 ml)
1 loaf sandwich bread (1)
butter for spreading

- In a bowl combine diced chicken, onion, celery, salt and pepper. Toss to combine. Add mayonnaise and lemon juice. Mix well.
- Butter slices of bread and put 2-3 oz (55-85 g) of filling on one slice. Spread filling and top with buttered slice.
- Using a sharp knife, remove crusts, cut in 4 triangles. Arrange on serving tray.

Fat Archies

½ cup shortening (125 ml)

½ cup granulated sugar (125 ml)

½ cup brown sugar (125 ml)

1 egg (1)

½ cup molasses (125 ml)

½ cup boiling water (125 ml)

2 tsp baking soda (10 ml)

2½ cups all-purpose flour (725 ml)

1 tsp cinnamon (5 ml)

1 tsp ginger (5 ml)

½ tsp nutmeg (2 ml)

½ tsp salt (2 ml)

• In a bowl, cream shortening, white and brown sugar, and egg until well blended. Beat in molasses. Combine soda with boiling water and add to creamed mixture, beating well.

• Measure flour, cinnamon, ginger, nutmeg and salt. Add dry ingredients to creamed mixture. Mix in to form a smooth and slightly sticky dough.

• Roll out on floured surface. Cut with 2-inch (5-cm) cutter. Place on greased baking sheets and bake in a 375⁰ F (190⁰ C) oven for 15-20 minutes. Transfer to cooling racks. Makes 4 dozen.

Pecan Squares

½ cup butter (125 ml)

½ cup brown sugar (125 ml)

1¼ cups all-purpose flour (310 ml)

½ tsp baking powder (5 ml)

½ cup chopped pecans (125 ml)

Topping

3 eggs (3)

1 cup dark corn syrup (250 ml)

½ cup brown sugar (125 ml)

½ tsp salt (2 ml)

1 tsp vanilla (5 ml)

1½ cups coarsely broken pecans (375 ml)

• In a medium mixing bowl, combine butter, sugar, flour, baking powder and chopped pecans. Work butter into ingredients with pastry blender or fingertips until crumbly. Press into a greased 9 x 13 (23 x 33-cm) pan.

• Bake in a 350⁰ F (180⁰ C) oven for 12-15 minutes.

• Beat eggs well. Add corn syrup, brown sugar, salt, vanilla and pecans.

• Spread over partially cooled base and bake at 350⁰ F (180⁰ C) for 30 minutes or until light brown and firm.

• Remove from oven. Allow to cool for 20 minutes and cut into squares or bars. When cold, sprinkle with icing sugar. Makes 36-40.

Raspberry Bars

1¼ cups all-purpose flour (310 ml)
½ cup butter (125 ml)
¼ cup granulated sugar (60 ml)
1 cup pure raspberry jam (250 ml)

Topping
2 eggs (2)
1 cup granulated sugar (250 ml)
2 cups shredded coconut (500 ml)
½ cup chopped almonds (125 ml)
1 tsp vanilla (5 ml)
1 tsp baking powder (5 ml)
2 tbsp flour (30 ml)

- Bottom Layer: Combine flour, butter and sugar in a medium bowl. Using a pastry blender or fingertips, mix until crumbly. Press into a greased 9 x 9-inch (23 x 23-cm) pan.
- Spread jam carefully over base.
- Topping: In a medium bowl, beat eggs until frothy. Add sugar, coconut, almonds, vanilla, baking powder and flour. Stir to combine well. Spread over jam layer. Bake in a 350° F (180° C) oven for approximately 30 minutes until set and lightly browned. Cool and cut in bars or squares. Makes 36.

Cupcakes with Jam Filling

¾ cup butter or shortening (175 ml)
1½ cups granulated sugar (375 ml)
2 eggs (2)
2½ cups sifted pastry flour (625 ml)
3 tsp baking powder (15 ml)

1 tsp salt (5 ml)
2 tsp grated orange rind (10 ml)
1 cup milk (250 ml)
1 tsp vanilla (5 ml)
3 tbsp strawberry jam (45 ml)

- In a bowl, mix butter or shortening, sugar, eggs, flour, baking powder and salt. Add ½ cup (125 ml) of milk and beat for one (1) minute.
- Add remaining milk, flavouring and orange rind. Beat for an additional 3 minutes until batter is creamy.
- Line muffin tins with cupcake papers. Spoon batter into papers ¾ full.
- Bake in a 350° F (180° C) oven for 20 minutes or until firm to the touch.
- Remove from oven and turn out on cooling rack.
- When cupcakes are cold, carefully remove a slice from the top. Place a dab of jam in centre and replace top. Makes 16 cupcakes.

Tweed Squares

½ cup butter (125 ml)

⅔ cup granulated sugar (150 ml)

1⅓ cups all-purpose flour (320 ml)

2 tsp baking powder (10 ml)

½ tsp salt (2 ml)

½ cup milk (125 ml)

2 egg whites (2)

3 squares semi-sweet chocolate, grated (3)

<u>Icing</u>

2 cups icing sugar (500 ml)

4 tbsp butter (60 ml)

½ tsp vanilla (2 ml)

2 tbsp milk (30 ml)

2 squares semi-sweet chocolate, melted (2)

Cream butter and sugar until light and fluffy. Combine flour, baking powder and salt. Add flour mixture alternately with milk to creamed mixture. Beat egg whites until stiff. Fold into batter. Sprinkle grated chocolate over batter and fold in. Pour and spread into a greased 9 x 9-inch (22 x 22-cm) pan. Bake in a 350⁰ F (180⁰ C) oven for 35 minutes. Cool and frost. Makes 36 squares

Beat icing sugar, butter, vanilla and milk until creamy. Spread over cooled squares. Melt chocolate in saucepan over low heat. Remove from heat. Cool slightly and spread over icing swirling to combine colours. Allow to cool and set completely. Cut in bars or squares.

Peter Rankin 2007

Baking Powder Biscuits

1 cup all-purpose flour (250 ml)   1 tsp salt (5 ml)
1 cup whole wheat flour (250 ml)   ½ cup shortening (125 ml)
4 tsp baking powder (20 ml)   ¾ cup milk (175 ml)

- In a bowl, measure flour, baking powder and salt. Using a pastry blender or fingertips, work shortening into flour until crumbly.
- Add milk all at once. Mix to combine into a soft ball. Turn out on floured surface and knead 6-8 times.
- Roll out to ¾-inch (2-cm) thickness. Cut in circles and place on ungreased baking sheet. Bake in 415⁰ F (210⁰ C) oven for 12-15 minutes until golden.
- Remove from oven. Serve warm or cold. Makes 12-15 biscuits.

Whole Wheat Bread

¼ cup lukewarm water (60 ml)   2 tsp salt (10 ml)
2 tbsp dry yeast (30 ml)   1 cup hot milk (250 ml)
1 tsp sugar (5 ml)   1 cup warm water (250 ml)
2 tbsp shortening (30 ml)   3 cups all-purpose flour (750 ml)
¼ cup molasses (60 ml)   3 cups whole wheat flour (750 ml)

- Combine lukewarm water and sugar. Add dry yeast. Whisk lightly and allow to sit for 5 minutes until frothy.
- In a large bowl, combine shortening, molasses, salt, milk and water. Allow to cool until mixture feels cold to the touch. Add dissolved yeast and mix.
- Combine flour and liquid mixture, mix to work in flour (dough will be soft).
- Turn dough out on floured surface. Sprinkle dough with flour and knead dough 20 times until dough is no longer sticky. (More flour may be required during kneading.)
- Place dough in a lightly greased bowl. Cover with a cloth and allow to rise until double in size.
- When dough has risen enough, punch down to let gas escape.
- Shape the dough into loaves and place in well-greased loaf pans. Allow dough to once again rise to double in size.
- Bake loaves in a 400⁰ F (200⁰ C) oven for 40-50 minutes.
- Remove bread from oven and turn out on cooling rack.

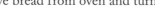

Peter Rankin 2007

Nancy's Wedding Feast

We invite you to imagine with us a wedding celebration in 1875. Meet the bride and groom as they are remembered by the young sister of the bride. Weddings are a major social event for all ethnic groups, the joy of music and dancing and food and the gathering of friends and relatives. In Mull River, a rural community in central Inverness County, this particular celebration was remembered for many years for its special pattern of dancing and the splendid wedding cake. So come along and share in the pleasure of Nancy's special day.

Nancy's Wedding Feast

"One piper for the tune; two, for the stepping; three, for the hope for long life; four, for the wish for good health." Aunt Jane said those words on her ninetieth birthday as she recalled the oft-stated proverb which explained the need for four pipers at the wedding in 1875 of her older sister Nancy.

"I remember them as if it were only yesterday that I first heard them." And then she added, "I'll remember them if I live to be a hundred."

And indeed she did. The last time she spoke them to us, she herself was celebrating her 101st birthday. "One piper for the tune, two pipers for the stepping; three pipers for long life; four pipers for good health."

The trim tiny feet of Aunt Jane moved in rhythmic recollection of the piping tunes.

Not only did our aged relative recall the words (half in English and half in Scots Gaelic) which clarified the reason her sister, Nancy MacFarlane, required four separate pipers at the celebration of her marriage to Donald "Christy" MacDonald, but she also retained many other details about that celebration of so long ago.

"I was just four going on five," said the reminiscing Aunt Jane, "but I can still see the feet of the bride and groom, with their fancy dancing slippers – so shiny – and oh, how they danced; how everybody danced." Her voice seemed young again as the memory of her sister's special day came alive in her mind.

With her recollection clearly focused on those events of the late summer of 1875, she continued, "it was old Kitty Livingstone, our grandmother's sister, who had given the traditional verse which identified that four separate pipers on four separate platforms were required in order to bring good luck to the newlyweds. Aunt Kitty believed in things like that, as did our grandmother. Indeed, Kitty had the power of the 'second sight' – without doubt, she did. So nobody would go against her. "With a little smile on her lips, she added, "even Papa paid attention to her although he had little time for superstition."

So, according to the recollections of Aunt Jane and other family members as well, there were four large wooden platforms built in the four corners of the small hayfield near the house. "At each in turn, a piper struck up a tune for the wedding reel and people took their places and danced all afternoon and well into the evening on that late summer day." After a pause as she gathered her memories, she continued. "There were many more than a hundred people who came for the celebration: neighbours and relatives and friends, some from far away. Oh, what a crowd! Even our great-grandmother came in her double-seated buggy with its canvas top. Her hair was tucked in an old-fashioned cap in the manner she considered proper. With her were cousins whom we rarely saw, for most of them lived away in "the Boston States."

With a look of delight in her faded blue eyes, she reminded us, "Ach, indeed, there was plenty for all to eat. So much food! Nancy had wanted a variety of dishes and lots of people at her celebration. Mama and Papa did as Nancy wished for they loved her dearly; she was their eldest daughter and the first of their nine children to marry. The tables were set out of doors in the apple orchard near the house. Each table had a white table cloth and so many dishes. Plain pine boards fastened to cut logs created benches on all sides. My other sisters and our first cousins from down the road waited on tables and kept filling the serving dishes with meat and vegetables and bread. With a twinkle of satisfaction in his eyes, Papa walked among the guests and greeted them with a cheery, '*Ciamur tha sibh*' (How are you?) and other Gaelic words of welcome. Many of the guests were more fluent in Gaelic than they were in English.

"Oh, Papa always tried to do whatever we asked of him, if we asked politely – and in Gaelic," Jane remembered. "He was a good, kind man. Before I was born, he even built a new house, the one where we are right now, because my two oldest sisters, Nancy and Sarah, told him they needed a more stylish house in order to attract and entertain suitors. They didn't want an old-fashioned building with fireplaces and low ceilings, but one built for stoves, with high ceilings and a long front hall going from the front door right through to the kitchen. And that is what our father and our brothers built with the help of Angus P. MacEachern, the house framer from River Centre."

Aunt Sarah used to laugh as she told the same story to us, as well. Although she had many suitors and was very attractive with her auburn red hair and ever-willing dancing feet, she never married.

"But Nancy got two men so that made up for me," Sarah used to say with a little laugh, and perhaps a little sadness in her eyes. She too had many stories of Nancy's wedding which she shared with us for she had been Nancy's bridesmaid and had lived at the old home all her long life.

As Aunt Jane took off her glasses and placed them on the table and closed her old eyes, she brought forth more vivid memories of that wedding celebration as though she could still see every detail after so many years. As the last person alive who had been present on that joyful day in 1875, she wanted us to remember it and to tell others about the people and the various aspects of the party. She continued, "Oh, my, my, he was good to us, Papa was ... and very jolly. He loved to dance as well. He even took me to dance in the second quadrille. I remember him also dancing with Nancy and my other sisters. Mama danced just one set with Papa and then returned to the kitchen to oversee the serving of the food. Ach, she was kind too, but much quieter and more strict with us than our father was. But she put a taste to the food that nobody else ever could. Dear Mama...."

Aunt Jane often told us of the variety of food which her mother and the older girls in the family had prepared. "Mother's sister, Aunt Grace, had returned for the occasion from her new home in London, Ontario. Along with other relatives, she cooked for days in our big kitchen and in the special outdoor cooking area built for the event. Aunt Grace had brought a description of a new way of preparing potatoes in what she called 'a salad' – a dish not previously known to the MacFarlanes. She had also learned how people in Ontario cooked lamb, with wild mint tucked around it.

"I remember how good that lamb tasted, even though I cried when Papa killed the little spring lamb I had helped to feed when it was small, but Aunt Grace cheered me up.

"She told me a funny story in Gaelic and taught me a new song. She was much more cheerful than her sister, our mother, and she kept the women in the kitchen laughing as she told stories of life in Ontario," Aunt Jane added to the recounting of that fabled day when four pipers played for Nancy's wedding.

It seems that one of the pipers was "the Black Piper" from nearby Mount Young; another was Hughie MacMaster from Judique Intervale; the third was James Campbell from across the river; and the fourth was Allan Gillis from Whycocomagh, a relative of our grandmother.

"No fiddles at weddings in those days and only the old-fashioned wedding reels. To be sure, they were nothing like the square sets people dance today," Jane noted. She had such a fine memory and gathered up all her recollections and those of other family members so that she could vividly describe all of the activities of that day more than eighty-five years earlier. Although she was very young at the time, every detail remained vivid; she must have recalled the details frequently through the years.

"Oh, the bridegroom was so handsome and had such black, black hair. You know he was Donald 'Christy' MacDonald, thought by all to be a very suitable 'catch' for Nancy. You know that the 'Christy' in his name is for his grandmother, Christy MacPherson, and is the way those MacDonalds were identified in order to distinguish them from other MacDonalds." With a smile on her face, Jane remembered her cherished brother-in-law: "He was young, and a good athlete, a merchant and a great dancer. He had a good education and could even have been a minister if he had wanted to do that. Mother used to say that his family had brought money with them when they came from Scotland. And oh, he could sing long songs in Gaelic and in English. He and Nancy were a handsome couple as they danced on each of the platforms in turn. He with his black curly hair and bright eyes and she with her long brown hair – all the way down her back – and her cheerful face, they were a picture of happiness. But, sad to say, he did not live very long, even though Aunt Kitty said that having four pipers playing at the wedding would ensure long life and good health. Tuberculosis took away his life just nine years after his wedding. He left behind those five dear little children, all so young. We all felt his loss."

As Aunt Jane remembered the bridegroom of so long ago, she reminisced: "He was so kind to me; gave me candy from their store, taught me to sing Gaelic songs ... and he and Nancy both danced with me that afternoon and laughed and laughed at my trying to follow their steps.

"Even though we all doted on Nancy's first husband, Donald 'Christy', and wept when he died, we came to like her second husband, John Smith, a fine, honest man, a widower when he and Nancy married. But there was no wedding celebration that time. They just went to a nearby community and were joined as man and wife in the minister's parlour. As some of you remember, Nancy lived to be nearly ninety and had a quick foot for dancing all her life. I miss her although she has been gone twenty years.

"But, oh, I almost forgot to speak about the cake – it was a marvel!" Jane remembered. "I can almost taste it still. Even though I was just a little girl, I was allowed to help to make it and put in the raisins which Papa bought at Uncle Archie's store in Whycocomagh. It was so sweet; and it had some rum in it so Mama wouldn't let me have a large piece, as she thought a little girl shouldn't have liquor. It was made months ahead and kept in a large crock set in the spring in the milk house. Oh, it was big and so beautiful – two layers it had – there was enough for everybody to have some. 'The Bride's Cake', Kitty Livingstone called it. I stood on tiptoes and held on tightly to the table as my sister and her husband cut the first slice. They each took a bite and then passed it to me. I was so excited I nearly dropped it."

Aunt Jane began to laugh as she remembered herself as a little girl with wedding cake in hand, "I was growing sleepy so I think I might have gone to take a nap. For that reason, I don't remember the 'Groom's Cake' which Donald's mother made with Nancy's help. But I heard about it. Most of all, I recall the people and the dancing and how happy the bride and the groom looked. I know that Mama and Papa were proud that they could give their daughter such a fine wedding feast. Even great-grandmother, generally so severe looking, smiled after Papa gave her a hot cup of tea with a measure of rum in it and then she joined in the singing of Gaelic songs."

Aunt Jane was intent on sharing her many memories of that celebration in Mull River long ago on a farm where she lived with her sisters and brothers and parents.

It must have been a great occasion, for she and her sisters (one of them my grand-mother) often spoke about it, recounting all the food and the people who came from all around and some from a distance (like Aunt Grace from Ontario). But it was the four platforms with the four pipers for dancing that seemed very important, as though that didn't happen very often – and never again at that farm house in rural Cape Breton, for all the other sisters (except Aunt Sarah) married in places far away. But the music was recalled as very good and the dancing wonderful and the verse about the pipers was repeated often, even though only the bride had a long life and good health. It seems to have been one of those fine moments in time which come to be the subject of stories told again and again. Everything seemed to come together to provide a memorable special day for Nancy and her family and friends.

I can still see Aunt Jane's blue eyes, so bright even in extreme old age, as she recounted the proverb, and her aged feet moved in a little dance step. I am happy to be able to picture with you that happy celebration of so long ago – Nancy's wedding feast.

Nancy's Wedding Menu
1875 Wedding

❦ MENU ❦

Nancy's Wedding Cake
Donald's Groom's Cake

Barley Soup

Roast Lamb
Roast Chicken with Potato Stuffing

Mashed and Baked Turnip with Cream
Boiled Potatoes
Aunt Grace's Potato Salad From Ontario
Boiled Salted Ham Sliced Thinly

Mock Cherry Pie
Mincemeat Pie
Apple Pie
Ginger Snaps

Scotch Shortbread
Country Loaf
Biscuits

Nancy's Wedding Cake

1½ lbs butter (700 g)
1½ lbs sugar (700 g)
12 eggs (12)
1 cup molasses (250 ml)
1 tsp salt (5 ml)
1 tsp soda (5 ml)
1 tbsp hot water (15 ml)
1½ lbs flour (700 g)

4 lbs raisins seeded (1.8 kg)
2 lbs currants (900 g)
1 lb candied citron (450 g)
1 tbsp ground cloves (15 ml)
1 tbsp allspice (15 ml)
1 tbsp nutmeg (15 ml)
1 cup dark rum (250 ml)

- In a large bowl, cream butter until soft. Add sugar and continue creaming until fluffy. Add eggs one at a time, beating after each addition. Mix soda in hot water.

- Combine the molasses, salt and soda mixture into creamed mixture.

- Measure flour in a large bowl. Add raisins, currants, citron and spices. Dredge fruit well in flour.

- Pour creamed mixture over flour mixture. Mix well, adding rum in two additions, and mixing well after each addition.

- Lightly grease two 8-inch (20-cm) and 3-inch (7.5-cm) deep square or round cake pans. Line each with two layers of parchment or brown paper and grease paper.

- Divide batter between the pans. Spread out batter using a spatula.

- Bake cakes in 275⁰ F (140⁰ C) oven for 2½ hours or until tester comes out clean. (Cooking time will depend on the size of the cakes.) Remove cakes from oven. Cool for one (1) hour in pans.

- Turn out cakes on cooling rack and remove paper. Cool cakes completely.

- Secure in plastic wrap and foil wrap. Place in a cool place for one (1) week, allowing cake to "mellow." Keep in refrigerator until serving time.

Donald's Groom's Cake

1 lb butter (450 g)
1 lb brown sugar (450 g)
9 eggs (9)
1 lb flour (450 g)
2 tsp mace (10 ml)
2 tsp cinnamon (10 ml)
½ tsp ground cloves (2 ml)
1 tsp baking soda (5 ml)

½ tsp salt (2 ml)
3 lbs currants (1.3 kg)
2 lbs raisins (900 g)
½ lb almonds blanched (225 g)
1 lb citron diced (450 g)
2 tbsp rum (30 ml)
½ cup cold strong coffee (125 ml)

• Cream butter and sugar until fluffy. Add eggs one at a time, beating after each addition.

• In a separate bowl, measure flour, mace, cinnamon, cloves, salt, baking soda, currants, raisins, almonds and citron.

• Spoon creamed mixture over dry ingredients with rum and coffee. Mix well to incorporate ingredients.

• Grease two (2) 8 x 8 x 3 (20 x 20 x 7.5-cm) pans. Line pans with greased paper.

• Divide the cake batter between pans, spreading to distribute batter.

• Bake cakes in a 275⁰ F (140⁰ C) oven for 2½ hours or until tester comes out clean.

• Remove from oven. Cool in pans for one (1) hour. Turn out on cooling rack and remove paper. Cool completely. Secure in plastic wrap and foil wrap. Store in a cool place for one (1) week, allowing cake to mellow. Put in refrigerator till serving time.

Barley Soup

3 lbs lamb shank (1.3 kg)
3 qts cold water (3 L)
2 tsp salt (10 ml)
1 tsp pepper (5 ml)
1 medium onion sliced (1)

½ small turnip diced (½)
2 medium carrots diced (2)
½ small turnip diced (½)
2 tbsp pot barley rinsed (30 ml)

- To make scotch broth stock, wipe meat and remove from bone. Cut in small pieces. Place meat and bones in large pot.
- Cover meat with cold water. Add salt, pepper, onion and turnip. Bring to a boil and skim fat off occasionally. Simmer for 2 hours. Remove from heat. Strain and reserve meat. Discard bones and vegetables.
- Return stock to pot. Add remaining carrot and turnip. Cook until vegetables are tender.
- Cook barley in 1 cup (250 ml) of boiling water until soft. Add to broth.
- Taste soup and adjust seasonings. Serve very hot.

Roast Lamb

4-5 lb leg of lamb (1.8-2.25-kg)
1 tbsp dried mustard (15 ml)
1 tsp salt (5 ml)
1 tsp black pepper (5 ml)
3 tbsp melted butter or oil (45 ml)

- Wipe lamb with damp cloth. Combine mustard, salt and pepper.
- Rub butter or oil over leg, rubbing into meat. Rub meat with combined seasonings.
- Place lamb on a rack in an open roaster pan. Roast in a 425⁰ F (220⁰ C) oven for 20 minutes. Reduce heat to 350⁰ F (180⁰ C) and continue cooking, allowing 20 minutes per pound. When cooked, remove lamb from oven and keep warm.

> **NOTE**
> To carve lamb, cut in thin slices at right angle to the bone, beginning in the centre.

Roast Chicken with Potato Stuffing

1 roasting chicken, 4-5 lbs (1.8-2.25 kg)
1 large onion sliced (1)
4 tbsp butter (60 ml)

Potato Stuffing
2 cups mashed potatoes (500 ml)
2 cups dry bread crumbs (500 ml)
2 onions chopped (2)
½ cup butter (125 ml)
1½ tsp salt (7 ml)
1 tsp black pepper (5 ml)
1½ tsp dry sage (7 ml)
2 tbsp milk (30 ml)

- Wash chicken.
- Remove gizzard and neck.
- In a medium bowl, combine mashed potato, bread crumbs, onion, butter, salt, pepper and sage. Combine well. Add the milk.
- Fill the chicken cavity with the stuffing. Truss the chicken by closing the cavity with poultry skewers.
- Place chicken in roasting pan and surround with sliced onion. Brush with melted butter.
- Cover the roast pan and bake for 25 minutes at 325⁰ F (160⁰ C). Remove cover, baste the chicken with drippings. Increase temperature to 350⁰ F (180⁰ C). Roast until golden brown. Complete cooking time should be 1½ hours.
- Remove from oven. Allow to rest in pan for 10 minutes. Transfer chicken to platter for carving and serving.

Mashed & Baked Turnip with Cream

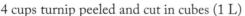

4 cups turnip peeled and cut in cubes (1 L)
1 tsp salt (5 ml)
Boiling water to cover
4 tbsp butter (60 ml)
2 tbsp brown sugar (30 ml)

¼ cup cream (60 ml)
½ tsp black pepper (2 ml)
Additional salt if needed
1 tbsp butter (15 ml)

- Place cubed turnip in medium saucepan. Cover turnip with boiling water, add salt. Bring to a boil, reduce heat to medium and cook covered until turnip is very tender. Drain.
- Return drained turnip to saucepan and mash to pulverize turnip. Add butter, brown sugar, cream, pepper and additional salt if needed.
- Spread turnip in a buttered 1-qt (1-L) casserole. Dot with remaining butter. Cover and bake in a 325⁰ F (160⁰ C) oven for 30 minutes. Serves 6-8

Boiled Potatoes

Select potatoes of uniform size. Scrub potatoes thoroughly. Cook potatoes in boiling salted water until tender. Drain and place in a serving dish.

> NOTE: Boiled potatoes were the most common way of preparing potatoes. They would be peeled at the table. Leftover potatoes were used in hash, fishcakes or fried with onion. It was a common practice to have cooked potatoes on hand, as they kept quite well and could be quickly turned into a substantial meal.

Aunt Grace's Potato Salad
(Ontario Recipe)

8 cold boiled potatoes peeled, sliced (8)
1 large cucumber peeled and sliced (1)
6 hard-boiled eggs sliced (6)
½ of a small onion diced (½)
Salt and pepper as needed

Dressing
3 egg yolks (3)
2 tsp mustard (10 ml)
1 tsp salt (5 ml)
2 tbsp melted butter (30 ml)
2 tbsp sugar (30 ml)
1 cup vinegar (250 ml)
½ tsp pepper (2 ml)
½ cup whipping cream (125 ml)

- In a large bowl, combine potatoes, cucumber, eggs and onion. Set aside.
- Place egg yolks in medium saucepan. Beat until smooth. Add mustard, salt, melted butter, sugar, vinegar and pepper.
- Place saucepan over a pot of boiling water (or use a double boiler).
- Cook over boiling water, stirring constantly until thick and creamy.
- Remove from heat. Cool completely. Fold cream into dressing. Pour over salad ingredients and allow to sit for two hours to incorporate flavours.
- Place salad in a large serving bowl. Serves 6-8.

Boiled Salted Ham

- Soak cured salted ham several hours or overnight covered with water. Discard soaking water and wash ham thoroughly.
- Trim off excess fat if desired.
- Place ham in a large pot and cover with cold water. Bring to a boil and simmer ham, allowing 25 minutes per pound.
- When ham is tender, remove from heat and allow to partially cool in water.
- Lift ham from pot. Remove the outside skin and fat.
- Score ham, stick whole cloves in ham. Dissolve 2 tbsp (30 ml) brown sugar in water to make a paste, and brush over ham. Bake ham for 30 minutes in slow oven.
- Serve ham cold thinly sliced.

Mock Cherry Pie

Sweet Pastry
4 cups flour (1 L)
1 tsp salt (5 ml)
2 tbsp granulated sugar (30 ml)
1 cup lard (250 ml)
½ cup butter (125 ml)
½ cup iced water (125 ml)

Mock Cherry Filling
1½ cups cranberries (375 ml)
¾ cup raisins (175 ml)
1½ cups granulated sugar (375 ml)
2 tbsp all-purpose flour (30 ml)
2 tbsp lemon juice (30 ml)
1 tsp grated lemon rind (5 ml)

- To make pastry, combine flour, salt and sugar in a bowl. Blend lard and butter into flour using a pastry blender or fingertips.
- Sprinkle iced water over flour mixture to moisten, and toss with a fork. When dough holds together, form into a ball. Wrap and chill for 30 minutes.
- In a medium-sized bowl, combine cranberries, raisins, sugar, flour, lemon juice and rind. Set aside.
- Divide pastry in half and roll pastry for bottom crust on a lightly floured surface. Place pastry round in pie plate.
- Spoon cranberry filling over pastry.
- Roll out remaining pastry. Using a pastry wheel or sharp knife, cut strips of pastry ½-¾-inch (1-2 cm) wide. Arrange strips in lattice work on top of fruit. Press edges of strips together and flute edges.
- Bake in a 375° F (190° C) oven for 50-60 minutes or until cranberries are soft and popped, and crust is golden. 10-inch (25-cm) pie.

Apple Pie

<u>Pastry</u>

3 cups flour (750 ml)

1 tsp salt (5 ml)

1 cup lard (250 ml)

4 -5 tbsp cold water (60 -75 ml)

<u>Filling</u>

6-8 tart apples, peeled, cored, sliced (6-8)

1¼ cups granulated sugar (310 ml)

1 tsp cinnamon (5 ml)

¼ tsp nutmeg (1 ml)

1 tsp lemon rind (5 ml)

1 tbsp butter (15 ml)

- To make pastry, combine flour and salt in a bowl. Blend lard into flour using fingertips, working lard into flour until mixture is crumbly.
- Sprinkle iced water over flour mixture to moisten and toss with a fork. When dough holds together, form in a ball. Wrap and chill for 30 minutes.
- In a bowl combine apples, sugar, cinnamon, nutmeg and lemon rind. Set aside.
- Divide pastry in half and roll pastry for bottom crust on a floured surface and line pie pan.
- Arrange apple slices in layers in the pie crust until all are utilized. Dot apples with butter.
- Roll out remaining pastry and place over apples. Press edges firmly together and flute. Slash two vents in centre of crust. (If desired, brush pastry with milk.)
- Bake in a 400⁰ F (200⁰ C) oven for 40-50 minutes until apples are tender and crust is golden.

Biscuits

2 cups all-purpose flour (500 ml)

4 tsp baking powder (20 ml)

1 tsp salt (5 ml)

4 tbsp shortening or butter (60 ml)

¾ cup milk (175 ml)

Milk for brushing

- In a medium bowl mix flour, baking powder and salt. Work shortening into flour with pastry blender or fingertips until coarse and crumbly.
- Quickly stir in the milk, tossing with a fork. Dough should be soft. Turn dough out on a lightly floured bowl. Knead a few strokes until smooth.
- Roll to ¾-inch (2-cm) thick. Cut with biscuit cutter. Place on ungreased baking sheet. Brush biscuits with milk.
- Bake in a preheated 415⁰ F (210⁰ C) oven for 12-15 minutes until golden. Makes 12-15.

Mincemeat

2 lbs lean beef cut in pieces (900 g)
1 lb beef suet (450 g)
5 lbs apples peeled and chopped (2.25 kg)
2 lbs brown sugar (900 g)
1 cup molasses (250 ml)
1 qt cider vinegar (1 L)
1 lb currants (450 g)
2 lbs raisins (900 g)
2 cups orange peel (500 ml)

1 cup citron peel (250 ml)
1 tsp salt (5 ml)
1 tbsp ground cinnamon (15 ml)
2 tsp ground cloves (10 ml)
1 tsp ground allspice (5 ml)
1 tsp nutmeg (5 ml)
1½ cups apple cider (375 ml)
½ cup brandy or water (125 ml)

- Place beef and suet in a large pot. Cover with cold water. Bring to a boil. Reduce heat and simmer until meat is tender. Remove from heat and cool without draining.
- Remove meat and suet, and chop or grind finely. Bring the meat stock to a boil and boil until reduced to one (1) cup.
- Add meat to stock with chopped apples, brown sugar, molasses, currants, raisins, vinegar, orange peel and citron peel, salt, cinnamon, cloves, allspice, nutmeg, apple cider and brandy.
- Heat ingredients gradually, stirring occasionally (to avoid sticking). Cook for two (2) hours to incorporate ingredients and flavour.
- Remove from heat. Ladle into sterilized crocks or jars. Store in a cool place.

Mincemeat Pie

2½ cups all-purpose flour (625 ml)
1 tsp salt (5 ml)
1 cup lard or shortening (250 ml)

¼ cup iced water (60 ml)
1½ cups mincemeat (375 ml)
(milk for brushing)

- In a medium bowl, mix flour and salt. Cut lard or shortening into flour using a pastry blender or fingertips until crumbly.
- Sprinkle water over pastry a little at a time, tossing with a fork. (Add just enough water to moisten.) Gather dough into a ball. Flatten into a disc. Wrap and chill.
- Divide pastry in two pieces. Roll one piece and line a 9-inch (23-cm) pie pan with pastry.
- Spread mincemeat in bottom pastry.

- Roll out remaining pastry and cover mincemeat, pressing pastry edges together. Flute edges. Make two slits in centre of pie. Brush with milk.
- Bake in a 375⁰ F (190⁰ C) oven for 40-50 minutes until crust is tender and golden.
- Remove from oven. Serve warm or chilled. Makes 9-inch (23-cm) pie.

Ginger Snaps

½ cup molasses (125 ml)

½ cup granulated sugar (125 ml)

3 tbsp lard or shortening (45 ml)

1 tbsp milk (15 ml)

2 cups all-purpose flour (500 ml)

½ tsp soda (2 ml)

½ tsp salt (2 ml)

1 tsp cinnamon (5 ml)

1 tsp cloves (5 ml)

½ tsp nutmeg (2 ml)

- In a large saucepan, heat molasses to boiling point. Remove from heat. Add sugar, lard and milk. Mix well.
- Combine flour, baking soda, salt, cinnamon, cloves and nutmeg. Add to molasses mixture and stir well to mix ingredients.
- Cover dough and chill. Roll out on a lightly floured surface to ¼-inch (5-mm) thickness. Cut out with floured cutter and place on a greased baking sheet. Bake at 375⁰ F (190⁰ C) for 10-12 minutes until crisp.
- Remove from oven. Transfer to cooling rack. Makes 3 dozen.

Scotch Shortbread

1 cup unsalted butter (250 ml)

½ cup brown sugar (125 ml)

2 cups all-purpose flour (500 ml)

¼ tsp salt (1 ml)

- Measure flour, sugar and salt in a medium sized bowl. Cut butter in cubes and, using fingertips, work butter into flour until crumbly.
- Pat mixture into a 9 x 9 (23 x 23-cm) pan. Prick all over with a fork.
- Bake in a 300⁰ F (150⁰ C) oven for 40-50 minutes until golden and firm.
- Remove from oven. Cool for 10 minutes and cut in bars.

NOTE
Shortbread has a distinctive texture, sandy and crumbly.

Country Loaf

1½ cups lukewarm water (375 ml)

2 tsp granulated sugar (10 ml)

2 tbsp active dry yeast (30 ml)

1 cup milk (250 ml)

¼ cup brown sugar (60 ml)

1 tbsp salt (15 ml)

¼ cup lard or shortening (60 ml)

4 cups whole wheat flour (1 L)

2 cups all-purpose flour (500 ml)

¼ cup bran (60 ml)

- Pour lukewarm water in a bowl. Stir in granulated sugar. Sprinkle with yeast and stir lightly with a fork. Let stand in a warm place for 10 minutes or until frothy, and yeast is dissolved.

- In a saucepan, scald milk and stir in brown sugar, salt and lard or shortening. Pour into a large mixing bowl and cool to lukewarm.

- Add yeast mixture to cooled milk mixture.

- Combine the two flours, bran and salt. Add half the flour to yeast mixture and beat well.

- Continue adding flour until dough becomes stiff and leaves side of the bowl.

- Turn dough out onto floured surface and knead, adding any remaining flour as needed so dough is not sticky. Continue to knead dough for 5 minutes or until dough is smooth and elastic.

- Place in lightly greased bowl. Cover with a cloth and set in a warm place to rise double in bulk, about 80 minutes.

- Punch down the dough. Divide in half and shape in two (2) loaves. Place in greased 8½ x 4½ (1.5 L) pans. Cover and allow to rise until double in bulk, 40-60 minutes.

- Bake in a preheated oven at 400⁰ F (200⁰ C) for 25-30 minutes or until loaves sound hollow when tapped. Turn out on rack to cool.

> **NOTE**
> When the Highland farmers grew their own wheat and ground it into flour on a stone or at the grist mill, it would be used to make a hearty and coarse loaf of bread. This recipe is an adaptation.

Peter Rankin 2007

The Road Ahead

Peter Rankin 2007

57

In southern inland Cape Breton, on a side road, just off the main highway from the Strait of Canso to Arichat and Sydney and near a stream known as River Inhabitants, sits a small graveyard – an obscure place for the burial of a woman born in Scotland to parents of some prominence.

Isabella McRae, the daughter of a distinguished Presbyterian minister, had married Capt. John Campbell, scion of a noble family related to the Duke of Argyll. After Campbell died unexpectedly in Jamaica, Isabella married Donald MacDonald, an employee on the Campbell croft, much to the displeasure of her relatives.

Isabella, her new husband, two of her seven Campbell children and a MacDonald son came to Cape Breton in 1830 as settlers, with other immigrants from the Isle of Skye. Life was difficult enough in a pioneer community, but MacDonald's fondness for liquor and his quick temper, resulting in many arguments made things much worse. In the end, MacDonald killed his wife in a rage. Murder was an unusual event in these early days of Cape Breton. At her graveside, we meet her son Charles James Campbell, a young man faced with a harsh reality.

The Road Ahead

A twenty-one year old youth stood silently at the open grave of his mother, on a small hill fifteen metres above the sullen-looking stream known as the River Inhabitants. The sky was overcast and the wind from the north. It was the 5th of November, 1840. A grove of hardwood trees, bare of their leaves, surrounded the recently cleared burial ground. Neither the location nor the weather had any warmth to them. Bare ground. The place seemed as forlorn as the events bringing him here were cheerless.

In his left hand, Charles James Campbell held a brooch pin in the shape of a Scottish thistle, his mother's favourite adornment. His other hand clutched a small leather-bound New Testament in Gaelic and English, a gift from his grandfather, a Presbyterian minister. Campbell's knuckles were white with anger and grief. His beautiful mother, Isabella McRae Campbell was dead. Wrapped in a shroud made from one of her own hand-woven shawls, she lay in the locally crafted pine box placed on the hard ground in front of him. She was about to be buried forever, one of the first to be interred in this cemetery located in the wilderness that was rural Cape Breton at that time of early settlement.

As he stood there, Charles James felt the anger toward his stepfather Donald Mac-Donald course through his whole body. He could barely stand still. He could not think of his mother as Isabella MacDonald, though she had married MacDonald in a civil ceremony shortly after the death of his own father, Capt. John Campbell. Her father and her brother, both Presbyterian ministers of a distinguished McRae family, had refused to perform a religious marriage ceremony for they strongly objected to her decision to marry a man who was her employee on the farm operated by the Campbells at Duntulum in the northern tip of the Isle of Skye. Of a different social class, MacDonald as well had a reputation for drinking and fighting. And now he was in jail in Arichat, the only town of any size nearby and the only location of an official of the Nova Scotia government. Charles James had resented his stepfather from the moment his mother brought him into the family circle and now he hated him for the violence that had torn their mother from them.

At his side stood his young brother Colin, sobbing as though he would never stop, his once cheerful twelve-year-old face streaked with tears. With the toe of his boot, Colin kept kicking at the clumps of near-frozen soil at his feet. With the brooch held tightly in his fist, Charles James put his arm around the lad's shoulders which were shuddering with grief. On the other side of the open grave, very much alone, was his nine-year-old half-brother, Duncan MacDonald, who had their mother's fair complexion and light brown hair. He looked bewildered for he had never been to a burial before, much less to that of a close relative. Circling the grave were residents of the River Inhabitants area. In the absence of a minister, their neighbour, old Donald MacLean read from the scriptures in Gaelic and led the assembled group in singing the twenty-third psalm. No one spoke words of comfort to the boys nor any words in praise of Isabella. The event was cheerless, much like the sky that November day.

A mood of disbelief hung over the small group as MacLean, an elder in his congregation back in Scotland, said the final words, "earth to earth ... dust to dust." Five days ago, who could have thought that the vivacious Isabella – "Bell" to her close friends – would meet such a terrible death! Her husband, it was rumoured, had hit Isabella with an oar again and again, as they made their way home from Arichat up the river in their small craft. Now being held by authorities in anticipation of a formal inquest, MacDonald had been drinking at various locations in the town and was said to have been furious at Isabella because she kept urging him to stop wasting their money on rum.

According to the Carter brothers, who pulled her lifeless body from the river after she had either fallen or been pushed over the side of the boat, Isabella had many bruises and a broken arm. She was barely recognizable. But MacDonald claimed she had fallen over and hit her head on a rock. Maybe the coroner and officiating judge would determine the actual cause of her demise. Already people were starting to express their concerns about what would become of the three brothers – their mother dead and her husband in jail.

Although his mother had come to be the legal wife of MacDonald, through words spoken by a Justice of the Peace in Scotland, Charles James had never felt that she should be called Isabella MacDonald. In his mind, she was still Mrs. Bell Campbell, the widow of Capt. John of Duntulum. As he watched the hastily-made coffin being lowered in the dark earth an ocean away from their home country and then covered over with shovels-full of sod mixed with the withered grass of November, he vowed to himself that as soon as he could he would erect a gravestone to the memory of his mother. On it, there would be no mention of MacDonald or the cause of her death. Then, to Donald MacLean, showing considerable grief himself, he said his thanks in Gaelic and asked if he might come to visit him soon for he needed some advice.

After pocketing the thistle pin and the Bible deep in the great coat that had been his own father's, he went to shake hands with all who had come, for he was the chief mourner and head of the household now. He thanked them in English or Gaelic as was appropriate for their backgrounds. He then pulled on his mittens, knitted for him last winter by his mother and he stood for one final moment at the mound of earth. He felt his heart harden like the sods at his feet. He knew now that he would return here, but only after many hard days and many roadways followed.

Slowly, with considerable reluctance, the small group began to move away from the grave site. They pulled their coats close around their bodies and pulled caps or hats firmly on their heads, for the weather was turning bitter. Not a ray of sun relieved the gloom of the afternoon. When the group came to the crossroads, not far from the burial site, some people turned left and others went right as they made their various ways home. Very little was said by anyone, although there was much on the minds of everyone. There seemed to be nothing to say, but people wanted to ask, "What would happen next? Did the boys have any money? Would Donald MacDonald be found culpable at the inquest to be held in two days? Who would ever have thought a murder could take place here, so far away from scenes of battle or conflict?"

With his full brother and his half brother walking slightly behind him, Charles James looked ahead to the narrow road which led to their house in Kempt Road, a small farming community of six or seven households. To the left, a wider and newly constructed road branched off toward West Bay and then to Whycocomagh, both communities on the Bras d'Or Lake. This new route seemed to summon him as had other roads called him when he was much younger, back in Scotland. Something about the broad highway interested him – a possibility of adventure or of something better, it seemed.

Before they had sold their sheep and cattle back in Skye and left for this dreary island of Cape Breton, Charles James remembered how he had looked down at the road leading from Duntulum toward the mainland home of his grandparents, Rev. John and Catherine McRae, in Kintail. How much now he wished he had gone to them rather than to this tree-filled country where the land seemed so closed in and life was difficult, with its heavy snows and short growing seasons. At least, if he had gone to his grandparents, he would not have had to put up with the drunken moods of Donald MacDonald and the frequently angry words directed to his mother.

Walking along the bumpy path to the log house constructed ten years ago when they arrived from Skye, Charles James spoke longingly to his younger brothers about the beautiful scenery along the road from the town of Portree to their old home croft at Duntulum. He recalled for them the treeless countryside and the high mountains and the great flocks of sheep. He wished himself back there so he could see the ample stone house where they had been so happy before his father, John Campbell, went to Jamaica in search of new opportunities for his family. Dying of yellow fever when he was just thirty-five, he left his widow and seven children nearly penniless. His pension from his army days ceased on his demise.

With keen recollection, Charles James imagined himself back in the garden of Duntulum on the day when the messenger arrived carrying a letter from Campbell relatives in Jamaica with the news of his father's unexpected death. He could still hear the sobbing as his mother gathered her seven children in the small sitting room to tell them that their father would never return.

Going back over the years since that day, he remembered well the argument which ensued when his charming, beautiful mother, Isabella, told her father and brother, both ministers, that she wished to establish a relationship with Donald MacDonald, a disbanded soldier who had been working as a shepherd on the croft. They knew, as Charles later learned, that MacDonald was overly fond of strong drink and could be brutal to those around him when he drank too much. They were not willing to perform the marriage rites, but her father stated that he would put a sum of money aside for her with the provision that the interest was to be used for the care of her children.

When a group of people from Skye decided to move to Cape Breton where they could own their own land, Isabella and Donald decided to accompany them. Their decision came after they heard from a distant Campbell relative who held the deed to the Duntulum croft that the rent would soon be increased. So, Isabella and her new husband and two of her Campbell sons and her young baby fathered by MacDonald sailed away from all that was familiar. Charles James could still see his mother standing at the rail of the vessel, covering her shoulders with a shawl fastened with the cherished thistle brooch given to her by her mother. The sun shining on the ocean in front of them seemed like a broad road to new opportunities. But he remembered how uneasy he felt as headed for an unknown country.

Not far along the road, Charles James, Colin and Duncan came to the small house where they had lived through the years of land-clearing and growing potatoes and selling timber. But those many months had been times of wrangling by their parents over money and liquor. As they entered the house, the realization struck that they were without parents. Their mother was in her grave and Donald MacDonald, their father and stepfather, was in jail awaiting a hearing to inquire into the cause of his wife's death. As he stood at the door, Charles James looked back to the road on which they had travelled from the graveyard and knew that soon, very soon, he would leave this place of sorrow and go back along the route to that new roadway to West Bay and Whycocomagh. Kempt Road in the River Inhabitants settlement would no longer hold him.

After doing the barn chores together and eating a supper of bread and cheese and warmed-over oatmeal, the two younger boys went to bed. They were exhausted from a day of so much emotion, so much sadness. But Charles James sat at the dining table and by candle light wrote letters to this grandparents and uncle back in Scotland to tell them the terrible new of Isabella's murder. They would have to convey the news to his brothers and sisters who were expecting to come to Nova Scotia whenever Isabella and Donald sent for them. It was important for the other Campbell children to know that they should not plan to leave Scotland.

C. J. (as he was often known) then penned a formal letter to Sir Colin Campbell, his father's cousin, who was also the Lt. Governor of Nova Scotia. Sir Colin had been fond of his mother who named one of her children for him. Indeed, he had warmly received Isabella two years ago when she travelled to Halifax to request his help in finding a position in the militia for her new husband. Although Sir Colin was surprised to learn of Isabella's new alliance with Donald MacDonald and of their decision to leave Scotland, he had signed a commission for her second spouse to be an officer in the local militia. As a former private in the Coldstream Guards, he had had some prior military experience. For his services, MacDonald was granted a small yearly stipend, which went for rum rather than for support of his family.

In his message to Sir Colin, Charles James stated that he would be leaving Kempt Road shortly, but future mail could be sent to him in care of a relative in Whycocomagh, Alexander Campbell. He also requested Sir Colin to help him find passage back to Scotland for his namesake, young Colin, and perhaps for little Duncan.

Putting his hand in his coat pocket before lying down near the fireplace, he wrapped his fingers around the thistle brooch. Tears came to his eyes, now that he was alone and he was overcome by a flood of memory. He recalled the many times he had seen his mother dressed for church with the brooch at her throat. She had pinned the piece of jewelry to the fabric of her dress when she prepared to go to see the Lt. Governor. He would always think of her fondness for that symbol of Scotland and for her quick steps as she danced to the pipe tune, the McRae Jig.

So much to remember! So much to cherish! And so much to put behind him! Recalling the determination that he felt in the final moments in the cemetery, he realized he didn't care whether or not he ever saw his stepfather again. In fact, he hoped the man would spend the rest of his life in jail for the murder he had committed. As for his half brother, maybe he too should go back to Scotland with Colin for he was a grandson to the McRaes just as much as he was. Or perhaps, he could go to live with relatives of his own father who lived some ten miles away. Overcome by weariness, he fell asleep by the fire.

When C. J. awoke the next morning, the horror of the events of the past five days was sitting in the front of his mind. How could this terrible thing have happened? Though he had often seen his stepfather in rages and even raise his hand as though to strike Isabella, he had never seen an actual blow. Still, in the early morning light of that dark, dreary November morning, he came to the realization that he could not undo the past, could not punish his stepfather and should not resent his young half brother, an innocent child. Charles James knew that he himself had to go down a new road and create a secure life for himself and for his younger siblings back in Scotland.

Aware of the location of his mother's small metal strongbox under the false bottom in her travel trunk, he went to it and opened it. Within she had placed a lock of his dead father's hair, a piece of lace from her wedding dress, letters from her father and Sir Colin and a sum of money. He knew that he had a right to take the money for it had come from his grandfather who had settled one hundred pounds on them all with the interest to go to Isabella, his daughter, now deceased. She had been saving the money to provide passage for her other children to come to Cape Breton. He knew now that he would use the bulk of the savings to give him a start in his life. But he would also give each of his brothers twenty pounds. Eventually, he might be able to bring the whole family together. For now, he would place the small metal box in his own chest and would cherish its contents.

Three weeks later, shortly after his stepfather had been judged suitable to be held for Grand Jury Court Session and returned to jail in Arichat, a letter arrived by messenger from Sir Colin with expressions of sympathy to them all, and a promise to find passage for Colin back to Scotland and for Duncan, too, if he wished to go. He recommended that the boys take a stage to Halifax and come to Government House so that he would find them a suitable vessel. He enclosed ten pounds of British currency to cover their expenses.

In addition, the Lt. Governor enclosed in the packet several letters of introduction for Charles to use as he needed and a line of credit authorizing him to order from a major Halifax wholesale merchandising firm. He strongly urged that Charles James Campbell prove the worth of his Campbell lineage and establish himself as soon as possible as a merchant in some community which was opening up for settlement, maybe on the Bras d'Or Lake. He reminded him that his facility in both Gaelic and English would stand him in good stead. With best wishes, Sir Colin urged him to send him reports about his progress.

Four weeks later, as the first snow of the season blew across the land, Charles James Campbell stood once again at the crossroads near Kempt Road. His brother Colin had gone to Halifax where the Lt. Governor found a berth for him to Scotland. Duncan, however, had chosen to remain with his MacDonald relatives in Cape Breton. They had parted with sadness, but promises of meeting again soon.

Behind C. J. was the log house where he had known only sadness. To the left was the road to the cemetery where his mother, Isabella (McRae) Campbell, known by some also as Mrs. Bell MacDonald, lay in her early grave. To his right was the new road to West Bay and Whycocomagh, which beckoned to him. With his clothes, some bedding and the small metal strongbox in a wooden chest on his shoulder and his mother's thistle brooch pinned to the inner fabric of his coat, he set forth on the road to the future. Never again would he be afraid and never again would he be lacking resources – those were his promises to himself. And so he set out on the road ahead....

Historical records show how quickly Charles James Campbell established himself in the new village of Baddeck on the Bras d'Or Lake where he settled in 1842. Within twenty years, through shrewd business practices and perhaps his connection with Sir Colin Campbell, he came to be the wealthiest inhabitant in Cape Breton. But he never forgot the burial site of his dear mother. In the 1850s, he purchased a fine gravestone to mark her final resting place. Incised at the top is a well-carved likeness of a Scottish thistle. The inscription states that this stone marks the internment location of Isabella Campbell, widow of Capt. John Campbell of Isle of Skye, and the daughter of Rev. John McRae of Kintail, Scotland. There is no mention of Donald MacDonald, her second husband.

Charles James Campbell's features are visible as incised in stone over the main doorway of the former post office in Baddeck. Across the road is the site of his former home, named Duntulum for the old croft on the Isle of Skye, recalled to this day by the name of Duntulum Street. Charles James assisted his siblings in Scotland and brought his sister Isabella over from Scotland in one of his own sailing vessels. Several of his brothers went on to careers in sheep husbandry and ministry in Australia and Tasmania. The court record regarding the trial of Donald MacDonald has not yet been located.

The Road Ahead

MENU

Barley Bree Soup

Kale Soup

Oatmeal Porridge

Scotch Eggs

Smoked Fish Pie

Stoved Chicken

Clapshot

Seaweed Pudding

Currant Cake

Scotch Pancakes

Oatmeal Scones

Barley Bree Soup

1 lb trimmed lamb neck (450 g)
1 oz pearl barley (25 g)
2 oz split peas soaked (55 g)
2 cups diced turnip (500 ml)
2 cups shredded cabbage (500 ml)

2 quarts water (2 L)
1 tsp salt (5 ml)
1 tsp pepper (5 ml)
2 onions sliced (2)

•   Cut lamb in chunks and place in a large saucepan with water, and bring to a boil. Skim. Add barley and split peas. Return to a boil and simmer for 30 minutes. Add turnip and onion. Simmer for an additional 1½ hours.

•   Remove meat from stock and coarsely shred. Return meat to saucepan. Add cabbage, salt and pepper. Cook for 20 minutes, stirring occasionally.

•   Skim soup if necessary. Taste and adjust seasoning. Serves 6-8.

Kale Soup

2 lbs kale leaves (900 g)
2 qts beef stock (2 L)
¼ cup oatmeal (60 ml)

Salt and pepper
1 cup cream (optional) (250 ml)

•   Remove thick ribs from kale leaves. Tear into pieces. Place in a large saucepan. Cover with stock and simmer uncovered until tender.

•   Stir in the oatmeal, salt and pepper. Simmer until soup has thickened and oatmeal is cooked.

•   Remove from heat and add cream, if using. Serves 6-8.

Oatmeal Porridge

4 cups water (1 L)
1 cup oatmeal (250 ml)
½ tsp salt (2 ml)

•   Bring salted water to a boil in a medium saucepan. Stir oatmeal into boiling water until the mixture is thickened, stirring constantly for about 3 minutes.

•   Reduce the heat and simmer uncovered for 20 minutes, stirring and scraping the bottom of the saucepan often to avoid sticking.

•   Remove from the heat. Serve in warm bowls with brown sugar or maple syrup.

> NOTE
> Oatmeal Porridge was a staple food enjoyed by the Scots in the past and still is today. Serves 6.

Scotch Eggs

6 eggs hard cooked (6)
1 lb sausage meat (450 g)
1 cup bread crumbs (250 ml)
2 tbsp chopped parsley (30 ml)

½ tsp thyme (2 ml)
½ tsp black pepper (2 ml)
1 [raw] egg (1)

- Peel eggs and set aside.
- Mix the sausage meat so it has a smooth consistency.
- Wet hands, completely wrap eggs with sausage meat, spreading meat evenly.
- Combine bread crumbs, parsley, thyme and pepper.
- In a bowl, lightly whisk the egg. Dip sausage-coated egg in egg mixture and roll in crumb mixture, coating eggs well with crumbs.
- Arrange eggs on a parchment-lined tray and refrigerate for several hours.
- To cook, place eggs on a lightly greased baking sheet and bake in a 375° F (190° C) oven for 25-30 minutes until coating is crisp and brown (turning several times during cooking process to avoid sticking).

> **NOTE**
> Scotch Eggs make a wonderful appetizer. Slice in half lengthwise and serve with mustard sauce.

Stoved Chicken

1 large chicken cut in pieces (1)
2 oz butter or oil (55 g)
2 onions sliced (2)
4-5 potatoes peeled and sliced (4-5)

1 tsp salt (5 ml)
1 tsp pepper (5 ml)
2 cups stock (500 ml)

- Heat butter or oil in large skillet. Brown the chicken pieces in skillet until crisp, turning occasionally.
- In a medium casserole, arrange a layer of sliced potatoes, top with a layer of onions. Season with salt and pepper.
- Arrange 4 pieces of chicken over vegetable and repeat layers ending with layer of potatoes.
- Pour the stock carefully over all. Cover securely.
- Cook in a 325° F (160° C) oven for 2 hours or until chicken and vegetables are tender.
- Serve with a salad and crusty bread. Serves 6.

> **NOTE**
> Stoved Chicken is an adaptation of a chicken dish cooked on the hearth.

Smoked Fish Pie

1 lb fresh haddock (450 g)
½ lb smoked haddock (or salt cod, soaked) (225 g)
1½ cups milk (325 ml)

2 tbsp water (30 ml)
1 bay leaf (1)
1 medium onion sliced (1)
2 tbsp butter (30 ml)
2 tbsp flour (30 ml)
2 eggs hard boiled (2) (optional)

1 tsp black pepper (5 ml)
5 potatoes peeled and sliced (5)
½ cup milk (125 ml)
4 tbsp butter (60 ml)
salt and pepper
½ cup grated cheddar (125 ml)

• Put fresh haddock and smoked haddock or soaked salt cod in a baking dish and cover with milk and water. Add bay leaf. Bake uncovered in 350⁰ F (180⁰ C) oven for 20 minutes.

• Remove from oven. Cool and flake fish. Strain the cooking broth and set aside.

• In a saucepan melt butter and sauté sliced onion. Add flour and cook, stirring continuously for one (1) minute. Add broth from fish. Bring to a boil. Reduce heat and cook until thickened.

• Arrange fish in a buttered casserole. Cover with sauce.

• Peel and slice eggs and arrange in sauce. Set aside to cool.

• Cook potatoes in salted boiling water until tender. Drain and mash. Add hot milk, butter, salt and pepper to taste.

• Cover fish with potato mixture. Form rough peaks with potatoes. Sprinkle with cheese.

• Bake in a 400⁰ F (200⁰ C) oven for 25 minutes until golden brown and bubbly around edges. Serves 6.

Clapshot

1 lb potatoes mashed (450 g)
4 tbsp butter (60 ml)
1 head kale trimmed and chopped (1)

1 tsp salt (5 ml)
1 tsp pepper (5 ml)
1 onion chopped (1)

• Cook the potato and kale separately in boiling salted water. Drain. Mash potato.

• Combine the hot potato and kale. Season with salt and pepper.

• Melt butter and sauté onion. Add to potato kale mixture. Spread mixture in a 2-quart (2-L) casserole. Cover securely and place in a 325⁰ F (160⁰ C) oven for 25 minutes until piping hot. Serves 6-8.

Seaweed Pudding

2 oz fresh carrageen seaweed (55 g)

1 quart whole milk (1 L)

2 tbsp sugar (30 ml)

- Wash the fresh seaweed and place in a saucepan with the milk. Slowly bring to a boil and reduce heat. Simmer for 30 minutes.
- Stir mixture occasionally until seaweed becomes gelatinous. Add sugar and stir to dissolve.
- Remove from heat. Strain into a bowl and leave to set in a cold place. Serves 6.

Currant Cake

½ cup butter (125 ml)

1 cup sugar (250 ml)

3 eggs beaten (3)

½ cup milk (125 ml)

2 cups all-purpose flour (500 ml)

3 tsp baking powder (15 ml)

½ tsp salt (2 ml)

1½ cups currants (375 ml)

- In a bowl cream butter. Add sugar gradually and cream until fluffy. Add eggs and beat until smooth.
- Combine flour, baking powder and salt. Toss currants in flour to coat.
- Add flour to creamed mixture with milk. Mix well and beat for 2 minutes until smooth.
- Grease and flour a round or square 10-inch (25-cm) cake pan. Pour batter in pan.
- Bake in a 350⁰ F (180⁰ C) oven for 40-50 minutes until tester comes out clean.
- Remove from oven. Cool in pan for 10 minutes. Turn out on cooling rack and cool completely.
- Wrap cake securely and allow to "mellow" for one day before slicing.

Scotch Pancakes

2 cups all-purpose flour (500 ml)
½ tsp salt (2 ml)
1 tsp baking soda (5 ml)
1½ tsp cream of tartar (7 ml)

½ cup granulated sugar (125 ml)
2 eggs beaten (2)
½ cup melted butter (125 ml)
1 cup milk (250 ml)

- In a bowl combine flour, salt, soda, cream of tartar and sugar. Make a well in the centre and add the lightly beaten eggs. Add the melted butter slowly to eggs, whisking the flour into egg mixture.
- Add milk a little at a time, beating well after each addition. The mixture should be smooth and thick.
- To cook, lightly grease the bottom of a heavy fry pan. Heat pan and drop one heaping teaspoonful of mixture on hot pan. Mixture will spread 2 inches (5 cm). Cook until golden on each side. Place on rack and cool.
- Scotch pancakes can be served with butter, preserves and marmalade.

> NOTE
> Small, light and tasty, these little pancakes were enjoyed as a bread product.

Oatmeal Scones

2 cups all-purpose flour (500 ml)
1 cup oatmeal (250 ml)
2 tbsp granulated sugar (30 ml)
2 tbsp baking powder (30 ml)
½ tsp salt (2 ml)

½ cup currants (125 ml)
½ cup melted butter or lard (125 ml)
2 eggs beaten (2)
½ cup milk (125 ml)

- Put flour, oatmeal, sugar, baking powder, salt and currants in a bowl. Mix and make a well in the centre.
- Beat eggs until frothy. Beat in melted fat and milk. Pour in well of dry ingredients. Stir to make a soft dough.
- Divide dough and pat in two (2) 6-inch (15-cm) circles. Transfer to greased baking sheet. Score each circle into 8 wedges.
- Bake at 400⁰ F (200⁰ C) until risen and golden brown, 15-18 minutes. Split and serve.

Iona Thanksgiving

Peter Rankin 2007

Iona, Cape Breton, is a site noted as the location where incoming immigrants and the Mi'kmaq once met and resolved their mutual suspicions of one another. The memory of this event survived in the oral tradition until a few details were finally recorded so future generations would be aware of an early time of thanksgiving.

The scene is depicted in a mural by Terry MacDonald that graces the Nova Scotia Highland Village visitor centre.

Iona Thanksgiving

1758

A native of the Island of Barra, Donald MacNeil (known as Donald Og, or Young Donald) served in the British Army during the battle for Louisbourg. After the capture of the Fortress, MacNeil was on board a British vessel pursuing a French ship through the Bras d'Or Lake, when he noted a fine and pristine location on the northern side of a narrow strait of water separating two headlands. It had all the natural characteristics that immigrants would seek as a location for a new settlement and there were no recognizable signs of the presence of people.

While on leave from his regiment, not long after this encounter, he sat by the peat fire in his stone house on the Island of Barra in the Hebrides and recounted for relatives his impressions of the land along the shore of the Bras d'Or Lake, far across the sea, in a place called Nova Scotia. Spoken in Gaelic, his words lingered for generations of firesides, as the account called out to kith and kin to seek the area now known as Iona, Cape Breton Island. In English his words detailed: "In addition to fuel found in the woods and the fresh water in the ground and the fish in the inland sea, you will find there more shelter from the north wind and better and earlier harvests and good fishing grounds." He described the location of the shoreline and the hills behind, on the large lake where the jutting headlands on the northern and southern sides come close to one another. He recommended that when the time came for them to leave their old home on Barra, his kinfolk should try to find this site and make a settlement there.

Donald Og MacNeil died in 1759, a casualty at the battle on the Plains of Abraham in Quebec; he never returned to the location so well described to his family and friends in Barra. The oral picture he painted of the place was remembered, as his words were transmitted to younger generations, only written down more than a century and a half after his visit there. Both in Scotland and in Cape Breton, his words survived through oral transmission.

And so it was that a group of MacNeils, just forty years later, set out to find the location so well recommended by the soldier from Barra. They had emigrated from

Barra in the late 1790s, early members of a great emigration from the Highlands and Islands of Scotland which was brought about by changing times in their ancestral lands. Taking up residence on the northern shore of Nova Scotia, at Arisaig, where relatives lived, they cherished in their hearts the words spoken by Donald Og and passed to them from the people who had heard him. They recalled as though having witnessed themselves the beauty and the good opportunities of the spot on the Bras d'Or Lake – fish and soil and fresh water and plentiful supply of wood. They speculated among themselves as to whether or not there really was such a place and whether it would still be available for new immigrants.

For many generations, the Mi'kmaq, a widely dispersed population of Aboriginal people, lived in the area which they called Mi'kma'ki, now called the Maritime Provinces. Hunting and fishing as a way of life, they moved from location to location as the seasons dictated. Although converted to Christianity in the 1600s, they retained a great respect for the earth and water and sky and preferred their nomadic way of life to that of the kind of permanent settlement pattern brought to their area from Europe. Not immediately opposed to Europeans coming to their area, they had nevertheless learned to be wary of incoming groups, whether French, English or Scots.

1801

In the late spring of 1801, four men of the group of MacNeils of Barra who had come to Arisaig, Nova Scotia, determined to go in search of the spot about which they had heard so much throughout their whole lives. After consulting with others in the area and looking at the available primitive maps of Cape Breton, they realized that they would be on a journey of several days before they would find the location recommended by their old neighbour and distant relative, Donald Og MacNeil, forty years earlier.

They knew that they had to take food and clothing and probably a tent of some sort with them. They secured a small boat, perhaps a shallop, a small boat with two sails. Also they took several axes in order to cut firewood and to fashion stakes to mark their claim to the land. Although the oral account does not give the food in detail, we know that they did take a supply of salt, probably to flavour the potatoes which would form part of their diet for the ten days or two weeks they would be away. The salt would also be useful if they were to cook fish found in the lakes or if they wished to try to preserve some of the products of the lakes. Very likely, they took some bread and cheese. A quantity of oatmeal for porridge would also be in the supply of food stored in a wooden chest which would have been placed in the small ship, along with a small kettle for boiling water. Although nobody knew for certain, they were told that there were probably no settlers along those shores of the Bras d'Or. To be sure, there were Gaelic-speaking Scots in other places on Cape Breton Island and a number of small groups of English-speaking Loyalists from New England in Ship Harbour and Port Hood and Mabou.

Thus, with some uncertainty about the forthcoming journey and with tearful farewells, Donald MacNeil and his son Rory, and Eoin MacNeil and his son John sailed away from Arisaig on a journey to Cape Breton. After a sail of two days or more they came to St. Peter's, where they knew they had to drag their boat across the isthmus separating the ocean from the lakes. Then, sailing slowly along the shores on both sides of the lake for three days in search of the location remembered in family tradition, they arrived at the legendary site. It was a reality – the two peninsulas reaching out toward one another, the wooded hillside, a fine beach, several small springs of fresh water and many fish in the water around them. The soil seemed deep and without many rocks. The promised land was a reality. The words of Donald Og were accurate and, perhaps, they had found a place to settle and raise their families.

Imagine a warm day in the late spring with a gentle breeze creating little waves on the waters of the great inland salt water sea known as the Bras d'Or Lake, the Arm of Gold! The strength of the sun warmed the faces of the travellers. In amazement, they looked all around at the various headlands, tree covered and without any signs of human habitation. At their feet, as they waded ashore, they saw schools of fish of several varieties. So much to take in! So much to be thankful for!

Drawing their boat above the high water line, they attached it by rope to a nearby tree. After some exploration up onto the hillside, they began to cut some small trees so as to fashion stakes for property markers. They made a fire on the beach in order to boil some water. They planned to cook some potatoes and maybe some fish for a meal; all seemed to be going well as they talked about what a fine place this would be for a new home for their families from the Island of Barra. They envisioned the planting of potatoes and kale and some barley and oats. They could move their wives and children here within weeks, or so they thought.

Around a headland to the south a canoe appeared and headed toward them. In it were a number of Mi'kmaq who were coming to the area to investigate the rising smoke. They came to challenge the MacNeils' right to claim the land. Donald MacNeil spoke some French, as did the Chief of the band and they conversed as well as they could in that language. The Mi'kmaq knew little of Gaelic and the men from the Isle of Barra knew nothing of the Aboriginal language. Donald had brought with him a document which seemed to give him and his companions the right to claim land, perhaps as a reward for previous military service. But, according to the account passed down through several generations, the Mi'kmaq were not impressed with such a piece of parchment; they said the land was theirs, not that of the King of England's, and it appeared as though a conflict was imminent.

In that tense moment Eoin MacNeil went to his knees in prayer, making the sign of the cross as was his custom. The Chief recognized this as a Christian ceremony, indeed Roman Catholic, as the Mi'kmaq were of the same persuasion, and all recognized that they were brothers in the faith. Donald took from the chest a crucifix which he stuck upright in the sand between them. By the placing of that symbol in front of the two groups, peace was established and they sat together on the shore near the small fire with its kettle prepared for cooking.

In recognition of the peacefulness of the moment, the Mi'kmaq brought from their canoe a number of eels which they had speared for their own sustenance. They put them in the pot which already had water boiling. Into the same pot, the MacNeils put salt from the supply they had brought with them. The meal was prepared and the Mi'kmaq much appreciated the fine taste the salt gave the eels and delighted in the potatoes. Cheese and bread were passed from one to another. With much satisfaction, the two groups of people feasted on the shared food and promised to be friends rather than to be enemies. Certainly, thanks were offered to God as all people crossed themselves in reverence to the crucifix positioned in the sand of the beach. A remarkable event on a quiet spring day long ago near the place in Iona where there is now a Roman Catholic church named for the renowned missionary, St. Columba, who came to Iona, Scotland from Ireland in the 500s.

Epilogue

With some reluctance as well as with renewed hopes, the four MacNeils set sail to return to Arisaig. Back along the shore line to the isthmus at St. Peter's and then along the coast of Cape Breton and across to Cape George, they went with what haste they could manage. They wanted to bring the good news to their families that soon they would return to the site above the beach, to mark out plots of land for each family, to clear land for planting and build a few temporary shelters. Then, they would find suitable transportation to bring families and their few possessions to their new home, where they would settle permanently. Others from Arisaig came with them and they were joined through the coming years by a number of families from the Isle of Barra who established farms on both sides of the narrows.

According to tradition, the Mi'kmaq assisted the new residents in becoming aware of the helpful plants found in the woods and of the varieties of edible berries and the usefulness of the maple trees in supplying sap for sugar. A willingness to live near one another in peace continued through the years. The story is a moving account of an early modest thanksgiving feast and was told again and again by descendants of the settlers at Iona and Grand Narrows until it was written down in accounts, such as that of the late S. R. MacNeil, and now visibly interpreted in a painting found at the Nova Scotia Highland Village at Iona, located near the beach where the two cultural groups met and agreed to live in peace.

1801

A Thanksgiving Feast

MENU

Mi'kmaq Eel Stew

Boiled Blue Potatoes with Salt

Dried Blueberry Cakes

Hot Cherry Drink

Mi'kmaq Eel Stew

2 eels skinned (2)
1 small turnip diced (1)
1 onion chopped (1)
6 potatoes cut in pieces (6)

1 tsp salt (5 ml)
½ tsp pepper (2 ml)
8 cups cold water (2 L)

•   Skin eels and cut in approximately 2-4-inch (5-10-cm) pieces. Place in saucepan. Cover with cold water and bring to a boil. Reduce heat and simmer for 30 minutes to tenderize and cleanse. Drain. In a large saucepan put diced turnip, onion, salt and pepper. Cover with cold water and bring to a boil. Simmer until turnip is partially cooked. Add the potatoes, eels and continue cooking until tender. Serve in bowls. Serves 6.

Blue Potatoes Boilded with Salt

6 large blue potatoes (6)
1 tsp salt (5 ml)
Boiling water (as needed)

• Wash potatoes to remove soil, and remove "eyes", small sprouts on potatoes. If potatoes are too large, cut each in half.
• Place potatoes in large saucepan. Sprinkle with salt and cover with boiling water. Bring to a boil. Cover the saucepan, reduce heat and simmer until potatoes are tender. Drain. Potato skins will loosen.
• Serve with eels, cod or meat dishes. Serves 6.

Dried Blueberry Cakes

Blueberries crushed and combined with grain. This mixture was formed into small cakes and allowed to dry in the sun. It could be eaten out of hand or with maple syrup. It was wrapped in bark to preserve its texture.

Hot Cherry Drink

Bark of the cherry or chokecherry tree, as well as twigs tied in little bundles were dropped in boiling water to make a hot drink. It was sweetened with maple sugar.

Maple Sugar

Sap from the maple trees was used as a sweetener and a beverage. Sap was also boiled down in earthen pots to make maple sugar cakes. This was considered a delicacy.

Peter Rankin 2007

Chez Douce: A Day in the Life of an Entrepreneur, 1815

Tens of thousands of people, as they come and go on the Canso Causeway, quickly pass a small graveyard near a lighthouse on the Cape Breton side. Few, if any, give any attention to the aged monuments. Although the name Belhaché survives on maps as the identification of a promontory in the area, it does not appear in the telephone directory and is unfamiliar to most people today. But Douce Belhaché and her young daughter, her only child, lie in that cemetery very near to the location of their former home in Port Hastings. The mother came to be a widow when her husband, Capt. Belhaché, was lost at sea. Douce remained in the area even after the death of her husband and came to be a successful entrepreneur. Although a lone woman without family in Cape Breton, she chose not to return to the shelter of her family on the Island of Jersey in the English Channel.

For years, legends have survived that a ghost walked the shore near the cemetery. Many believed that it was Douce Belhaché looking for the return of her shipmaster husband. But the greater story is that of her management of her own affairs and contribution to the development of an economy in the days when Cape Breton Island was being settled by immigrants from many places. She is the very first female entrepreneur known in that part of Nova Scotia.

Chez Douce: A Day in the Life of an Entrepreneur, 1815

A soft wind from the southwest was clearing the early morning fog from the Gut of Canso and a pleasant sunny day seemed to be in the offing. A layer of thin clouds, however, suggested that rain and wind would arrive within twenty-four hours. For now, the sailing ships anchored just off the shore were riding easily in the calm waters. Their spars were reflecting in the slightly rippled surface of the sea. Already on several of the vessels, sailors were busy, readying to set sail for distant ports with their loads of timber, salt fish in barrels and casks of farm butter.

The first smoke of the day was rising from the stout chimney of the one-and-half storey house midway up the hill from the shore of Plaster Cove. With its first storey of cut stone and the next level of wood, it varied from the other all wooden and log houses in the small community. Within the dwelling, Douce Belhaché was ready for the tasks of the day. Her breakfast of freshly baked bread and wild strawberry jam and tea had been prepared by her housekeeper, Sarah Hubert, a distant cousin. Together, they sat at the table in the corner of the kitchen, speaking in the language of their birthplace, the Isle of Jersey. The tongue, a mixture of English and Norman French, was to be heard as well in their morning prayers as they gave thanks for food and life.

Douce, a widow now for more than a decade, expected several business associates during the day. Her late husband, whose ship foundered near Phial on the coast of Madeira, had left home on a spring morning much like this – the sky clear and the wind gentle. But many months later, word came from one of the other Channel Islands captains that debris from the Belhaché ship, *L'Esperance*, had washed up on the coast of Madeira. A vicious storm had swept that area in July and brought disaster to several schooners. Douce, already anxious about his long absence, acknowledged that her fading hope for Philippe's return was, like his ship, dashed asunder.

After the women finished at the table, Sarah cleared away the pewter serving dishes and cups and plates edged with a bronze lustre glaze. The pitcher of the same pattern had been a wedding gift from Douce's parents when she and Philippe married back on the Channel Island of Jersey, in 1786. It was a cherished keepsake which brought memories of the sturdy stone house in St. Aubin where roses climbing stone walls were in bloom at this time of the year. That fleeting image passed quickly from Douce's mind as she reminded Sarah that Philip Ingouville would be at the house for a noon meal and that he and his daughter might remain over night before they set sail for their home at Sydney Forks at the head of Spanish Bay on the northeastern coast of Cape Breton. Ingouville, also a native of Jersey, had first arrived on this coast in 1788, the same year as the Belhachés. As friends and distant kin, they had been business associates for many years. His ship was lying at anchor in the harbour beyond the Belhaché wharf.

Douce returned to her bedroom for a few minutes to put on her standard white blouse and long dark blue skirt. Across her shoulders, she arranged a shawl newly woven by John and Isabella Buck in their weaving house just across the yard. Her boots were black leather, imported from France. Although a widow, Douce had long ago put aside the usual garb of sorrowing women and carefully adjusted on her head a bright white lace cap embroidered with gold thread. Her carefully combed hair was arranged in a tight bun at the nape of her neck. The image which looked back at her as she stood in front of the mirror was that of a middle aged woman with eyes still bright blue and laugh lines surrounding them.

After being certain she was ready for the day's undertakings, Douce went to a small room at the front of the house. Here the windows with their small panes allowed a view from the promontory below, coming to be called Belhaché's Point, all the way to Ship Harbour. She noted which vessels were preparing to set sail and which flags flew from their masts. She knew that later in the morning she would need to go down the hill to the wharf to confirm the number of casks of butter which she was shipping to Newfoundland and to examine the contents of the barrels of goods which were arriving from Liverpool, England. She would need the bills of lading to bring to her bookkeeper, Jean Langlois, who had a small office near the wharf.

Before she took her place at the oak desk imported from England many years ago, she paused by the hearth, in front of the grate wherein burned coal from Glace Bay, at the other end of Cape Breton. On the wall above was a small silhouette portrait cut from black paper by André Jervais. It was the outline of the face of a young child with thick curly hair, her only child and her namesake who was buried on a little hill on the promontory jutting out into the Gut of Canso. At least her burial site was known – her husband was but one of many sailors who drowned in deep water.

Douce Elizabeth Belhaché had died of fever at the age of six years and eight months, now almost twenty years ago. No day started without the mother putting her fingers to the outline of the face she had known so well. This day, she reminded herself that she must order a memorial stone with her late husband's name to be placed next to the child's marker at the cemetery near the sea at Belhaché's Point. The salt water of the nearby Atlantic Ocean, so much a part of their lives, continually rolled to the shore just beyond the grave.

But, for now, she must give her attention to documents newly arrived by messenger from the Justice of Peace in the area. Her request for another grant of land at Ship Harbour, now more often called Port Hawkesbury, had been approved by the Governor of Cape Breton. She had realized that she should apply for that piece of land when she became aware that the Paint and Bailleul families were establishing new yards for building ships in that cove. It had become evident to her that sometime soon she might need to build there herself so as to be nearer the activity.

In addition, she received a letter of permission to ship more plaster from the inlet where she owned the rights to excavate the soft rock. She had a request from the farming district of Mabou down the coast for a small shipload, where the plaster would be used, after being burned in a lime kiln, to sweeten the somewhat acidic soil of that area. She quickly wrote a letter to John Baillie who had a flat boat on which the mineral could easily be loaded. In her clear handwriting, she requested a price from him for transporting the valuable product to Mabou Harbour. It would be but one of several missives in her own hand which would be delivered later on in the day by a trusted messenger whom she paid well to respect the confidentiality of her business correspondence.

As the sun, now high in the sky, came through the front windows, she paused as Sarah brought to Douce cups of hot chocolate and plates of warm rolls and several slices of local cheese. As they shared the small mid-morning repast, they discussed what food they would need to import from the larger markets in Halifax. It was too early for the first new potatoes from the Isle of Guernsey, but perhaps they should place an order for the time when they did arrive at one of the wholesalers in Halifax. The climate on the Channel Islands was much more conducive for harvesting early vegetables than that on Cape Breton with its frequent late frosts. They listed several other items for the household.

After they finished the hot chocolate, Douce listened with her head nodding approval to Sarah's request to hire two of the young MacKinnon boys in the area to help with whitewashing the exterior walls of the house and barn, and their sisters to help with washing the blankets and painting the floors. It was time for the yearly thorough housecleaning. Sarah also reported that she had heard that some of the farmers along the shore in Judique were planning to bring spring lambs to Plaster Cove at the end of the week. They were said to be in good shape. Douce made a note to herself to send a message to one of the farmers there, whom she knew well, to offer him a suitable price. The lambs would sell well in Newfoundland, and she was sending butter and timber to St. John's at the end of the next week on one of the Ingouville ships. Fresh lamb might go as well.

Before Sarah went back to the kitchen hearth to begin preparations for the noon meal, Douce shared with her the thought that she might build a house at Ship Harbour now that she had been granted a piece of land there. Sarah was pleased with the idea, for she had young nieces living there whom she much liked. The two women had a deep confidence in one another and knew that their relationship was much more than employer and employee, and very important as two women living alone in a house in a seaport where sailors came and went. Sarah knew where Douce kept a loaded pistol in a drawer in the desk in the drawing room should an occasion arise where such a weapon was needed.

As Sarah rose to return to the kitchen, Douce asked her to go across the dooryard to the weaving house of the Bucks and to ask Isabella to come over for a few minutes. Douce had arranged for Isabella and John Buck to come from Scotland more than ten years previously. As skilled weavers, they prepared yard goods for sale, often to newly-arrived immigrants who required more clothing or bed coverings. But they were also able to weave fine linen from flax thread imported from Ireland. Much of this product Douce used in her own house or sent as gifts to her cousins in Arichat and Quebec or occasionally gave to the wives of ship captains who arrived with their husbands at her wharf from places in the United States. The end of the war between Great Britain and the United States had brought many vessels to the Gut of Canso, and more and more families accompanied the sea captains.

After a few minutes, Isabella Buck knocked at the door of the room Douce used as her office. With Isabella's Lowland Scots accent and Douce's soft Channel Island voice, their conversation in English still amused both of them as they heard the different sounds in each other's words. Douce commented on how much she liked the new shawl which she was wearing around her shoulders, woven from cotton and fine wool. She told Isabella that she thought such an item was very marketable, and wondered if Isabella and John could plan to weave more of the fabric and engage a young girl to make the shawls under their direction. She thought there might be many requests for them. Isabella was pleased with the idea for she preferred that kind of weaving to just making yards and yards of homespun.

Douce also asked Isabella if they needed a larger space for their two looms and spinning wheels. She felt that it might be time to expand the business a bit. Isabella had a good judgment and took care of the business aspects of their weaving, while John cared for the looms and for setting up the patterns for the warp. Their older children were now able to look after the sheep they raised so that they had a supply of the best wool for their work. Isabella agreed that a larger building would allow them to expand and to take on an apprentice or two, thus providing some employment for young women in the area. Douce said that she would speak to Alex MacKinnon, the carpenter, and ask him to undertake the work.

Isabella left after sharing a merry joke with Douce that grew out of the misunderstanding of English words by recent Scottish Gaelic-speaking people. They thought that a male sheep was a "bull sheep," since they had learned the word bull as related to cattle. The laugh lines around the eyes of Douce Belhaché were well exercised as she enjoyed her conversations with Isabella and John, her neighbors and employees. She started to write a preliminary deed by which she would transfer the land on which they lived and worked in order to recognize the fulfillment of their agreement with her to weave for her household needs and for her export business. She appreciated their excellent work and their diligence.

As the day progressed, the long, thin clouds were starting to diminish the light of the sun. The wind was shifting to the west and small white caps were beginning to be seen on the strait between Cape Breton Island and mainland Nova Scotia. Douce noticed that the liquid in the barometer was starting to fall, an indication that inclement weather was approaching. But nothing could diminish her pleasure as she welcomed to her home her long-time friend and very distant relative, Philip Ingouville, and his daughter, Ann, who had been born about the same time as her own child. She rejoiced as Ann greeted her as "Tante Douce" and kissed her on both cheeks. The question passed through her mind as to what her own child would have looked like at this age. But she quickly asked them to sit down and, with much interest, she asked Ann about her engagement to be married.

Although Douce and Philip lived at different parts of Cape Breton Island, and road travel was sometimes all but impossible, they did visit several times a year and were often in correspondence concerning business matters. Douce was able to negotiate very profitable arrangements with Philip who operated a large farm at Sydney Forks and employed many people. He also had several vessels coming and going across the Atlantic and she found that he could always find room on his vessels for the large shipments of dried cod which she could provide for markets in Europe and South America. They both knew that for generations their relatives had participated in a cooperative shipping relationship. Philip enjoyed his negotiations with Douce and never took advantage of her. They were respectful of each other as persons and as business associates.

Almost the same age, they had seen Cape Breton come to be an important part of the growing import-export business which was so beneficial to the Channel Islanders. They had lived through the early days of the island coming to be a colony with its own governmental officials located in Sydney. And now they were witnessing the arrival of many immigrants, often on the Channel Island boats, from Ireland and from Scotland. Occasionally, they spoke about what life would have been like if they had remained on the Isle of Jersey. Philip had been so bold as to ask her once why she didn't go back after her husband didn't return from his journey to Madeira with his shipload of lumber and fish. With a look of pain in her usually happy eyes, she reminded him that her only child lay buried here and she chose to stay where her life had also been happiest and not just the saddest. She revealed as well that she enjoyed the challenge of continuing the business that she and her husband, Philippe, had started.

As Douce and Philip Ingouville and his daughter Ann sat to the noon meal in the dining room of the sturdy house above the wharf, Douce saw that her good friend looked quite unwell. But she mentioned nothing to him then. After their meal and some good stories shared in Jersais dialect, Ann went next door to the weaving house to select a piece of fabric which Douce wished to give her as a wedding gift. Douce and Philip went to the small room across the hall and quickly settled their business matters.

Douce then told him that she was considering bringing a Methodist minister from either England or the Channel Islands to the area, for she felt that it was time to establish a church, so the community could welcome people of different denominations. She added that she had very much enjoyed the service conducted by an itinerant Methodist minister several weeks previously. Ingouville agreed with the concept and said that he would make inquiries through his agents overseas. And then he told her that he was not feeling as well as usual and thought he might go to Halifax to consult a doctor. Furthermore, he wanted her to know that their agreements were in good shape and his agent would continue to honour them even if he were ill, or.... He didn't finish the sentence. Douce, however, realized the import of his words and his loyalty to her was gratifying.

Believing that they should lift anchor today and start the journey home, the Ingouvilles refused Douce's offer of hospitality for the night, much to her and Sarah's disappointment for they had prepared for them. But with promises of coming again soon, Philip and Ann Ingouville departed. They quickly found their way down the hill and a small boat carried them back to their schooner.

For some time, Douce sat looking at the strait as the Ingouville ship left the port. She asked Sarah to bring her a glass of Jersey wine and to share one with her. Together, they reviewed the events of the day and looked to what had to be done during the rest of the week. Now that the spring had come, Douce knew that she needed to make a trip to Arichat to consult with some of the ship owners there. Her cousins there were expecting her to remain with them for several days. For now, she would go to the wharf to be certain that all was in order with the items to be exported and with those that arrived from overseas.

Putting a warm cloak on over the shoulders, she left her house and started down the hill. Looking across the sky, she saw that the clouds were increasing. Her competent eye began to calculate how the changing weather would affect the ships about to leave port. But looking to the ground as well in order to keep her feet on the walking path, she noticed that the first wild strawberries of the season were in bloom in the field. Wild strawberry preserves were one of the delights of the coming summer season and one of the first berries she and her husband had enjoyed when they came to these shores as a young recently married couple.

At the brow of the hill, she came to the stones piled up thirty years earlier when she and Philippe and their young baby first came to this hillside to live. These were left over from the construction of their house. Here and there among the stones, she noticed the very last of the mayflowers in bloom, the scent of the tiny blossoms carried in the damp air of the afternoon. It was such a haunting fragrance, so unlike anything she had known in her childhood home even though other flowers were abundant there. But the sounds of voices from the wharf below reminded her that she needed to hasten on to the business of the day. So she left the signs of spring behind in the knowledge that she would revisit them as she returned. Pulling her shawl tightly around her, she hurried on. She had business to conduct and papers to sign.

Thus may have gone the day of an early entrepreneur of Cape Breton Island, Douce Hubert Belhaché, a very capable woman, a survivor. The winds of time have carried away the tangible traces of her life, but her influence may still be felt as we walk along the shorelines of history and legend.

Channel Islands

MENU

Cauliflower Cream Soup

Crab Cakes with Coriander

Chicken Liver Pâté

Jersey Pork Chops with Cider

Crêpes Stuffed with Spinach

Bubble and Squeak

Gâche aux Pommes
(Apple Cake)
Wild Strawberry Preserves

Plum Chutney

Cauliflower Cream Soup

1 medium cauliflower (1)
1 large onion diced (1)
2 tbsp butter (30 ml)
2 tbsp ground almonds (30 ml)
4 cups chicken stock (1 L)

½ tsp salt (2 ml)
½ tsp pepper (2 ml)
½ cup cream (125 ml)
1 tbsp toasted almonds (15 ml)
1 tbsp chopped chives (15 ml)

- In a large saucepan melt butter and sauté onion until soft.
- Divide cauliflower in florets and add to onion mixture. Add ground almonds, chicken stock, salt and pepper.
- Bring to a boil. Reduce heat and simmer for 30 minutes or until cauliflower is tender.
- Strain and reserve stock. Pass cauliflower through a sieve to puree. Return to saucepan with reserved stock. Simmer for 5 minutes.
- Add cream, toasted almonds and chives. Serves 6.

Crab Cakes with Coriander

1 lb crab meat (450 g)
8 oz bread crumbs (225 g)
1 medium onion chopped (1)
2 tbsp butter (30 ml)
2 egg yolks (2)

2 tbsp chopped coriander (30 ml)
½ tsp black pepper (2 ml)
2 tsp lemon zest (10 ml)
Oil or butter for frying

- In a bowl combine the crabmeat and bread crumbs. Set aside.
- Heat butter in skillet and sauté onion until soft. Remove from heat. Cool and toss into crab mixture with egg yolks, coriander, pepper and lemon zest.
- Shape the mixture into 8 cakes, rounding and shaping with hands.
- Place cakes on a lightly floured tray and refrigerate for several hours.
- Heat oil or butter in skillet. Place crab cakes in skillet. When bottom of cake is crisp and firm, turn and cook other side until crisp, approximately 5-7 minutes.
- Remove from skillet and serve with a crisp salad. Serves 4-6.

NOTE
Crab mixture will be very soft. Refrigerating cakes before cooking is very important.

Chicken Liver Pâté

½ cup butter (125 ml)
1 medium onion finely chopped (1)
8 oz chicken livers (225 g)
1 clove garlic crushed (1)
½ tsp salt (2 ml)

1 tsp pepper (5 ml)
1 tsp tarragon (5 ml)
2 tbsp brandy (30 ml) [optional]
¼ cup clarified butter (60 ml)

- In a medium skillet, melt 3 tbsp (45 ml) of the butter. Stir in onion and, over a medium heat, cook until onion is soft. Stir in chicken livers. Cook for 5-6 minutes until browned on all sides.
- Add garlic, salt, pepper and tarragon. Reduce heat and cook for 2 minutes.
- Remove from heat. Cool slightly. Pass through a sieve or puree in food processor.
- Cool to lukewarm. Beat in remaining butter and brandy, if using. Pour into earthenware terrine or small casserole.
- Melt clarified butter over a low heat. Using a spoon, skim and discard the froth from surface of butter.
- Carefully pour the melted butter over pâté, discarding the milky residue.
- Chill pâté for 6 hours. Serve with fresh bread or crackers.

NOTE
This pâté will keep for 5-6 days refrigerated.

Jersey Pork Chops with Cider

4 large pork chops (4)
1 tbsp melted butter (15 ml)
1 large onion sliced (1)
Pork pan drippings
2 tbsp butter (30 ml)

2 tbsp flour (30 ml)
1¼ cups cider (310 ml)
3-4 sage leaves (3-4)
Salt and pepper

- Brush the pork chops on each side with melted butter. Sprinkle with salt and pepper. Arrange in a baking pan and cook in a 400⁰ F (200⁰ C) oven for 20 minutes, turning once. Remove from oven and keep warm.
- Combine drippings from pork with butter and cook the onion until soft. Sprinkle in the flour and cook for one (1) minute, whisking continuously.
- Add cider, sage leaves, salt and pepper to onion. Bring to a boil, stirring. Reduce heat and simmer until thickened.
- Pour sauce over chops. Return to a 350⁰ F (180⁰ C) oven for 10 minutes.
- Serve with apple sauce. Serves 4.

Crêpes Stuffed with Spinach

<u>Crêpe Batter</u>
1 cup all-purpose flour (250 ml)
2 eggs (2)
2 cups milk (500 ml)
2 tbsp melted butter (30 ml)
Pinch salt and pepper

<u>Sauce</u>
2 tbsp butter (30 ml)
2 tbsp all-purpose flour (30 ml)
2 cups milk (500 ml)
½ cup grated Swiss or cheddar cheese (125 ml)
½ tsp salt (2 ml)
½ tsp pepper (2 ml)

<u>Filling</u>
10 oz fresh spinach leaves (280 g)
8 oz cream cheese (225 g)
1 tbsp curry powder (15 ml)
¼ tsp pepper (1 ml)

- Make crêpe batter: Beat eggs in a bowl. Stir in flour, melted butter, milk, salt and pepper. Beat ingredients until smooth and creamy. Allow to sit for 30 minutes.
- Heat an 8-inch (20-cm) crêpe pan and brush with oil. Pour approximately 2 tbsp (30 ml) of batter in pan. Spread batter. Cook, turning once. Remove to cooling tray and continue. Makes about 12 crêpes.
- Cook the spinach. Drain, squeezing out excess water. Roughly chop spinach and put in bowl.
- Stir curry powder and cheese into spinach with pepper.
- Divide the mixture between 12 crêpes. Roll each and place in a rectangular casserole.
- To make sauce, melt butter and add flour, stirring until smooth. Gradually add milk. Bring to a boil. Reduce heat and simmer, stirring continuously until thickened. Season with salt and pepper. Remove sauce from heat. Add half the cheese to sauce, mixing well. Ladle sauce over crêpes, and sprinkle with remaining cheese.
- Bake in a 350⁰ F (180⁰ C) oven for approximately 20 minutes or until bubbly.
- Remove from oven. Serves as a luncheon dish, or accompaniment to cold meats. Serves 4-6.

Peter Rankin 2007

Bubble & Squeak

2 lbs potatoes peeled (900 g)
1 lb cabbage (450 g)
4 tbsp butter (60 ml)

4 tbsp cream (60 ml)
1 tsp salt (5 ml)
1 tsp black pepper (5 ml)

- Cook the potatoes and cabbage separately in boiling salted water. Drain.
- Mash the potatoes, adding butter, cream, salt and pepper. Chop the cooked cabbage and add to the potatoes. Mix thoroughly.
- Cooking in a frying pan allows the bubble to squeak.
- Melt 1 tbsp (15 ml) of butter in a large frying pan. When piping hot, spoon in the cabbage and potato, pressing it down. Soon it will make bubbly and squeak sounds.
- Cook for 5 minutes and cut into large wedges, turning each wedge and pressing down to form a solid piece. Spoon onto serving plates.

Gâche aux Pommes
(Channel Apple Cake)

1 lb cooking apples peeled and diced (450 g)
1½ cup all-purpose flour (325 ml)
1 tsp baking powder (5 ml)
½ tsp salt (2 ml)
1 tsp cinnamon (5 ml)
½ tsp allspice (2 ml)
½ tsp ginger (2 ml)

¼ cup mixed peel (60 ml)
½ cup chopped walnuts (125 ml)
¾ cup butter (175 ml)
¾ cup brown sugar (175 ml)
3 eggs (3)
2 tsp lemon zest (10 ml)
1 cup sultana raisins (250 ml)

- Cook diced apples in a little water until they are barely soft. Cool completely.
- In a bowl, combine flour, baking powder, salt, cinnamon, allspice, ginger, raisins, peel and walnuts. Set aside.
- In a large bowl, cream butter and sugar until fluffy. Add eggs and lemon. Beat well.
- Fold dry ingredients into creamed mixture alternately with the apples. Mix to combine.
- Grease and flour an 8-inch (20-cm) round cake pan. Spread batter in pan. Bake in a 325° F (170° C) oven for one (1) hour 15 minutes or until tester comes out clean.
- Remove cake from oven. Cool in pan for 10 minutes. Turn out on rack to cool. Cut in slices to serve.

Plum Chutney

6 lbs plums (2.7 kg)

1 lb cooking apples peeled and chopped (450 g)

1 cup raisins (250 ml)   1 tbsp salt (15 ml)

4 large onion sliced (4)   6 chopped garlic cloves (6)

1½ quarts cider vinegar (1.5 L) 1 tbsp ground allspice (15 ml)

3 lbs sugar (1.3 kg)   Juice and zest of lemon

- Cut plums in half and remove stones. Place in a large cooking pot with apples, onions, raisins, cider, sugar, salt, garlic, allspice and lemon.
- Mix well to combine. Place on heat. Bring to a boil, stirring constantly. Reduce heat and simmer for 2-2½ hours until thick, stirring occasionally.
- Pour into sterilized jars and seal. Store in a cool place. Makes 4 quarts (4 L).

> **NOTE**
> Chutney is a wonderful accompaniment to cold meats, cheese and pâtés.

Wild Strawberry Preserves

4 cups strawberries (1 L)

½ cup water (125 ml)

4 cups granulated sugar (1 L)

- In a medium saucepan, mix berries, water and sugar together. Let stand overnight.
- The following day, bring to a boil. Reduce heat and cook for 20-25 minutes until thickened.
- Ladle into sterilized jars. Seal with paraffin wax.
- Store jars in a cool dark place.

> **NOTE**
> Cultivated strawberries can be substituted. Berries must be very ripe, cut in pieces and crushed before cooking. Makes 6 cups.

Peter Rankin 2007

Earth - Sky - Water - Spirit: The Funeral of Chief Thomas Toma

The saltwater lake at the heart of Cape Breton Island is generally known as "The Bras d'Or Lakes" as there are several parts to it although all part of the whole – officially named Bras d'Or Lake. There is uncertainty about how it got its name, but many link it to the early French explorers who remarked on the sheen of the sun on the waters as being like an "arm of gold." The area of the lake is nearly 1,100 square kilometres. The length is almost 100 km, its widest place 50 km from shore-to-shore. As there are but two narrow natural entrances on the northern end, there is very little rise in the tide on most of the system. A canal was constructed on the southern end which connects the lake with the Atlantic Ocean through a system of locks.

For the Mi'kmaq, the lake has been part of their lives for many hundreds of years. Their major settlements are all on its shores. The Mi'kmaq named the lake Pitawpo'q or "salt water." The spiritual centre of the Mi'kmaq nation is Potlotek, or Chapel Island, as it known today, where the Grand Council meets and where there is a yearly pilgrimage in honour of St. Anne, grandmother of Jesus and patron Saint of the Mi'kmaq.

Escasoni (or Eskasoni, as it is spelled today) is an area long favoured by the native people for its good fishing and hunting. Though they journeyed around the island of Cape Breton in seasonal pursuit of fish and game, they maintained a settlement at Escasoni during the year and returned there often.

The lake for many generations was a major route for travel in the days before roads were common. The Mi'kmaq in their canoes and later inhabitants in small sailboats and dories and then in larger vessels powered by steam, went from one end to the other and from side to side as they exchanged goods and met in small communities for social occasions. Today, the lake is almost entirely without commercial shipping save the freighters that serve the gypsum plant near Little Narrows, but there are many recreational boats in the summer time. The sun still creates a golden sheen.

Earth - Sky - Water - Spirit:
The Funeral of Chief Thomas Toma

Come with us on a cold, gloomy day at the start of the year 1834, to the top of a high hill where we can look out over the great expanse of the Bras d'Or Lake at the widest spot. See the distant hills to the west where the sun sets into the Gulf of St. Lawrence and where eagles fly in great numbers. Look to those small ragged mountains to the northeast where the ocean enters the lakes. Closer, you can pick out the low-lying hill above the Mi'kmaq community of Eskasoni. Turn your head southward and see the low-lying island that is a sacred meeting place of the Mi'kmaq, Chapel Island. Behind us, for sixteen kilometres extends the spruce-covered forest, the earth that is eastern Cape Breton Island. Feel the red soil frozen beneath your feet, the solid ground, our great parent. Be aware of the breath of the Great Spirit of life on your face and receive it in your heart.

Look up! Through a break in the clouds, the sun comes through and shines on the water below us creating an arm of gold, a *bras d'or*. High above us now, two bald eagles are flying in easy circles as they ride on the air currents. Here is nature at its full at its best.

From this vantage point in your mind, journey with us back in time to a solemn occasion in Cape Breton history, recorded in the annals of the day. We have a fine place from which to watch and reflect on the event unfolding; sense the importance of joining earthly life with the eternal life as the Mi'kmaq do in their ceremonies.

From this spot, where the splendour of creation is so evident, we can watch a solemn procession of canoes along the shoreline in front of us as they travel from the northeast to the southwest, from Eskasoni to Chapel Island. Hear the steady beat of many drums in the distance and catch the sound of women singing a dirge. Watch the rythmic motion of the paddles as the hollowed hemlock with the body of the late chief, Thomas Toma, within, is slowly transported on two canoes lashed together. This is a procession of great dignity as many elders and relatives and friends accompany their respected leader on his final journey across the Bras d'Or Lake, so familiar to him in his lifetime.

For many weeks now, as the autumn of 1833 turned into early winter, family and friends kept watch at the bedside of the ancient and revered elder, Thomas Toma. Nobody still on earth can remember him at his birth or even as a child. A few recall him as a young man full of vigour. It is said that Thomas is more than 100 years of age – perhaps he has reached his 103rd year. All know, however, that he is the son of the former chief, Thomas Toma the first of that name, of ancient lineage in the hierarchy of Mi'kmaq families.

Recall as we stand here, warmly clothed and in silent appreciation of the solemnity of the event, that the man has lived a long and distinguished life and travelled many times in his canoe from place to place around this lake, its many inlets and bays, and even across to mainland Nova Scotia and Prince Edward Island. As we do now, he looked to the sky to see the eagles in flight and to watch the signs foretelling the weather of the coming days. Although a strong person by all accounts, he was not the great hunter and warrior that his father had been, but in times of conflict he led through careful wisdom and quiet conversation. From the State of Maine, to the island of Newfoundland and to the shores of Quebec and New Brunswick, he was noted for his fairness in making judgments. Now he is united again with the Great Spirit from whom he drew his life and his inspiration.

Although various remedies were brought to his bedside by noted healers, the leaves and the bark of the ash trees, the pith and dried foliage of the beech trees, and other traditional medicines seemed to bring him some comfort, but no healing. The dried root of the moccasin plant, served to him in a warm potion, had no curative effect. Mi'kmaq incantations and Christian prayers were said around him as family and friends, even strangers who knew him but by reputation, travelled from distant places to be with him and his family in the time of his slow decline and coming death. In the Mi'kmaq tradition, in times of great illness and death, nobody should be alone, but always in the presence of caring people.

Word of his coming demise was carried a great distance. Like a tall pine tree in the forest, he was reaching his end and would soon fall to the ground and come to be mingled with the earth. Messengers on foot and in canoes had carried the news through the whole of the Nation of the Mi'kmaq, to small encampments in the eastern United States and to the bays of Newfoundland.

One by one, his children and nephews and nieces, his relatives from far and near, and the distinguished elders from throughout the Mi'kmaq Nation, Mi'kma'ki, have gathered at his dwelling and have come to his side in order to seek his forgiveness for any insults they have offered to him. As is their ancient custom, they have asked for his peace in order to calm any troubled spirits around them. According to the long-established ritual of *apiksiktaq* or the act of mutual forgiveness, they wish to share with him their pardon and their giving of blessing as they have received his.

If we had stood on this height above the Great Lake during the past days and weeks, with our feet on the ground and eyes to the water below us, we would have seen in-dividual canoes and groups of sailing craft passing in front of us, as people near and far came to the winter home of the chief out of respect and brought gifts of food and coverings made from animal skins.

For weeks, women have been preparing meals and other items necessary to care for the physical needs of the great number of people arriving for the coming funeral. Preserved moose and caribou and rabbit and dried berries have been brought from storage. Carefully prepared furs have been spread in large tepees. Water in large caldrons has been kept from freezing as bonfires blazed day and night. Such food as could be prepared ahead for the great feast which would follow the funeral has been packed in birch bark and placed in baskets for transport to the traditional site on the sacred island sixty-five kilometres along the lake.

And the day came when, in the presence of his sons and grandchildren and his other near kin, the great chief breathed his last. With appropriate prayers and sayings from both traditional liturgies and those of the Roman Catholic church, they reverently prepared his body for its final journey and burial. At the top of the mountain, a tall hemlock where one was nearest the great creator, was felled, trimmed and hollowed out to be his resting place. The proper clothing for a distinguished leader has been placed around his body and other items of significance for his heritage, his faithful adherence to the Christian Church and his long life have been gathered near him.

Now, after four days of solemnly keeping watch and reciting prayers at his residence, the hemlock trunk has been carefully placed on two canoes lashed together. Eight strong young men, each from the various parts of the Mi'kmaq Nation, have taken paddles in hand and have started a rhythmical raising and dipping in the frigid lake. From our hilltop vantage point, we can see the procession now coming along in great precision. We can hear a drum in slow rhythm befitting the occasion.

As the solemn gathering of canoes comes closer, we can see those in which twelve distinguished elders are being transported. In the air, now we can hear the solemn funeral hymn continuously sung by six young woman of the Nation. They are singing in their own language and traditional form. See, there, in the second canoe after those carrying the body, is Chief Thomas Toma's eldest son and his son-in-law Francis Gregoire and his much younger half-brother Noel Toma. They are dressed in their finest clothing with the tall decorated hats on their heads.

As the procession moves with a slow, rhythmical pace from our right to our left, we are surprised by the bursting forth of bright rays of sunlight through dark clouds. Two eagles are seemingly following the group of travellers. At respectful distance to the rear, we see the boats transporting the rest of the mourners and those carrying some of the food which will be served after the funeral mass to be held at Chapel Island. Already gathered at the holy spot, many members of the nation and public officials of Cape Breton Island are awaiting the arrival of the group from Eskasoni. One after another the vessels pass by. Only in the distance now do we hear the hymn being sung and the sound of the oars keeping time – a drum beating out its message of sadness and calling people to the final ceremony.

We know as well that following the funeral, all of the assembled people will share stories of the deceased and of other distinguished elders of the past as they enjoy a fine feast of traditional, nourishing food. For it is the belief that this is a time to celebrate life as well as one to commemorate the recently departed. After some hours of eating and sharing in the traditions of their ancestors, the people will slowly depart by canoe and on foot as they return to their homes. They will have gathered in great respect to Chief Thomas and have followed the proper procedures and traditions.

Before we depart from our vantage point from we which we have watched this historic procession, we may well stop and reflect on how privileged we have been to be witnesses of a great and solemn event. We know that those shafts of sunlight coming from the heavens were somehow or other the approval of the Great Spirit – an arm of gold indeed, spreading across the great assemblage and bathing in its light the hollowed-out hemlock carrying its precious burden. So much we have seen in such a short time!

Now we can leave the hard-packed soil of this hillside on Cape Breton Island. But we know that we have been nourished with the gifts of earth and sky and water and prevailing spirit as we make our own ways home. This great funeral procession of the late chief Thomas Toma will remain in our memory – an event of January 1834.

Afterword: An account of this procession, written by a person who witnessed it, is found in a short-lived newspaper of the time, The Cape Bretonian.

Chief Toma's Funeral

❧ MENU ❧

Braised Moose Roast

Eel Stew

Pheasant Pie

Mi'kmaq Hash

Venison Stew

Indian Fry Bread

Cherry Cakes

Indian Corn Pudding

Cranberry Tea

Hot Cherry Drink

Braised Moose Roast

1 4-lb roast of moose (2 kg)
¼ lb salt pork cut in strips (115 g)

Marinade

1 tsp black pepper (5 ml)	4 tbsp brown sugar (60 ml)
1 tsp cinnamon (5 ml)	½ cup white vinegar (125 ml)
6 whole cloves (6)	¼ cup oil (60 ml)
1 tsp dry mustard (5 ml)	

* Trim all membrane from roast. Wipe with a damp cloth.
* Lard the roast with pork. Pierce the roast with a pointed knife or skewer two inches (5 cm) apart. Insert the strips of pork, pushing down with tip of knife.
* Place the roast in an earthenware container.
* Combine all marinade ingredients and pour over roast. Marinate the roast for 24-48 hours. Keep in cold place, turning frequently to allow marinade to penetrate meat.
* Remove roast from marinade and place in a roaster. Roast in a 350° F (180° C) oven for 1½ hours or until meat is tender.

Eel Stew

2 eels skinned (2)	1 tsp salt (5 ml)
1 small turnip sliced (1)	½ tsp pepper (2 ml)
1 onion chopped (1)	6-8 cups cold water (1.5-2 L)
6 medium potatoes quartered (6)	2 tbsp butter (30 ml)
2 cloves garlic (2)	

* Cut skinned eels in approximately 2-inch (5-cm) pieces. Place in saucepan. Cover with cold water and bring to a boil. Reduce heat, simmer and cook for 30 minutes to tenderize. Drain.
* In a large saucepan put turnip, onion, garlic, salt and pepper. Cover with cold water. Bring to a boil. Reduce heat and simmer until turnip is partially cooked.
* Add potatoes, eels and butter. Continue cooking until all are tender. Adjust seasoning if necessary. Serves 6.

Pheasant Pie

Pastry for double-crust pie
2 pheasants (2)
2 onions sliced (2)
2 ribs celery chopped (2)
6 peppercorns (6)
1 tbsp salt (15 ml)
2 bay leaves (2)
1½ quarts water (1.5 L)

Sauce
½ cup butter (125 ml)
1 tsp salt (5 ml)
½ cup flour (125 ml)
1 tsp pepper (5 ml)
4 cups broth (1 L)
1 tsp dry mustard (5 ml)
1 cup cream (250 ml)
2 cups sliced mushrooms (500 ml)

- Skin and clean pheasants. Trim and wash thoroughly in salted water. Sponge dry. Place pheasants in a large cooking pot. Cover with water. Add onion, celery, peppercorns, salt and bay leaves.
- Bring to a boil. Reduce heat and simmer covered for 2½ hours or until meat is tender. Remove meat from bones and set aside.
- Strain broth and reserve for sauce.
- To prepare sauce. Melt butter in medium saucepan. Add flour and cook for one (1) minute.
- Add broth, mushrooms, salt, pepper and mustard and cream. Cook, stirring until thickened.
- Arrange pheasant pieces in a 2-quart (2-L) casserole. Add sauce and combine. Cool.
- Roll pastry to shape of casserole. Place over pheasant mixture, turning edges of pastry under, and crimping edges. Make a cut in centre for steam to escape. (Brush with egg if desired.)
- Bake in a pre-heated 400⁰ F (200⁰ C) oven for 25-30 minutes until crust is golden and filling is bubbly. Serves 6-8.

Mi'kmaq Hash

2-inch square salt pork (5 cm)
1 large onion sliced (1)
6 medium potatoes quartered (6)

1 tsp salt (5 ml)
½ tsp pepper (2 ml)
3 cups water (750 ml)

> NOTE
> Other root vegetables such as turnip or carrots could be added to this hash for variety.
> Serves 4-6.

- Cut salt pork in cubes and fry in a skillet to render the fat. Add onion, potatoes, salt and pepper.
- Place in a saucepan. Cover with water and cook uncovered until potatoes are tender. Remove from heat. Stir gently. Taste and adjust seasoning if necessary.

Venison Stew

NOTE

Venison was a favourite of the First Nations people. They supplied venison to the early settlers in return for salt pork, flour and sugar.

3 lbs venison shoulder leg cut into 2-inch (5-cm) cubes (1.3 kg)

2 cups water (500 ml)

4 tbsp cider vinegar (60 ml)   3 allspice berries (3)

1 bay leaf (1)   2 cloves garlic (2)

2 tsp dried sage (10 ml)   1 lb field mushrooms (450 g)

6 juniper berries crushed (6)   4-oz piece of salt pork cubed (115 g)

NOTE

Vegetables such as potato, carrots and turnip can be pre-cooked and folded into stew.

• Place the venison in a large earthenware casserole. Combine water, vinegar, bay leaf, sage, crushed juniper berries, allspice berries and garlic. Pour over venison and marinate overnight.

• Remove meat from marinade and pat dry. (Reserve marinade for later use.)

• In a heavy casserole, brown cubed pork to extract the fat. Brown the venison on all sides over a high heat.

• When meat is browned, add the reserved marinade. Cover and cook in a pre-heated 300° F (150° C) oven for 1½ hours. Add mushrooms and continue cooking for an additional hour until all is tender. Serves 4-6.

Indian Fry Bread

2 cups flour (500 ml)   1 tsp salt (5 ml)

3 tsp baking powder (15 ml)   ¾ cup milk or water (175 ml)

• Mix flour, baking powder, salt and milk or water together.

• Gather into a ball and knead until dough is elastic on a floured board.

• Divide into small balls. Pat with hands into circles. Punch hole in centre of each.

• Heat 4 tbsp (60 ml) of oil in a large skillet. Fry cakes 5 minutes on each side. Remove from skillet. Cool slightly.

• Serve fry bread to accompany meat dishes. Makes 12.

Cherry Cakes

Wild black cherries and chokecherries were a popular food. The cherries were cooked, combined with grain sweetened with honey or maple syrup, formed into small cakes. They were stored for winter use in a birch bark container.

Indian Corn Pudding

5 tbsp yellow cornmeal (75 ml)
1 cup milk (cold) (250 ml)
1½ cups hot milk (375 ml)

2 tbsp sugar or honey (30 ml)
1 egg (1)

- In a small saucepan, mix the Indian cornmeal and cold milk until well combined. Stir in the hot milk and sugar or honey.
- Cook over medium heat, stirring continuously until mixture thickens. Beat egg and add to pudding mixture.
- Pour mixture into a buttered 1-quart (1-L) casserole. Place casserole in a pan with 1 inch (2.5 cm) of hot water. Bake in a 325⁰ F (160⁰ C) oven for 40-45 minutes until mixture is firm and tester comes out clean.
- Remove from hot water bath and serve warm or cold. Serves 6.

> NOTE
> This is a more modern version of Indian Corn Pudding. It reflects new cooking techniques used.

Cranberry Tea

No specific quantities were given for this tea; however, I have taken the opportunity to improvise a recipe. YL

6 cups cranberries mashed (1.5 L)
8 cups boiling water (2 L)

¾ cup maple syrup (175 ml)

- Mash cranberries until they are a pulp. Pour boiling water over berries and simmer for 20 minutes, stirring occasionally.
- Remove from heat. Cool for one (1) hour and strain through a cheesecloth.
- Discard pulp. Place juice in a large container and sweeten with maple syrup.
- Use as a drink. Can be enjoyed hot or cold.

Hot Cherry Drink

The First Nations people were innovative and understood nature. This cherry drink was made with the bark of cherry and chokecherry trees, along with twigs tied in little bundles, dropped in boiling water and sweetened with maple sugar. This would have made a soothing drink for pleasure as well as for medicinal purposes.

Peter Rankin 2007

The Deserted Hilltop

Throughout the hills and valleys of Cape Breton, in large towns and isolated homesteads, stories of supernatural happenings have been shared at firesides for generations. Regardless of the ethnic origins of the people telling the scary stories and of those listening to accounts of ghosts and strange happenings as the here-and-now is suspended, all present are drawn into a mysterious world – at least for a time. The tales often sent small children to their beds with fear in their hearts. The following story comes from several sources. Its locale has been identified as being variously in the northern and the eastern, as well as the western corners of the island. But the events recounted here are as "true as I'm sitting here." The names of the members of the Dewilde Family are confirmed in census records. This tale is related here as though in the words of Alois Dewilde. Based on an oft-told tale, The Deserted Hilltop is for reading aloud.

The Deserted Hilltop

In my ninth year, we came to live on the hilltop farm in the spring of the year after the First World War ended. After struggling to earn a living for our family in the coal mines in Inverness and then in Sydney Mines, my father decided he could no longer work underground in the dark and damp. As recent immigrants from Belgium, we were grateful to have escaped the terrible destruction in our old village in Europe, but had yet to find a place in Cape Breton where we felt we belonged.

One day, our father, Mathieu Dewilde, a strong and cheerful man in those days, announced: "The Dewildes did not cross the ocean to live under it. We will go to live on a farm where we will be out in the air and free of bosses. I believe I have found us a place to live." Although it was a rundown property with a reputation as a hard-luck farm, we thought we had finally found a location in which to put down roots. After loading our clothes and other possessions in the back of our half-ton truck, we put the dirt of the coal town behind us and set off down the highway.

At the end of a road which climbed a steep hillside, the cleared land was surrounded by a forest of tall, dark trees on the slopes below, the farmhouse and barn in the middle of the field. Sagging fences stretched out in several directions. From every window in the house, there was a wide view out over the valley. In the distance, when the weather was clear, we could see the ocean out past the entrance to the mines.

"I think we can make a good home here," my father said to our mother. She seemed to agree and said we needed to do some planting first and then work on the house to make it more comfortable.

"We'll plant flowers in front just like at my grandfather's old cottage in Belgium." She spoke mostly in Flemish which we understood as well as we did English.

All five of us children were as eager as our parents to make a go of the place. Although we were all under ten years of age, we helped around the farm as much as we could. A few weeks after our arrival, we planted some potatoes and turnips and kale in a garden which a neighbour at the foot of the hill ploughed for us. Willingly helpful, he nevertheless shook his head in disbelief when my father assured him that we intended to live on the property which had been deserted for seven years.

With some money left from his years of working underground, our father bought several head of cattle and a few sheep. Using money saved from her sewing for neighbours when we lived in one of the row houses at the mines, our mother purchased several apple trees and a cherry tree, "for pies," she said with a laugh, as though there would be fruit right away. And she planted seeds in the soft ground right next to the house.

"Soon it will be just like in Belgium," she said with her usual hopeful outlook. All in all, we were making a new start.

Although the place was buffeted by strong winds almost daily and it had a somewhat eerie feeling to it when the rain clouds obscured the view, our first months there were very happy. The garden was growing and the chickens were laying eggs and the cows and sheep prospered as the new grass came up in the fields. We even laid out an area for playing ball in the flat space of the dooryard between the house and the barn.

At the end of the summer, our mother began to teach us at home, as it was six miles to the nearest school. Most of our instruction was in Flemish, but together we began to teach her some English. Often we laughed at her way of saying words such as tree and water and potato. But since we all wanted to learn how to read and write and do figures, we spent many hours together in a warm, bright corner of the kitchen.

Our parents remained in good cheer as they seemed glad to be away from the dirt and the unpleasantness of the mining towns. They helped us to make the best of our isolation in this new location. To be sure, we missed having children of our own age to play with, but we were busy in the garden and in the barn and in doing our lessons. A few people came to visit, most of them out of curiosity to see who would live on the old farm on the hilltop. But, by and large, we were quite solitary. As long as we had one another and things were going well, we didn't seem to mind.

One day in September, our neighbour at the foot of the hill came by to say that he could use my father's help in harvesting his oats and would pay him a small amount for each day's work and would also give us some of the hay crop for our cattle during the winter. As well, his wife had some need for our mother's skilled fingers in sewing clothes for their children. With this additional income and provisions, our father said, "We are going to have enough to see us through the winter. The Dewilde family will be all right."

That evening, he taught us some card tricks and told us funny stories about his younger years. We all laughed and laughed and enjoyed cookies before going to bed. As a final treat, in Flemish, he told us an old story about goblins at Halloween which he had heard from his grandfather when he was a child. Full of the delight of the evening, we quickly went to sleep.

Although September's winds were very blustery at times, there were also many days of sunlight and open skies. The leaves on the hardwood trees on the hillsides below the farmstead turned golden, then bronze and then fell to the ground. Bereft of the foliage, the maples and birches began to look very stark and quite dark. But we were all busy at our tasks in the section of the kitchen set aside as a classroom. At first, we didn't mind the gloomy skies and the way the trees were looking very foreboding without their green leaves, even when the frost finally came to the hilltop and nipped our mother's flowers which slowly turned black. Increasingly, we remained inside except when we went with father to the barn to help with the chores.

In early October, the weather changed abruptly. Early sleet swept across the field and rapped at the windows. Sometimes, it even awakened us in the night as though it wanted to come inside. The wind blew constantly, first from one direction and then from another. Leaves blown from the trees in the dooryard turned black on the ground. For long periods, clouds with dark brown edges, hung low over our farmstead and prevented our seeing the valley or the sea beyond.

After we dug the potatoes and turnips and pulled the onions and harvested the last of the kale, we spent almost no time playing ball in the yard. My sisters, Marie and Frances, spent many hours drawing pictures of sunny days and of little sheep in the fields. My brothers, Matt Jr. and Alphonse, and I were able to help our father in the barn and were learning from him the elements of shoe repair. His father had instructed him in the craft, many years before, back in Belgium.

As the days grew colder, we brought our school table and chairs closer to heat of the kitchen stove. Our mother prepared stews and special breads while she was listening to our lessons. At times, it seemed as though the strong gales wanted to blow right through our house. Indeed, it seemed as though some strong force wanted to push us over the edge of the hill, away from the flat field where our house and barn stood.

Although the events of the Halloween evening in our first (and only) autumn on the hilltop happened more than eighty years ago, they are never to be forgotten. Late in that day as twilight came, the blasts of the wind from the west shifted to the north. The setting sun began to go down behind the trees on the slopes in the distance, leaving behind a red sky and its rays tinged the black clouds with a strange hue. The colour of the sky was reflected in the mirror which hung on the wall over the kitchen sink. As a result, the whole room seemed to take on a dark red tone, reminiscent of dried blood – a very odd occurrence.

Our father went early to the barn to finish the evening chores in the cow stable and to bring the fresh milk across the yard to the house. Believing he would soon return, we all sat down at the kitchen table for a meal of Belgian pancakes and jam. As the redness of the sky darkened, the wind began to increase and seemed to come from all quarters of the sky at once. And then... then, a huge flock of great black birds flew into our yard and landed on the bare ground between the house and the barn where we had played ball. We had never seen anything like them previously. The five of us and our mother gathered at the kitchen windows and watched in astonishment as the birds screeched and filled the air with terrifying cries and began to dance around in a strange formation.

On flapping wings, they rose up into the air and then came back down, again and again. Each time they landed, they seemed to become larger and more frightening. And then... then, they slowly changed their shapes into those of strange creatures with hands and long noses, instead of claws and beaks. The feathers on their heads turned into scraggly strands of straw-colored hair.

Though the darkness increased, it was still permeated with a red tone from the final rays of the setting sun. In the gathering dusk, we watched as the figures danced around and around in a circle. Their voices still sounded like the cries of birds. In their claws, now like hands, branches which they had snatched from nearby trees, turned into brooms with which they seemed to sweep the earth.

In the wind, we thought we could hear a tune played on a distant fiddle whose strings were so badly tightened that the sound was discordant. Louder and louder was the noise. Our mother, generally so calm and cheerful, began to scream and scream. She called and called for our father to come from the barn. Then, in a panic, she forced us to leave the windows and to go with her down into the cellar through a trapdoor set in the middle of the kitchen floor.

There in the darkness, we huddled together as our mother tried to allay our distress despite her own. Above us, the wind continued to batter the house. The cackling of the birds, or whatever they were, echoed in every corner of the dark, dank cellar. Again and again, one after another, each of us called to our father, but there was no response. We had no idea what had happened to him. The night was full of eerie, disturbing sounds.

Near dawn, the night became still. No wind; no calls of birds; no discordant sound of a distant fiddle. As the silence continued, we followed our mother back up to the kitchen and looked out into the yard. We could see no sign of the birds or whatever those frightening figures had been. In the light of the early morning, all that we saw was our father sitting on the stump of a tree outside the cow stable. His hair, once brown, had turned white over night. His face was the colour of wood ash, a look of total exhaustion across his whole body.

Slowly, he rose and came to the house. As he came through the door, he said to our mother, "We are leaving here now." And that morning, we left the hilltop with our few possessions placed in the back of our pickup truck and our animals herded ahead of us down the steep road. Our father never returned to the place he had felt was so full of promise and he refused to tell us what he had seen or heard. We took up residence at another old farm some miles away, but the joy of life was gone from our father's face and his walk. He never regained his former good cheer nor did he ever again tell us jokes or show us card tricks.

Through the years, others have gone to the hilltop, if only for brief visits. But I would advise the curious to stay away, particularly on Halloween. With horror, I remember the events we witnessed at the farmstead those many years ago when I was but a boy of nine.

Belgian Cuisine

MENU

Soupe à l'Oignon

Terrine de Campagne

Mushroom Hash with Eggs

Thick Belgian Waffles
With Wild Berry Sauce

Liver and Onions

Jardinière de Légumes

Potato Pancakes
(Galettes de pomme de terre)

Mousse au Chocolat

Clafoutis
(Cherry Pudding)

Soupe à l'Oignon

4 tbsp butter (60 ml)

1½ lbs onion thinly sliced (675 g)

2 tsp sugar (10 ml)

1 tbsp flour (15 ml)

6 cups beef stock (1.5 L)

½ tsp salt (2 ml)

1 tsp pepper (5 ml)

Thick slices of bread

4 tbsp grated Swiss cheese (60 ml)

• Melt butter in a large saucepan and add onion and sugar. Over a low-medium heat cook the onion very slowly for 20-30 minutes until golden brown, stirring occasionally. Do not burn.

• Stir the flour into the onion mixture and cook over a low heat for 5 minutes, stirring well to prevent burning or sticking to bottom of pan.

• Add the beef stock, salt and pepper. Bring to a boil. Reduce heat and simmer 15-20 minutes. Taste soup and adjust seasoning if necessary.

• Toast slices of bread lightly on both sides. Sprinkle with grated cheese.

• Place a piece of toast in each serving bowl and ladle the hot soup over the top. Serves 6.

> **NOTE**
> Bowls of soup can be placed in a hot oven or under broiler to melt the cheese.

Terrine de Campagne

2 lbs fresh pork shoulder, ground (900 g)

1 lb veal, ground (450 g)

1 lb chicken, ground (450 g)

2 onions chopped finely (2)

4 tbsp brandy (60 ml)

3 eggs (3)

2 tsp salt (10 ml)

1 tsp pepper (5 ml)

2 tsp dried thyme (10 ml)

4 tbsp chopped parsley (60 ml)

• Put ground meats in a large bowl. Add chopped onion, salt and pepper.

• Combine brandy and eggs. Work into meat mixture with herbs. Using a wooded spoon, work mixture until it is smooth.

• Butter a large terrine or two heavy loaf pans. Fill with mixture. Pat down and cover securely.

• Place terrine or pans in a pan of hot water. Place in a 325⁰ F (160⁰ C) oven and cook for 1½-2 hours or until firm to the touch.

• Remove from oven. Cool partially and turn out. Cool completely and allow to set before serving.

• To serve, cut in slices and serve with pickles and mustard.

Peter Rankin 2007

Mushroom Hash with Eggs

6 slices bacon diced (6)

3 tbsp butter (45 ml)

1 tbsp olive oil (15 ml)

1 lb mushrooms sliced (450 g)

2 medium onion chopped (2)

2 cloves garlic minced (2)

2 large potatoes peeled and diced (2)

1 tsp salt (5 ml)

½ tsp pepper (2 ml)

1 tsp summer savory (5 ml)

6 eggs (6)

Salt and pepper

½ cup cheddar cheese (125 ml)

- Cook chopped bacon in a large skillet until crisp. Remove bacon from skillet and set aside. Discard fat.
- Heat butter and oil in skillet. When hot, add mushrooms and cook until mushrooms are golden and liquid is evaporated. Remove mushrooms from skillet and set aside.
- Place onion, garlic and potatoes in hot skillet (add oil if necessary). Sauté until potatoes are barely tender.
- Combine bacon, mushroom and potato, and arrange in a 2-quart (2-L) casserole.
- Break eggs over hash. Sprinkle with salt, pepper, summer savory and cheese.
- Place casserole in a 350⁰ F (180⁰ C) oven and bake until eggs are firm and cheese is bubbly, approximately 20 minutes.
- Remove from oven and serve with sliced tomatoes. Serves 6.

Thick Belgian Waffles

1¾ cups all-purpose flour (425 ml)

1 tbsp baking powder (15 ml)

½ tsp salt (2 ml)

1 tbsp granulated sugar (15 ml)

3 large eggs (3)

¾ cup melted butter (175 ml)

1½ cups milk (375 ml)

- In a medium bowl, measure flour, baking powder, salt and sugar.
- In a separate bowl, whisk eggs. Add melted butter and milk, and whisk to combine.
- Make a well in centre of dry ingredients and pour in the liquid ingredients. Gently whisk together until combined, and mixture has a bubbly texture.
- Spoon a ½ cup (125 ml) of batter (or amount recommended by manufacturer) onto the waffle iron. Spread batter to ¼-inch (5-mm) of the edge of grid.
- Close the lid and bake until waffle is golden brown. Serve immediately or keep warm in a single rack on baking sheet in 200⁰ F (100⁰ C) oven. Makes twelve (12) 6-inch (15-cm) waffles.

Wild Berry Sauce

1 cup blackberries (250 ml)

2 cups blueberries (500 ml)   1¼ cups granulated sugar (310 ml)

1 cup water (250 ml)   1 tsp lemon zest (5 ml)

• In a medium saucepan, combine berries and water. Simmer for 20 minutes until berries are soft. Add sugar and lemon zest. Continue cooking until slightly thickened, 15 minutes.

• Remove from heat. Cool. Serve chilled with Belgian Waffles.

Liver and Onions

4 large slices calves liver (4)   2 onions sliced (2)

Salt and pepper   1 tsp vinegar (5 ml)

3 tbsp flour to coat (45 ml)   ¼ cup white wine or water (60 ml)

3 tbsp butter (45 ml)   2 tbsp cream (30 ml)

1 tbsp olive oil (15 ml)

• Season the slices of liver with salt and pepper, and dredge in flour to cover completely.

• Heat butter and oil in a large skillet. Add sliced onion and cook to soften. Remove from skillet and keep onions warm in a casserole.

• Place liver in skillet over a medium-high heat to seal. Turn liver halfway through cooking (the middle should be pink).

• Remove liver from skillet and keep warm. Add vinegar, wine or water to juices in skillet. Bring to a boil, scraping the base. Return onions to pan. Add cream and simmer one (1) minute

• Remove from heat. Pour sauce over liver and serve. Serves 4.

Peter Rankin 2007

Jardinière de Légumes

2 sweet potatoes sliced (2)
1 lb carrots cut julienne (450 g)
1 medium turnip cut julienne (1)
4 large parsnips sliced (4)
1 lb green beans (450 g)
2 onions sliced (2)

4 tbsp butter (60 ml)
1½ cups chicken stock (375 ml)
1 tsp salt (5 ml)
1 tsp black pepper (5 ml)
2 tsp summer savory (10 ml)
whipping cream (optional)

- In a large saucepan, melt butter. Sauté vegetables, tossing occasionally for 10 minutes. Add stock, salt, pepper and summer savory. Toss vegetables.
- Cover saucepan. Reduce heat and cook until vegetables are tender.
- Add cream, if using. Stir gently. Taste, adjust seasoning and serve. Serves 6-8.

Potato Pancakes
(Galettes de pomme de terre)

2 lbs potatoes (900 g)
3 eggs (3)
1 large onion finely chopped (1)
1 tbsp flour (15 ml)
1 tbsp chopped chives or parsley (15 ml)

½ tsp salt (2 ml)
½ tsp pepper (2 ml)
¼ tsp grated nutmeg (1 ml)
6 tbsp cooking fat or oil (90 ml)

- Peel potatoes. Grate them coarsely with a grater. Put grated potato in a strainer. Rinse well under running cold water. Drain and sponge dry. Transfer to a bowl.
- Break the eggs into bowl of grated potato. Mix well together. Add chopped onion, flour, chives or parsley, salt, pepper and nutmeg. Stir the mixture thoroughly.
- Divide potato mixture into equal-sized portions and shape them into small cakes, using spoon to shape them.
- Heat fat or oil in a large skillet. Add potato cakes and fry until golden brown on both sides, turning once during cooking.
- Serve very hot to accompany a meat or salad dish. Serves 4.

Mousse au Chocolat

4 oz bittersweet chocolate (115 g)	2 egg whites (2)
5 tbsp butter room temperature (75 ml)	¼ tsp salt (1 ml)
3 whole eggs (3)	2 tbsp granulated sugar (30 ml)

- Chop chocolate and place in a small bowl. Place bowl over a saucepan of hot water (not boiling) without stirring for several minutes until melted.
- Remove chocolate from heat. Blend the butter into the hot chocolate using a wooded spoon. Cool slightly.
- Separate the 3 eggs. Add yolks one at a time to chocolate.
- Combine 5 egg whites and beat with salt until soft. Add the sugar, continuing to beat until stiff peaks form (egg whites will be shiny).
- Spoon a small quantity of egg whites into chocolate. Mix in using a spatula.
- Add remaining whites in two additions, working quickly as you fold whites into chocolate.
- Pour into a serving bowl and chill for several hours. Serves 4.

Clafoutis
(Cherry Pudding)

3 cups fresh cherries (750 ml)	Batter
1 tbsp lemon juice (15 ml)	¼ cup all-purpose flour (60 ml)
2 tbsp granulated sugar (30 ml)	3 tbsp granulated sugar (45 ml)
	¾ cup milk (176 ml)
	2 eggs (2)
	2 tsp lemon zest (10 ml)

- Combine cherries with lemon juice and sugar. Spread in a buttered 1½-quart (1.5 L) baking dish. Set aside.
- In a bowl, measure flour and sugar. Slowly whisk in the milk until blended. Add eggs and lemon zest. Whisk until combined and smooth.
- Pour batter over cherries. Bake in a 375⁰ F (190⁰ C) oven for 45 minutes or until set and puffed around the edges. Tester inserted in centre should come out clean.
- Serve warm or at room temperature with pouring cream. Serves 4-6.

NOTE
Clafoutis can be prepared using other firm fruit such as apricots, gooseberries and blackberries.

Peter Rankin 2007

Picnic with Healthy Hilda
A Reminiscence in the First Person

"Down-East Days" are those days in the late spring and the summer when the humidity is low, the temperature moderate and the breeze gentle but steady. Large cumulus clouds move across the sky and as they pass between the sun and the earth, shadows are created on hillsides – children love to try to keep up with the patterns as they pass over fields and beaches. With clear air, it seems as though we can see forever over hills and valleys to other hills. Those are glorious days for picnics in high places where people can feel close to the sky and the sun and the earth. Hilda MacDonald was a person who treasured those special days. Let us find one of those mornings and go with Hilda and others to the top of Cape Mabou in happy recollection of a Down-East Day.

Picnic with Healthy Hilda
A Reminiscence in the First Person

"Come, let us go on a picnic. I haven't been to Cape Mabou in years." With those words on a fine August morning in 1958, Miss Hilda MacDonald began to organize an outing to the top of the ridge of nearby hills known as Cape Mabou. "We used to go blueberry picking there when I was a girl," she added. "Perhaps, we'll find some ripe berries."

We knew that although all of the families had left their farms, and the place was bereft of human residents, many fields were still open and acres of wild berries offered their fruit to the sky and the birds – and humans. "I don't think anybody will care how many berries we pick for our personal use," added Hilda.

"Let's go in the morning tomorrow so we can have lots of time for looking around. You'll bring your car and I'll ask Lena MacKay to go with us." Lena had grown up on a farm on Cape Mabou and knew the names of the people who used to live on each property. I knew her as a jolly person, full of fun and ready for adventure; she could also be counted on to bring delicious baking from her own kitchen.

In answer to Hilda's question about who might go with us, I mentioned that my cousin Bob was visiting while on a vacation and was a cheerful person who loved to go to new places, particularly if they were off the beaten path.

"Perfect," replied Hilda, "and let's ask my cousin Grace who is at her own house here in the glen while she is taking time off from her job in Boston." And then she added, "She is a little timid, but good company, nevertheless."

My Ford station wagon was new that year and had lots of room for people and for picnic baskets and whatever else was needed.

"I'll bring a big supply of nutritious picnic fare, and let everybody else bring whatever they like," Hilda announced as we established the time for setting forth. Although I knew that we all hoped she would have fried chicken and ham in her picnic basket, I was quite sure she would bring something she deemed more healthy. Others, however, might bring food that Hilda would not recommend as appropriately nutritious.

It needs to be said that there is more behind the phrase "nutritious food" than is immediately evident. Hilda was "Miss Hilda MacDonald" to most people. A retired teacher, she was also known as "Healthy Hilda" by her former students at Teachers College in Truro, where she taught biology, nutrition and public health to generations of teachers-in-training. Now age 75, she was still very agile and much given to walking and to "good food, properly prepared and served." She often added, "Nutrition includes the food, the cooking, the dishes and the company."

She gained the nickname "Healthy Hilda" for her constant teaching to her students that they needed to have food from the major food groups each day. She was also firm in directing that they should not overcook vegetables and eat as much salad and fruit as possible. She seemed to be a living example of the benefits of careful diet for she was trim, agile and full of energy.

Several of her students whom I had met said that they were also told by her never to take strong tea and to learn to say, "No thank you" when offered beer or alcoholic beverages or desserts made with too much sugar and processed flour. It was also rumoured on campus that she avoided anything other than polite conversation with people of the opposite sex. So stories about Healthy Hilda and her diet and personal habits were numerous. In her presence, however, her students and most other people were always polite and attentive.

After a career of nursing and public health teaching, she came back to our area in her retirement where she had maintained a family home for many years. She came each year for a month or so, but was now in residence almost all year long. Her cottage was well maintained and surrounded by beautiful flowers and some fruit trees. With very few close relatives in the district, and with a somewhat reserved attitude, she was always addressed as Miss Hilda by her neighbours. People were amused by her maintaining a very strict schedule of meal times and rising and sleeping and by her never taking snacks between meals. "No tea and cookies for me; just water, please," she would say when she went to call on friends and neighbours. She offered visitors to her veranda warm, weak tea and thin slices of fruit.

While Hilda was in her seventies and Lena in her mid-fifties, the rest of us were in our late twenties. There was quite an age difference among us as we set forth the next morning for Cape Mabou, but we felt no barriers and shared jokes with one another. It was a beautiful summer day to go in search of a good picnic site and blueberries. We were all interested in going to the top of the high range of hills with its extensive fields, its once productive land and its great views out to the ocean and to other distant places. Miss Hilda was a lively conversationalist who always wanted to search out our opinions about things that mattered in the world. She assiduously avoided gossip of any sort, but kept up a lively discourse with whomever she met.

While my cousin Bob thought that cold beer was a proper part of any picnic and I thought the same of a bottle of good wine, we realized that we would not be able to bring along any of our favourite beverages. Instead, we brought iced tea – one container had strong tea while the other held a weaker brew, Miss Hilda's style.

Lena MacKay was noted for her very fine homemade white bread and her very tasty, but very sweet chocolate brownies and butterscotch squares. In many circles, she was viewed as an excellent cook, but not in Healthy Hilda's opinion. "I think Lena uses too much refined white flour and much too much sugar and butter in her cooking." Although Lena respected Miss Hilda's view, she did decide to put a supply of her good sugar cookies and squares in her lunch box. As well, she also brought a white linen tablecloth and napkins and other useful items.

Grace had a basket filled with oranges as well as with plums from the tree in her family's farmyard. We all wondered what Hilda had tucked away in her large picnic hamper and hoped there would some of her famous oatmeal bread – "made with honey and very little salt," she would often report. Clearly, though, she wanted to surprise us for she made no reference to the contents of her large wicker basket.

At the appointed time, we all gathered at Miss Hilda's house in the glen, for we knew of her insistence on punctuality. After joyful greetings, we prepared to set out on our adventure. The day was warm with a light breeze and big fluffy clouds – a "Down-East Day," we all agreed. The humidity was so low that it seemed you could see almost forever. With all the baskets stowed in the back, we set off singing the only Gaelic song we all knew – "*Ho ro mo nighean bhoideach*" and we sang it again and again. Then, Miss Hilda told us about a trip she had made through the Grand Canyon many years earlier, in 1904, when she was only nineteen years old. Strange to say, she had met a neighbour from Cape Breton there. She was riding on a mule in company with other people in her party when she came across Angus MacQuarrie who was helping to build a wider road in that area as an entry way to a proposed National Park. "And I haven't seen Angus since that day – more than fifty years ago. I was surprised to come across him so far from home. I nearly fell off my mule when he recognized me and spoke to me in Gaelic." And then she added a little sadly, "I wonder if we would know one another now. He is a bit older than me, but still quite well, I believe."

"Turn up this road and watch out for sharp turns," Lena advised. The words were barely out of her mouth when the road became steep and narrow; on a sharp right angle bend, we met a lumber truck coming down with a load of logs piled high. Quick twists on the steering wheel and a move to the very edge of the road where there were no guard rails and some fancy manoeuvring by the truck driver prevented a collision. We were all quite jostled about – there were no seat belts in those days. But no damage was done to our vehicle or our lunch baskets.

"Sharp turns always bring surprises," said Lena, "but they don't have to be so frightening. I was quite scared, but the driver is Roddie Allan's son, as good at the steering in a truck as on the dance floor." We all agreed that we would hope to meet him the next time at a square dance and not a quick turn in a steep road.

Miss Hilda, however, was laughing and laughing – her wig, which everybody knew about but nobody ever mentioned, had slipped down as the car veered sharply. She announced, "People would think I had been drinking if they saw me now." Her remark was so out of character in describing a scene which we couldn't imagine that we all joined in her mirth. And she proceeded to straighten the hairpiece again.

The truck moved on down the road, but we paused for a few minutes at the edge of the road and looked into the ravine below.

"Not quite the Grand Canyon, I expect," said Grace, "but too far down for me." She moved to the other side of the back seat as she was quite frightened of heights. "I didn't realize how steep this road is. But I'll be all right when we reach the top." And we began to sing "On Top of Old Smokey" as we found our way around curves in the road, and were quite enjoying one another as we made up verses about the steep road to Cape Mabou.

Without further misadventure, we arrived at the flat plateau where the community of Cape Mabou had once been. As we drove along for several miles, Lena told us, "Archie MacKay lived over there, a relative of my father." And, as we went past a little grove of poplar trees, she announced, "There is where Cape Mabou College was; that is what we used to call our one-room school house. I went through grade five here. We had a fine teacher. Her name was Maggie Angus Rory the Turner. She lived with her parents in a lovely big house right over there near those tall trees. All gone now." And then we came to the place where Lena lived as a child. She promised us that there would be lots of berries there so we turned in and drove right to the middle of a big field. "We grew lots of hay and oats here," reminisced Lena. "But the soil is sour now and fit only for wild berries. Such a change."

While some of us took the picnic baskets out of the back of the station wagon, Bob went off in the direction where Lena told him there was a fine spring of fresh water in a little gully. He came back to us with his face all washed and his hair combed and several small stones which he thought contained flecks of gold in them. He had found them where the fresh water gushed out of the ground. Lena quickly said with a laugh, "If we had known there was gold on this property we would never have sold it and moved away." We all laughed. She added with a bit of sadness in her voice, "My father prospected for gold in Alaska when he was young, but without any success." Miss Hilda wanted to know more about what Bob saw in the rocks and questioned him about the geology of the Cape. "Lots of rocks in the field when my father ploughed it," Lena stated. "We never thought there might gold in 'these here hills', or anything worth studying. Guess we were wrong."

As we took the various containers of food from the picnic baskets, Bob described a little bit about the geological structure of the ridge and the role of glaciers in this region, much to Miss Hilda's satisfaction. Rejoicing in the fresh air and then seeing all the food set out, we all realized at once that we were hungry. "Time for lunch!" I announced.

"Where's the dinner bell?" Hilda struck the side of a metal dish with a spoon and said, "Let's have the picnic right now!" And the spoon clanged against the dish – CLANG! CLANG! CLANG!

Grace spread out Lena's white linen cloth on the grass. Miss Hilda brought out tall crystal glasses for the iced tea. Linen napkins were distributed and crockery plates put on the cloth – all a great deal more elegant than most of us were used to when we went on picnics. But Healthy Hilda believed in a certain style. From her big hamper, she brought forth several varieties of fruit, all carefully washed and lettuce and carrots from her own garden. Her fine dark bread was thinly cut. She commented favourably on Lena's white bread biscuits, but I noted she didn't taste them.

Celery with cream cheese and tiny cherry tomatoes were passed around. But Healthy Hilda's outstanding contribution was a potato salad made with oil and chunks of local salmon which she had cooked in the morning. On the top was a garnish of devilled eggs and parsley. In a small jar enclosed in a much larger crock packed with ice, was her own salad dressing.

"The ice prevents any spoilage as it has some cream in it," she carefully mentioned, as though she were speaking to a class of students. Alas, there was no fried chicken or ham – neither of them in high regard in Miss Hilda's list of healthy foods.

We feasted, enjoying every bit of the food; the beautiful day, the clean air, the elegant setting all contributed to our satisfaction. With lots of conversation about life on Cape Mabou in years gone by, we talked all through the meal. The iced tea in tall glasses was refreshing and particularly tasty, garnished with fresh mint Bob found near the spring. For dessert, we had plums from Grace's tree and other fruit as well. And then we enjoyed a square or two and several sugar cookies. Even Miss Hilda took one. "But don't tell anybody how much I liked it," she noted wryly.

"A good feast," pronounced Miss Hilda. "They don't call me 'Healthy Hilda' for nothing, you know." We all laughed with her, for we were not aware that she even knew of the label. Her constant good cheer was a delight as we sat together at our picnic outing on Cape Mabou.

"And now we can get our exercise by searching out the blueberries. There seem to be many all around us, and quite ripe too," Grace observed. We filled containers with them as we went back and forth across the field.

"Eat them right now" suggested Miss Hilda, "or wait until you reach home. Don't wash them now; they'll keep their freshness longer and taste better. And don't put the covers on tightly. Let the berries have the fresh air. Just like us, they'll be much fresher in this fine Cape Mabou air." With the blueness around our mouths showing how much we enjoyed the tasting, we also put many cupfuls in several large containers for enjoyment later and as a reminder of our picnic.

As the puffy afternoon clouds moved across the blue sky and made shadows on the former hayfield as they passed in front of the sun, we sat together as Miss Hilda told us more of her journey to the Grand Canyon and of her adventures as a nurse during the First World War. We tasted a few more berries and finished the iced tea, still garnished with the fresh mint.

"I didn't even miss my usual bottle of beer," mused Bob, as he lay back on the grass. Miss Hilda laughed and said, "A little bit now and then is all right, but just remember the brain cells you damage with alcohol." Although retired for many years, she was still the teacher.

With some reluctance, we realized it was time to go home. But before we left, we watched with delight as several white-tailed deer passed leisurely across the field. Going back down the steep road, we sang a song which we made up about a picnic with every food group present and even included a line about wigs that slipped. We called our ditty " HH's Picnic on Cape Mabou." With some reluctance, but with good memories, we said so long to one another and promised to go again.

It seems like yesterday as I think of the delicious food and the pleasant company and beautiful location as we went with Healthy Hilda that day at Cape Mabou. An ordinary event really, but an extraordinary memory.

A Healthy Hilda Picnic

MENU

Assorted Raw Vegetable Platter
Celery, Cherry Tomatoes with Cream Cheese

Potato and Fresh Salmon Salad
with Creamy Vinaigrette Dressing

Devilled Eggs

Hilda's Oatmeal Honey Bread

Lena's Baking Powder Biscuits

Butterscotch Squares
Chocolate Brownies
Brown Sugar Cookies

Hilda's Fruit Basket
Oranges, Plums, Wild Blueberries

Iced Tea with Wild Mint

Potato and Poached Salmon Salad

4 cups cooked potatoes cubed (1 L)
3 green onions chopped (3)
½ cup chopped celery (125 ml)
1 cup cooked garden peas (250 ml)
1 lb poached salmon (450 g)
1 tsp salt (5 ml)
1 tsp pepper (5 ml)

Salad Dressing
1 tsp dry mustard (5 ml)
½ tsp salt (2 ml)
3 tsp sugar (15 ml)
3 egg yolks slightly beaten (3)
¼ cup vinegar (60 ml)
2 tbsp olive oil (30 ml)
¾ cup cream (175 ml)
½ tsp black pepper (2 ml)

- In a medium bowl, toss together diced potatoes, onions, celery, cooked peas, salt and pepper.
- Remove skin and bones from salmon. Break into large pieces and arrange over potato mixture. Set aside.
- To prepare dressing: In a small saucepan, mix together mustard, salt and sugar. Add egg yolks, vinegar, olive oil, cream and pepper.
- Place saucepan over a basin of hot water. Stir and cook over boiling water until mixture begins to thicken. Cool completely.
- When serving, pour dressing over salad and toss carefully with a fork. Serves 6.

Devilled Eggs

6 hard-cooked eggs peeled (6)
3 tbsp mayonnaise (45 ml)
1½ tsp wet mustard (7 ml)

½ tsp salt (2 ml)
Few grains cayenne
Paprika for sprinkling

- Peel eggs and cut in half lengthwise. Remove yolk and arrange whites on a platter.
- Using a fork, mash yolks until smooth. Add mayonnaise, mustard, salt and cayenne. Mix well.
- Using a pastry bag with a large tip or spoon, fill shells. If using spoon, shape the filling with back of spoon. Sprinkle with paprika. 12 devilled egg halves.

Hilda's Oatmeal Honey Bread

2 cups boiling water (500 ml)

1 cup regular rolled oats (250 ml)

½ cup liquid honey (125 ml)

2 tsp salt (10 ml)

2 tbsp butter (30 ml)

2 tbsp regular dried yeast (30 ml)

1 tsp sugar (5 ml)

½ cup lukewarm water (125 ml)

5 cups all-purpose flour (1.25 L)

- Place rolled oats in a large bowl. Pour boiling water over oats and let stand for 30 minutes, stirring occasionally to cool ingredients.
- Meanwhile, place lukewarm water in a small bowl. Sprinkle in sugar and yeast. Whisk lightly to dissolve. Allow to rest in a warm place until frothy.
- To rolled oats mixture, add honey, salt, butter and yeast. Add flour and beat thoroughly. (Dough should be firm but soft. Beat in more flour if necessary.)
- Remove from bowl and knead for 3 minutes on a well-floured surface. Return to bowl and let rise until double in bulk in a warm place, approximately one (1) hour.
- Divide dough in two pieces. Shape into two loaves and place in well greased pans. Allow to rise again until double in bulk.
- Place loaves in a preheated 375^0 (190^0 C) oven. Bake 60 minutes until bread shrinks from side of pan and sounds hollow when tapped.
- Remove from oven. Turn out on cooling rack.

Lena's Baking Powder Biscuits

2 cups all-purpose flour (500 ml)

4 tsp baking powder (20 ml)

1 tsp salt (5 ml)

4 tbsp shortening or butter (60 ml)

¾ cup milk (175 ml)

Milk for brushing

- In a medium bowl mix flour, baking powder and salt. Work shortening into flour with pastry blender or fingertips until coarse and crumbly.
- Quickly stir in the milk, tossing with a fork. Dough should be soft. Turn dough out on a lightly floured bowl. Knead a few strokes until smooth.
- Roll to ¾-inch (2-cm) thick. Cut with biscuit cutter. Place on ungreased baking sheet. Brush biscuits with milk.
- Bake in a preheated 415^0 F (210^0 C) oven for 12-15 minutes until golden. Makes 12-15.

Butterscotch Squares

½ cup butter (125 ml)

1 cup brown sugar packed (250 ml)

1 egg (1)

1 tsp vanilla (5 ml)

1 cup all-purpose flour (250 ml)

1 tsp baking powder (5 ml)

¼ tsp salt (1 ml)

1 cup chopped walnuts (250 ml)

- Melt butter in a medium saucepan. Add sugar to melted butter and mix well. Add egg and vanilla, and stir to combine.
- Add flour, baking powder, salt and nuts to creamed mixture. Mix well.
- Pour into a lightly greased 8 x 8-inch (20 x 20-cm) pan. Bake in a 350⁰ F (180⁰ C) oven for 30 minutes until tester comes out clean. Remove from oven and cool. Sprinkle with icing sugar and cut in 25 pieces.

Chocolate Brownies

½ cup butter (125 ml)

¼ cup cocoa (sifted) (60 ml)

2 eggs (2)

1 cup granulated sugar (250 ml)

¾ cup all-purpose flour (175 ml)

¾ cup chopped walnuts (175 ml)

¼ tsp salt (1 ml)

- In a medium saucepan, melt the butter and add the cocoa, stirring well. Remove from heat. Set aside.
- In a medium bowl whisk egg until frothy. Add sugar, flour, nuts and salt. Pour cocoa mixture over all and stir to combine.
- Pour batter into a greased 8 x 8-inch (20 x 20-cm) pan. Bake in 350⁰ F (180⁰ C) oven about 30 minutes until edges begin to show signs of pulling away from sides of pan. Remove from oven. Cool and frost.

Cocoa Coffee Icing

4 tbsp butter (60 ml)

2 cups icing sugar (500 ml)

4 tbsp cocoa (60 ml)

2 tbsp warm coffee (approximately)

- Combine all ingredients in a bowl and beat until glossy, adding more coffee if necessary.
- Spread on brownies. Allow to settle before cutting in 25 squares.

Brown Sugar Cookies

1 cup butter, room temperature (250 ml)

1 cup brown sugar (250 ml)

¼ cup granulated sugar (60 ml)

1 egg (1)

1½ tsp vanilla (7 ml)

2 cups all-purpose flour (500 ml)

1 tsp cream of tartar (5 ml)

1 tsp baking soda (5 ml)

¼ tsp salt (1 ml)

- In a bowl, cream butter until light and fluffy. Add sugars and continue creaming for 4 minutes. Beat in the egg and vanilla.
- Measure flour, cream of tartar, soda and salt. Add to creamed mixture. Mix well.
- Shape dough into 1-inch (2.5-cm) balls. Arrange on ungreased baking sheet. Press with a fork to flatten.
- Bake in 350⁰ F (180⁰ C) oven for 8-10 minutes until golden. Remove from oven and transfer cookies to cooling rack. Makes 5 dozen.

Iced Tea with Wild Mint

8 cups strong hot tea (2 L)

2 tbsp granulated sugar (30 ml)

8 cups ice cubes (2 L)

8 lemon slices (8)

Sprigs fresh mint

- Place hot tea in a large bowl. Add sugar and stir to dissolve. Add ice cubes and lemon slices. Allow tea to sit until very cold.
- To serve: Place a few ice cubes in tall glasses. Add iced tea and one lemon slice. Garnish with sprigs of fresh mint. Serves 8-10.

Peter Rankin 2007

Pentecost - Spirit - Flame - Manna
Feeding the Five Thousand

*I*n its oral or recorded history, each community has individuals who alone or in groups have participated in happenings which were seminal in helping to define that location. In Cape Breton, few communities have seen so many people come together and participate in such an emotionally moving event as the outdoor communion in Whycocomagh in 1853. More than five thousand people were so deeply affected that for generations they spoke to one another of the living presence of the Holy Spirit, as Rev. Peter MacLean spoke and prayed and distributed the elements of communion on a hillside.

For three hundred years, Scottish Presbyterians, in Scotland, mostly Gaelic-speaking, had held these worship services out of doors, first in secret as they were persecuted by the established church, and then in remembrance of those who dared to be different, to think in new ways, to be nonconformists. In Cape Breton, with generations of the practice behind them, worshippers congregated at sites such as what is now the Stewartdale Cemetery to hear the Word, sing the psalms and engage in theological discussions in the Celtic tongue. While the sacrament was the emotional high point of this communion, known in Gaelic as the Sàcramaid, only those finally deemed worthy by elders, and by themselves, were issued a communion token which permitted them to receive the bread and wine. Few of these tokens survive. Those that do are treasured by families or museums or congregations. Such "Tokens of Grace" are used as the title of a recent book on the outdoor communions by Dr. Laurie Stanley-Blackwell.

Now, one hundred and fifty years later, the folk memory is fading, but the place is still holy to many and it is said that the lives of people of the current generations are different due to the insights their ancestors gained on that day. We may go to the site today and ponder what the events meant. For some, it may be helpful to read about the experience of the early Christians in the Book of Acts on a day called "The First Pentecost" when people "spoke in tongues" and saw small flames appear on the heads of those present.

Pentecost - Spirit - Flame - Manna
Feeding the Five Thousand

Aig gach ni tha trath.... For everything there is a season.... (Eccl. 3.1)

*S*tand today on a quiet hillside in Stewartdale, outside Whycocomagh, Cape Breton. A cemetery site for more than one hundred and seventy years, it was once the location of the MacLean Church, built as a place for Presbyterians to assemble in worship and named for an early minister, Rev. Peter MacLean. It was a United Church of Canada sanctuary when it burned fifty years ago.

Read the names on the tombstones. MacDonalds and Campbells, MacQueens and MacKinnons, MacLeans and Morrisons, MacFarlanes and Rosses – and so many more, many of them born on the Isles of North Uist, or Skye or Tiree or Mull in the early 1800s. If those alive in 1853 could speak today, what a tale they would tell of the remarkable event in October that year! Listen... perhaps we can still hear the story from long ago. Then, as now, the wind blows freely across the slope down from the mountains above. The view to Whycocomagh Bay is expansive. The blueberry bushes still grow and the mayflowers bloom in their time. "For everything there is a season" indeed. The voices of the participants in the events on this site will tell us much.... Hear their story.

For the sharing of news, there is a season....

On a Sunday morning in the summer of 1853, members of the Presbyterian Congregation of Whycocomagh and area had met as usual for more than two hours of preaching and prayer in Gaelic, singing the Psalms in that favoured Celtic language without musical accompaniment, giving careful attention to teachings recited so persuasively from Holy Writ. In the small frame church standing where roads from Campbell's Mountain, Skye Glen, Whycocomagh Village and Mabou met, the three hundred and fifty congregants heard the announcement of great good news. Their revered former minister, Rev. Peter MacLean, "Mr. Parag" as he was known far and wide, would return in the autumn after being in Scotland for six years. His letter had just arrived from overseas after weeks on board a sailing ship. He wished to be the preacher at the outdoor communion service to be held here on the outskirts of Whycocomagh in October. Hearing of his plan, all present rejoiced.

Known for his powerful oratory in Gaelic, his intense dedication to his people and his persuasive sharing of "the Word of God," MacLean would draw people from all around Cape Breton Island. Hundreds and hundreds would wish to be present at this five-day long event. In keeping with long-standing tradition, the preaching and teaching and receiving of the Sacrament of the Lord's Supper would take place on the hillside above the church. The Presbyterians here, as well as those in Scotland and parts of the United States, shared in the Lord's Supper just once a year as a climactic conclusion to several days of spiritual preparation.

After the welcome announcement, the service was concluded with a persuasive benediction. Before people went out into the noontime sun, the Clerk of the Session of the congregation, John MacQueen stood in his place and requested the people to remain for a few minutes so that some planning might begin. Although people wished to go to their own homes or those of relatives for dinner before returning for the obligatory afternoon service, they all knew that many visitors, relatives and friends and strangers, would arrive for the time of Sacrament and to hear Mr. Parag. John MacQueen reminded the parishoners, "We need to plan for at least two thousand faithful souls. Tents can be set up outside the church; benches can be made from rough lumber around the edge of the hill; the communion table will have to be taken to the top of the hill and the booth where the ministers will stand to preach will need to be repaired. We will need to order communion tokens." There was much to think about and to do.

As they left the sanctuary, the men and women of the congregation began to plan how to provide food for the meals during the day and in the evening and who would serve the food. Others volunteered to look to providing tents and benches; all realized that they needed to begin to provide for the sheltering of those who were coming for the days of prayerful preparation, lectures and reflection prior to the time of the great communion. In small groups, in the churchyard, people carried on conversations about the tasks to undertake.

For welcoming visitors, there is a season....

The good news spread around the Island, to Sydney and Cape North, to Mira and Baddeck, to Grand River and Margaree, to West Bay and all communities in be-tween. "Rev. Peter MacLean will return from Scotland for the time of Sacrament in Whycocomagh." In remote glens as well as in small villages, people began to prepare for the journey to Whycocomagh. Some would go by boat, others by buggy and oth-ers on foot. But all felt summoned to the time of intensive religious observances and learning. As well, in many a household, family members began to spend more time each day in prayer and in hearing the Bible read or recited in Gaelic or in English. They wished to prepare their hearts and their understandings for this time of soul-searching and renewal. In Presbyterian communities around the island, a sense of anticipation was everywhere.

All through the summer, in Skye Glen, Whycocomagh, Dunakin, Mull River, Head of the Bay, Ainslie Glen, North and South Sides of the Bay and River Denys, people were starting to consider how family members could attend the five-day event and at the same time tend to the farm tasks. As well, they knew their relatives coming from a distance would expect a place to sleep. Farmers had to decide what animals they would slaughter so as to have sufficient food at the house and at the gathering place. Extra butter was churned, well salted and set aside in a cool spring, pork and beef was salted and placed in barrels, as was fish from the rivers and the lakes. People dug potatoes and turnips a bit early and set the harvest aside in large baskets.

Barrels of flour were brought to farmhouses from the stores in the villages so that an ample supply of bread and biscuits, shortbread and pies, and cookies made specially for children could be baked in the weeks just before the event.

As September came along, and the time of the open-air gathering drew nearer, mer-chants ordered from Halifax extra quantities of tea and raisins, sugar and flour and peppermint candies. People who sold rum and wine looked to supplement their supplies, as their sales would also increase during the "time of Sacrament" even though this was a time of religious observance.

At the site, rough benches and canvas tents began to be erected. The women of the congregation came to clear understanding with one another about who was going to serve the food at the noon and evening meals for people who would have come any distance. Large cauldrons for boiling vegetables and salted fish were placed on stone hearths over fire pits. Devices for cooking meat on outdoor fireplaces were constructed by local blacksmiths. Dry firewood was stacked near the places for food preparation. Loose hay was piled in nearby groves of trees so that there would be sustenance for the horses. Wooden barrels bound with iron were brought and placed near the spring just down the hill from the church so they could be filled with fresh water each day. Other people scrubbed and whitewashed the church for it would be used for special prayer meetings and preaching in English. As well, the booth from which the ministers would deliver their sermons and recitations was repaired and whitened. So much to do; so many people busily engaged! All the while daily life went on, just not in the usual routine. Almost daily, messages arrived from friends living in distant places – they were coming to the services. So much to do, so many people to feed and house!

One week before Peter MacLean was expected to arrive and the great event to begin, the people of the Whycocomagh Congregation of the Presbyterian Church gathered at noon between the morning Gaelic service and the afternoon English worship time, to consider their preparations. John MacQueen, Clerk and Senior Elder, commended them for all that had been accomplished and reminded them of what had yet to be done. His wife, Alexis, met as well with the women so that households would know what food they should bring and who was to cook each day. All details were shared with the congregants so that everybody could assist visitors to the area. Young people were requested to see to the care of the horses and to ensure that buggies would be well-attached to trees in case a heavy wind should come up. They would also bring spring water as needed. The households where the several visiting ministers would stay were all located near the site of the church. Mr. Parag would find accommodation with the MacQueens who were good friends and had a large comfortable house in the village. As people left after the English service, all agreed that everything seemed in order. Although many were tired, they looked forward to the time of meeting old friends and eagerly looked forward to hearing the fiery, inspired preaching of Mr. Parag.

For gathering and for hearing the Word, there is a season....

On Sunday evening, word came by a messenger on horseback that Rev. Peter MacLean had arrived from Scotland, had left Sydney for Whycocomagh by sailing packet across the Bras d'Or Lake and would be in Whycocomagh by the next evening, God willing. The word spread quickly, "Mr. Parag is coming, Mr. Parag is coming! Thanks be to God." So much elation and anticipation! All rejoiced and were grateful that this opportunity of being in his presence one more time was actually going to happen. Evening prayers in households throughout the district were unusually fervent.

The weather had been threatening on Sunday, but began to clear on Monday. As Tuesday dawned with bright skies and gentle winds, horse-drawn buggies and farm wagons filled with people appeared on the roads from every direction. People arrived on foot as well, weary of their journeys. From the hilltop above the church site, observers could see dozens of small sailboats coming into Whycocomagh Harbour. And the time of preparation for the celebration of the Lord's Supper began with worship services, with the singing of the psalms and with lectures by elders, ministers and Mr. Parag.

By Wednesday evening, every house in the area had visitors. Distant cousins and old friends were sleeping on feather beds on floors and even in haymows and school-houses. Some came ready to camp on the site in tents of their own. Surely, such a crowd had never previously been seen anywhere on the island. People greeted one another in Gaelic and English in between services and times of prayer. During the noon meals, all began to catch up on news of kinfolk in other places. The food in great abundance was spread out on plank tables; nobody went away hungry.

By noon on Thursday, it was very evident that many more people than expected had made the trip to Whycocomagh. Somebody estimated that at least five thousand were present, men and women and small children, aged grandparents and young people, preachers and teachers. Even travelling merchants could be seen, locating their buggies some distance away from the church. They were willing to make money selling rum and finery to anyone so inclined. The shoreline was covered by boats drawn up on the beach. As well, the area for tying and feeding horses had to be increased and more hay brought from nearby farms.

The response of the crowd was dramatic. Such quiet! Such deep prayer! Such persuasive and committed preaching from Peter MacLean! After a particularly poignant sermon about sin and the saving power of Jesus, tears could be seen in the eyes of men and women, young and old. So began the great Pentecostal experience recalled for generations, a time of such blessing that many families came to experience a new way of life.

The local women, meanwhile, reluctantly realized that they would have to go home, one by one, and bake more bread and prepare more pies. The men knew they would have to slaughter more lambs and old sheep as well. They leaders of the congregation gathered for a few minutes following the afternoon services before they went home to milk their cows and tend to other farm chores. They agreed that the people present in such numbers would require increased provisions, for their physical sustenance as well as spiritual nourishment. They were reminded that, "the Lord will provide" – "How?" was the question in many minds.

For unexpected wonders, there is a season....

Those who arrived early at the site the next morning were surprised to see a number of wicker baskets on the steps of the church. Piled within were small pieces of some sort of bread. The food was soft and sticky and a little sweet. Nobody knew where the donations had come from, but all found the bread very satisfying. The form of cooking was unknown to them, but was most welcome in helping to feed the more than five thousand individuals gathered during the day at the various places on the hillside where lectures and sermons and times of reflection were taking place.

Although no explanation for these baskets of unusual food is recorded, a quiet oral tradition in several of the valleys adjacent to the church is that the "little people," the fairies, supplied the nourishment. One of the elders of the congregation, Neil MacLean, a man of much knowledge about natural healing potions from wild plants had, it was said, once helped the little people when several of their members were very ill. And so, some people believe, the small folk helped out in a time of need. Others say that the sticky substance was manna from heaven, the same as reported in the Old Testament of the Bible. Still others have suggested that the Mi'kmaq, who were not Presbyterians but lived near the area, showed good neighbourliness in a quiet way. Manna? Secret recipe? Shortbread? Whatever the origins, the baskets appeared unexpectedly on the doorsteps of the church each morning thereafter during the celebrations. The feeding of the multitude was indeed a miracle, for nobody at that 1853 gathering was hungry.

In addition to the memory of the feeding of so many thousands, later generations recalled the unusual blessings which their parents and grandparents experienced during those days. People recounted the manifestation of the Holy Spirit. Not only, it is said, were individuals willing to confess freely their addiction to liquor or to ask forgiveness for cheating their neighbours, perhaps by secretly moving boundary markers, but others were moved to reveal how sinful they had been in other aspects of their lives. It was said indeed that a "feeling of great peace settled around all."

Tradition also recalls that as Rev. Peter MacLean began to preach his final sermon loudly and earnestly in Gaelic, some people in the gathering started to speak out in languages they did not know. Those present were reminded of the happening at the first Pentecost as described by Luke in the Book of Acts where some were inspired "to speak in tongues."

Then, on that hillside, so quiet today, but filled with more than five thousand people assembled that day, small flames began to dance on the heads of white-haired elders.

Others said they saw this visible representation of the Holy Spirit on the tops of the bonnets of pious old ladies and around the faces of children. Some individuals seemed to be in a trance as they raised their hands to heaven. Accounts vary, but all concur that something very unusual occurred that day.

For saying farewells, there is a season....

A spirit of great energy spread among the congregants. Many of those present remembered the time as one of unusual blessing. They told their children and their children's children with such assurance that the account comes to us today. After the final benediction, many were in tears as they reluctantly began to leave for their homes in distant parts of Cape Breton. But they went certain that the spirit of God had been present in abundance and manifest in unusual ways. Although he was clearly tired from preaching and teaching for so many hours and so many days, Mr. Parag passed through the crowds shaking hands and wishing "*beannachd Dhe leibh*" ... "blessings on you" to former parishioners and others who had been deeply inspired by his words. Most knew that they would not meet again on earth and wept with that realization on their hearts.

For searching for meaning, there is a season....

Certainly the event was the largest gathering on record of Cape Bretoners singing the psalms of David in Gaelic, a time when more than five thousand people were fed with loaves and fishes and manna. Many years later, one elderly man spoke about the events of October, 1853, when he was just a young person: "It was a true Pentecostal experience, I have no doubt."

Today, the quiet hillside is the final resting place of many who were present at "The Great Communion," including John MacQueen and his wife Alexis. They can no longer speak of what they knew and felt and experienced. Nor can they tell us how the people of the congregation prepared so much food and provided so much hospitality. As we go to the hillside and stand on the highest point, we can ponder what happened when the Rev. Peter MacLean returned here to preach and teach and wonder at the scale of such a community undertaking.

Aig gach ni tha trath ... and a time for everything under heaven.

Whycocomagh 1853

Pentecost – Spirit – Flame – Manna

MENU

Scotch Broth in Cauldron

Whole Lamb, Spit-Roasted

Hip of Beef, Pit-Roasted

Potatoes & Turnip Cooked in Cauldron

Steamed Salmon

Marag

Pickled Eggs   Spiced Beets

From Community Pantries:

Dundee Cake   Rice & Raisin Pudding
Spice Cake   Bread Pudding
Oatmeal Cookies
Blueberry Pie

Scotch Brown Bread Biscuits
Bran Bread
Bannock

Scotch Broth

3 lbs lamb (1.3 kg)

½ cup pot barley (125 ml)

3 quarts water (3 L)

2 tbsp butter (30 ml)

1 cup diced carrots (250 ml)

1 large onion diced (1)

1 cup diced turnip (250 ml)

½ cup chopped celery (125 ml)

2 tsp salt (10 ml)

1 tsp pepper (5 ml)

• Wipe meat and cut in 1-inch (2.5-cm) cubes. Put meat and bones in a large soup pot. Cover with cold water. Bring to a boil. Add barley. Reduce heat and simmer for 1½ hours or until meat is tender. Remove bones and skim off fat.

• Melt butter in skillet. Sauté vegetables for 5-8 minutes. Add to soup with salt and pepper. Cook until vegetables are soft and barley is tender. Serves 6.

> **NOTE**
> If soup is too thick, add more water and adjust seasoning if necessary.

Whole Lamb, Spit-Roasted

A fire pit would be created with large rocks. Fire would be lit in the centre. A whole lamb would be suspended above the pit on a metal bar supported on tripods. The lamb would be secured to the metal bar. The fire would be lit in the pit and, as the meat began to cook, the metal bar would be turned by hand using a crank allowing the meat to cook evenly. This would take several hours. When cooked, the lamb would be removed from the heat and allowed to settle for a period of time before slicing and serving.

Hip of Beef, Pit-Roasted
One (1) large beef hip 60-80 lbs (28-38 kg)

A large pit would be dug out and lined with large rocks to hold back gravel and protect soil area.

In centre of pit, an area would be designated to prepare fire, allowing a walking space for workers. The beef hip would be placed and secured on a raised stand 3-4 feet (1-1.3 meter) above the fire area. (The stand was constructed of iron.)

The fire would be lit and allowed to reduce to coals. As the meat heated and roasted, it required occasional turning to assure even roasting.

Two men, using pitchforks and wearing gloves, would turn the meat occasionally to allow for even cooking. When cooked, beef would be removed from the heat and allowed to settle for a period of time before slicing and serving.

Potatoes & Turnip Cooked in a Cauldron

One (1) very large cast iron cauldron
50 lbs potatoes peeled (25 kg)
25 lbs turnip peeled and sliced (13 kg)
1 cup salt (250 ml)
Water as needed to cover

Prepared potatoes and turnip would be placed in large cauldron, covered completely with water and sprinkled with salt.

Cauldron would be suspended from a tripod, and fire would be lit below cauldron in an area outlined with rocks to secure fire. Cauldron would be brought to a boil (fire would be tended to keep water boiling). Vegetables would be tested using a large fork when cooked. Cauldron would be removed from tripod, water drained and vegetables would be served to accompany meat.

Steamed Salmon

1 3-4 lb salmon (1.3-1.8 kg)
2 tsp salt (10 ml)
1 tsp pepper (5 ml)

1 onion sliced (1)
2 bay leaves (2)
Cold water for covering fish

• Rinse salmon thoroughly. Place salmon in a large fish poacher or roaster. Sprinkle with salt and pepper. Add sliced onion and bay leaves.
• Cover with cold water and simmer (do not boil), allowing 8-12 minutes per pound. When tested with a fork, fish flakes.
• Lift carefully from stock and place on a heated platter. Salmon was frequently served with an egg sauce.

Peter Rankin 2007

Marag

4 cups rolled oats (1 L)
1 cup standard oat meal (250 ml)
2 tbsp salt (30 ml)

2½ tsp pepper (12 ml)
4 cups ground suet (1 L)
3 cups finely chopped onion (750 ml)

• In a large bowl combine rolled oats, oatmeal, salt, pepper, suet and chopped onion. Mix well to combine ingredients.

• To make Marag: (Use plastic casings purchased from meat company.) Tie a secure string on bottom before filling. Insert a large open funnel in casing opening and fill casing with marag, packing filling firmly in the casing using a plunger. Fill casing and tie top securely with string.

• Pierce casing all over with sharp skewer.

• Place marag in large roaster of rapidly boiling salted water. Reduce to simmer.

• Place a weight on top of marag in roaster.

• Steam for 3 hours, turning frequently and pierce several times with skewer to reduce pressure. Remove from water and place on cooling rack. Cool completely.

• To serve Marag: Cut in slices ½-¾-inch (1-2-cm) thick. Place slices in hot skillet and fry, turning once until crusted and heated through. Serve with eggs or potatoes.

Pickled Eggs

12 hard-cooked eggs (12)
3 cups white vinegar (750 ml)
4 tbsp granulated sugar (60 ml)
1 tsp salt (5 ml)

1 tsp mustard seed (5 ml)
6 whole cloves (6)
2 bay leaves (2)

• Cook eggs. Remove shells and set aside.

• In a saucepan, combine vinegar, sugar, salt, mustard seed, cloves and bay leaves. Bring to a boil and simmer for 15 minutes. Cool slightly.

• Place eggs in a large sterilized jar. Pour vinegar mixture over eggs, making sure eggs are completely covered. Place lid on jar and refrigerate for 7 to 10 days before using.

• Pickled eggs can be enjoyed with cheese and crusty bread.

Spiced Beets

3 lbs small beets cooked (1.3 kg)

1 cup water (250 ml)

5 cups vinegar (1.3 L)

2 cups granulated sugar (500 ml)

1 tbsp cinnamon (15 ml)

1 tsp whole allspice (5 ml)

1 tsp whole cloves (5 ml)

• Cook beets in boiling water until tender. Plunge in cold water and strip off skins.

• In a large saucepan, combine water, vinegar, sugar, cinnamon, whole cloves and whole allspice (tied in a piece of cheesecloth). Bring to a boil and simmer for 15 minutes.

• Slice beets and pack in sterilized hot jars. Fill jars with liquid. Seal and process 20 minutes in hot water bath.

• Store jars in dark cool place.

Dundee Cake

1 cup butter (250 ml)

1 cup granulated sugar (250 ml)

4 eggs (4)

1 cup sliced almonds (250 ml)

2½ cups all-purpose flour (625 ml)

1 tsp baking powder (5 ml)

½ tsp salt (2 ml)

2 cups golden raisins (500 ml)

1½ cups currants (375 ml)

½ cup citrus peel (125 ml)

2 tbsp orange juice or milk (30 ml)

For Decoration: 1 cup peeled whole almonds (250 ml)

• In a large bowl, cream butter and add sugar slowly until light and fluffy. Beat in eggs one at a time, beating for two minutes. Stir in almonds.

• In a medium bowl measure flour, baking powder, salt, raisins, currants and citrus peel. Add to creamed mixture and mix thoroughly. Add orange juice or milk, and combine well.

• Fill a pan 10 x 10 x 3 in. (25 x 25 x 7.5 cm) greased and lined with brown paper or parchment paper. Spread batter well and cover with whole almonds.

• Bake in a 325⁰ F (160⁰ C) oven for 1½ hours or until tester comes out clean. Remove from oven, cool in pan for 30 minutes. Turn out on cooling rack and cool completely.

• Wrap cake securely and allow to mellow for a few days at room temperature.

> NOTE
> If cake browns too quickly, lay a sheet of foil over surface.

Rice & Raisin Pudding

½ cup short grain rice (125 ml)

1 quart milk (1 L) ½ cup granulated sugar (125 ml)

½ cup raisins (125 ml) 1 tsp vanilla (5 ml)

¼ cup butter (60 ml) ¼ tsp salt (1 ml)

3 eggs (3) Cinnamon and nutmeg for sprinkling

• In a medium saucepan, mix rice with 2 cups (500 ml) milk. Cook over a medium heat, stirring constantly until rice is tender. Add raisins and butter. Remove from the heat.

• In a bowl, whisk eggs. Add sugar, vanilla, salt and remaining milk. Stir into hot rice mixture.

• Pour into a buttered 1½ quart (1.5 L) baking dish. Sprinkle top with cinnamon and nutmeg.

• Set baking dish in pan and fill half full with hot water. Bake in a 325⁰ F (160⁰ C) oven for 30 minutes or until set. Serves 6

• Rice pudding can be served warm or cold. Serve with whipped cream, if desired.

Bread Pudding

1 quart scalded milk (1 L) 3 eggs (3)

2 cups day-old bread cubes (500 ml) 4 tbsp melted butter (60 ml)

¼ tsp salt (1 ml) 1 tsp vanilla (5 ml)

½ cup sugar (125 ml) ½ tsp cinnamon (2 ml)

• Place bread cubes in a large bowl. Pour scalded milk over bread. Whisk eggs. Add salt, sugar, butter, vanilla and cinnamon. Mix to combine.

• Pour into a buttered 1½ quart (1.5 L) casserole. Set casserole in pan and fill pan half full with hot water.

• Bake 50-60 minutes in a 325⁰ F (160⁰ C) oven until knife inserted comes out clean. Remove pudding from water and allow to settle before serving either hot or cold.

> NOTE
> Bread pudding is a very old dessert, and was developed to utilize dried bread. It has become very popular, and is now frequently called bread and butter pudding.

Oatmeal Cookies

1¾ cups all-purpose flour (425 ml)
1 cup brown sugar (250 ml)
½ tsp baking soda (2 ml)
½ tsp salt (2 ml)
1 tsp cinnamon (5 ml)

½ cup melted butter (125 ml)
½ cup melted lard (125 ml)
1 egg beaten (1)
1 tbsp molasses (15 ml)
¼ cup milk (60 ml)
2 cups rolled oats (500 ml)
1 cup raisins (250 ml)

- In a large bowl, combine flour, sugar, baking soda, salt and cinnamon.
- In a separate bowl, combine melted butter and lard, beaten egg, molasses and milk.
- Mix liquid ingredients with dry ingredients and toss in rolled oats and raisins. Stir to combine.
- Arrange heaping teaspoons on greased baking sheet about 2 ins (5 cm) apart. Flatten slightly with a fork.
- Bake in a 350⁰ F (180⁰ C) oven until edges are brown, approximately 12-14 minutes.
- Remove from oven. Cool slightly and transfer to cooling rack. Makes approximately four (4) dozen.

Scotch Brown Bread Biscuits

2 cups whole wheat flour (500 ml)
1 tbsp baking powder (15 ml)
1 tsp salt (5 ml)
½ cup butter (125 ml)
¾ cup milk (175 ml)

- In a medium bowl measure flour, baking powder and salt. Using a pastry blender or fingertips, work butter into flour until crumbly. Add milk and mix to a soft dough.
- Spoon out dough and shape in small balls (about 2 ounces of dough).
- Place balls on greased baking sheet and flatten lightly with palm of your hand.
- Bake in a 400⁰ F (200⁰ C) oven for 12-15 minutes.
- These brown bread biscuits resemble bread rolls.

Bannock

3 cups all-purpose flour (750 ml)
1 tsp salt (5 ml)
2 tbsp baking powder (30 ml)

2 tbsp granulated sugar (30 ml)
3 tbsp lard or shortening (45 ml)
1 cup milk (250 ml)

- In a bowl combine flour, salt, baking powder and sugar.
- Using a pastry blender or fingertips, work lard or shortening into dry ingredients until crumbly.
- Pour in milk. Stir with a fork and form into a ball. Turn out on floured work surface. Knead about 10 times.
- After kneading, form dough into a circle and place on ungreased baking sheet. Pat dough to one (1)-inch (2.5-cm) thickness. Score into triangles.
- Bake in a 400^0 F (200^0 C) oven for about 20 minutes, until well browned.
- Bannock can also be cut in circles and baked.

Spice Cake

½ cup shortening (125 ml)
½ cup granulated sugar (125 ml)
½ cup molasses (125 ml)
2 eggs (2)
2 cups flour (500 ml)
3 tsp baking powder (15 ml)

½ tsp baking soda (2 ml)
½ tsp salt (2 ml)
1 tsp cinnamon (5 ml)
¼ tsp cloves, allspice and ginger (1 ml)
¾ cup buttermilk (175 ml)

- Cream shortening and sugar until light. Add molasses and beat well. Whisk in the eggs one at a time, beating after each addition.
- In a bowl measure flour, baking powder, soda, salt and spices.
- Add alternately with milk to creamed mixture, beating after each addition.
- Pour batter in greased 10-inch (25-cm) cake pan. Bake in a 350^0 F (180^0 C) oven for 40-50 minutes or until tester comes out clean.
- Remove from oven. Cool in pan for 10 minutes. Turn out on cooling rack and cool completely.

Bran Bread

2 cups bran (500 ml)
2 cups whole wheat flour (500 ml)
¾ cup brown sugar (175 ml)
1 tsp soda (5 ml)

2 tsp baking powder (10 ml)
½ tsp salt (2 ml)
1 egg (1)
1¾ cups buttermilk (425 ml)

• In a large bowl combine bran, flour, sugar, soda, baking powder and salt. Mix to combine ingredients.
• In a separate bowl, whisk egg with buttermilk. Add to dry ingredients, mixing only enough to combine ingredients.
• Pour into a greased 9 x 5 x 3-inch (23 x 13 x 7.5 cm) bread pan. Bake in a 350⁰ F (180⁰ C) oven for one (1) hour or until tester comes out clean
• Turn out on cooling rack. When cool, wrap securely and allow to mellow for one (1) day. Serve as bread to accompany meal.

Blueberry Pie

Pastry
4 cups all-purpose flour (1 L)
1 tsp salt (5 ml)
1 cup lard or shortening (250 ml)
¼ cup butter (60 ml)
½ cup iced water (approx.) (125 ml)

Filling
4 cups blueberries (1 L)
¾ cup granulated sugar (175 ml)
4 tbsp flour (60 ml)
2 tsp lemon juice (10 ml)
1 tsp grated lemon rind (5 ml)
Milk for brushing
Sugar for sprinkling

• In a large mixing bowl measure flour and salt. Combine well. Using a pastry blender or fingertips, work lard and butter into flour until crumbly.
• Sprinkle water over flour mixture a little at a time tossing with a fork. When moist gather dough in a ball.
• Flatten dough into a disc. Wrap and chill for 30 minutes.
• Divide dough in half. Roll out one piece and line a 10-inch (25-cm) pie pan.
• In a medium bowl combine blueberries, sugar, flour, lemon juice and rind. Spoon into prepared pie shell.
• Roll remaining pastry and place on top of blueberries. Press down sides of pastry. Cut away excess and crimp edges of pie. Make two 1-inch (2.5-cm) cuts in centre of pie. Brush with milk and sprinkle with sugar.
• Bake in a 400⁰ F (200⁰ C) oven until fruit is bubbly and crust golden, 35-40 minutes. Makes a 10-inch (25-cm) pie.

Peter Rankin 2007

The Child is Father of the Man: Jacob Ross in Glace Bay

Located on the eastern tip of Cape Breton Island, Glace Bay received its name "Ice Bay" from the French when the island was under their control. Coal mining was carried on for many years, but came to be a booming industry in the mid-1800s. A fishing fleet operated out of the harbour as well. By 1901, the community had grown sufficiently to be incorporated as a town as people were attracted by the opening of new mines and by the potential for small businesses. New residents came from the rural regions of Cape Breton and mainland Nova Scotia, from Newfoundland, from many countries of Europe and from China. The census records in 1910 show that 52 per cent of the population had arrived in the previous ten years.

With its many ethnic groups and various religious organizations, Glace Bay quickly came to be a multicultural community. For children, such as Jacob Ross, the subject of this story, there was much opportunity to be aware of the customs of people from many distant places. Although most young people went to work in the coal mines or for the several railway lines operating in and out of Glace Bay, others found their way to various locations across the continent. Both women and men often found new opportunities for themselves in many professions, in business and politics. Outmigration has been a fact of life in this community for several generations. However, the celebrations of Old Home Week see people returning home to renew old ties.

While the Jacob Ross in this story is created from an amalgam of accounts of several young people of the early 1900s, the names of his companions are all to be found in the recording of families in the census of 1910 for Glace Bay, and they are all of the right age to be in this story.

The Child is Father of the Man: Jacob Ross in Glace Bay

From the time he came into the world, Jacob Ross was a child full of curiosity. Indeed, his parents, Mary and John Ross of Glace Bay, Cape Breton, agreed they had a child who was unusually interested in his surroundings. Of course, he was a delight to his grandparents who believed they had a very bright descendant and they came often from their farm twenty-five miles away to be with him.

As John and Mary Ross were both always busy waiting on customers who came to their small general store at the corner of Commercial Street and Pitt Lane, Jacob from a young age grew up surrounded by shelves full of groceries and hardware. The family had living quarters in one of the two small apartments on the second floor of the building, above the store, but as a baby, Jacob was generally to be found confined in a large laundry basket placed on one of the counters.

As he had need of more space, his parents cleared away a section of the store, not far from the sacks of flour and the barrel of molasses and there placed a good-sized baby pen built with the help of Joe Nolan, a carpenter who lived with his parents in the other apartment over the store.

As Jacob began to crawl, they enlarged his space so that he was able to watch everything that was going on and look at everybody who came into the shop. Not the least bit shy, he started to speak at any early age and seemed to think it was his responsibility to start a conversation with every customer who came across the threshold. People were amused by him and responded with sentences sometimes in English, often in Gaelic or German.

The jangle of the bell, occasioned by the opening of the door, was Jacob's signal for pouring out a stream of syllables. Always in good cheer, he was more than content to look at the bunches of onions hanging from the beams and point them out to all who would look. Old and young, male and female, were drawn to him and engaged him in conversation. Some brought him small toys which made him laugh and encouraged him to speak even more. When picked up by the customers, he wanted to examine the buttons on their coats or the caps on their heads.

An only child, with parents busy measuring out brown sugar into paper sacks or weighing flakes of dried cod on the scales, Jacob learned early to be self-assured and independent. Two or three apples rolling across the floor were a source of amusement for some minutes, particularly if he was able to give them a push with his fat little hands. As for food, he liked a variety, and the more colour the substance had the better. To be sure, he sometimes squashed his serving of potato with his little hands and experimented with throwing it to the floor to see what would happen, laughing with glee at the sound of the vegetable splattering on the linoleum. But just as well, when he sat in his high chair at meal times, he liked to smell the slices of an orange or the blue berries from his grandparents' farm before tasting them. Always inquisitive, he explored his world as thoroughly as he could.

Long before he could speak whole sentences, he would hold out his hands and point at turnips brought in from a farm in nearby Mira or at fresh beans fresh from his grandpa's farm in Sydney River. To pull on a pair of men's suspenders hanging from a peg on the wall of the store and then to watch them bounce back into shape was enjoyment out of the ordinary. He always had something to say when a woman with a big hat with artificial flowers came to buy yard goods or rubber boots. He wanted to hold the flowers in his hands. Sometimes he was disappointed but more often than not he charmed the ladies so much they indulged him.

Born in 1901, Jacob was growing up in a community that was increasingly multicultural. As more and more people arrived in Glace Bay to work in the mines or on the railways or to open small businesses or establish tailoring shops, the Ross store began to keep ingredients that met the needs of people from Russia and Poland, from Germany and Italy, from Newfoundland and Belgium, from China and from the Acadian districts of Nova Scotia. Salami and garlic and poppy seeds appeared on the counters alongside carrots and dried cod.

The small houses of people who worked in the offices of the coal mines or in various shops lined the road in one direction from the corner where the Ross Store was situated. In the other direction, rows of company houses constructed for the miners extended in a long line down the hill toward the shore and the pithead. Many of the mining families did most of their shopping at stores operated by the coal company, but some came to look for certain ethnic foods which the Rosses supplied. Book-keepers and teachers and the wives of carpenters and shoemakers found most of the things they required at Ross's General Store. Jacob welcomed everybody with the same enthusiasm and a happy smile. Indeed his friendliness may have attracted customers.

Before he was old enough to go to school, he used to ask to spend some time with Joe Nolan and his parents in their apartment over the store. Natives of Ireland, they spoke with an accent unlike that of Jacob's parents and they made a different kind of stew which Jacob relished. He even stayed with the elder Nolans for some hours while Joe was at work as a builder of wooden crates for the railways. Upon returning to the store or his parents' apartment, he had many comments to make about what the Nolans told him of their old home in Ireland.

At least once a week, Jacob's grandfather, Abraham Ross, arrived in Glace Bay from the farm at Sydney River with produce from his garden or fresh eggs or homemade butter to be sold by John and Mary. On those occasions, Jacob often asked if he could go for a walk with his grandpa down to the shore or up along the nearby brook. While they went along the roadways, they carried on a continuous conversation about everything they saw – the young boy and the old man. After one such excursion, Abraham Ross commented to his son and daughter-in-law that while he was not certain just what Jacob would become in his adult years, he believed it would be something special. "He has such a curiosity about everything and a genuine interest in everybody we meet," the grandfather observed.

For Jacob's mother, Mary, Abraham's statement confirmed what she was seeing in her son. Although she was constantly busy with customers in the store, she always kept her eye on Jacob and noticed with pride the way he was growing up. He continued to have the same curiosity he had shown as a much younger child. From the time he came to be seven years old, his parents permitted him to wander around the neighbourhood since he enjoyed looking at the new buildings being constructed and talking with all the people he met on the street. As before, everyone seemed to respond with interest to the friendly young lad.

After he came to be seven or so, during vacations from school, Jacob wandered around Glace Bay, talking to all whom he met and looking at the buildings which were being constructed. In 1910, when he came to be nine years old, he announced that he wanted to help around the store. While he was a bit too young to wait on the customers, he liked meeting people; his presence encouraged the patrons to buy. His friendliness as a child continued to be part of his personality, as was his curiosity about the world around him. After a time, his parents asked Joe Nolan to build a small cart by which Jacob could convey for delivery the groceries or hardware purchased in the store to the homes of customers. Painted a bright red with a black metal handle, the wagon much pleased Jacob and he felt he was helping his parents. So, around the neighbourhood he went, parcels piled high. From these excursions, he came home with accounts of what he had seen at the various houses and the various languages he had heard.

The long, long days of summer in 1910 were a delight for this child of nine. When not pulling the delivery wagon while he conversed with the customer who walked at his side, he was free to spend time with his friends exploring the various sections of Glace Bay. While some boys would go to work in the mines by the time they were twelve years old, July and August found most young people wandering the shoreline in search of treasures washed up on the beach, or going swimming in the brook that ran through the centre of the town to the sea, or wandering through the woodlands which surrounded their community. Organized activities were yet to be a part of the social life of children, and family vacations were not yet common; few shopkeepers took any time off. Children were free to roam and explore.

And so it was that young Jacob and the other lads who lived nearby spent hours listening to the roar of the sea as heard in shells held up to their ears, or picking unripened apples from the wild trees growing along the brook and throwing them at each other, or searching for mushrooms in the woods. While seated on hillsides looking out to the sea, many of them had stories to tell of the faraway places where they had been born and from which they had left with their families in order to come to live in Glace Bay. There were descriptions of Poland and Russia and Newfoundland as well as of journeys across the ocean.

As warm summer afternoons waned and a hunger came upon the boys, they would go as a group to whichever family was nearest, in the hope that they would be given cookies or a piece of apple pie. Often, they were invited to remain for a whole meal. Most families were large; a few more mouths to feed placed no great strain on the resources of the particular family. The parents knew that as long as the young people were together they were probably safe from any harm. Feeding them was a kind of insurance that they would stay together and look after one another.

For many of the group of friends, the food was just food, nourishing and satisfying. But for Jacob, the various dishes were a source of fascination. There was such a variety, so many different smells, so many ways of mixing foods, all so different from his usual fare at home. Both of his parents had grown up in farm homes where Gaelic was spoken and the diet was primarily meat or fish and potatoes and other vegetables according to the season. Homemade white bread was part of every meal in those houses.

Thus Jacob had many stories to tell his parents. Living next door in the first of the miners' row houses were the Boones from Newfoundland. They delighted in sharing their favourite way of serving cod which they called "brews." Jacob loved the texture and the aroma of Elizabeth Boone's fish dinners. John Boone, who was the same age as Jacob, expected to join his older brothers and their father, Samuel, in the coal mines within a few years, but for the time being, he was free to roam with Jacob.

Across the street lived Harry and Hester Cohen, recent immigrants from Russia. Their son, Archie – who had what Hester called "a good Scotch name" – was learning to read the Old Testament in Hebrew. As he looked at the words in the ancient language in front of Archie, Jacob was quite amazed at the shape of the letters. Harry, who much approved of the boy's interest in learning, said to Jacob, "you have a good Jewish name, the same as my grandfather's, back in Russia." The Cohens were going from community to community throughout the rural regions with a horse and a wagon to sell clothes and other goods to people who lived far from stores. Once in a while, they took Jacob with them and shared their Russian variety of bread and meat with him. They had a hope someday that they might open a Kosher meat shop – another concept of food supply which intrigued Jacob Ross.

Some days, Edward Kowalski's father, François, took the boys out into the woods to search for mushrooms and other edible plants. Edward was the same age as Jacob and well recalled his family's recent trip on a large vessel as they sailed from Poland. While Edward took much interest in his father's shoemaking business, his older sister, Fanny, was hoping to be a teacher. Edward's older brothers were already experienced handlers of the pit ponies that pulled the carts full of coal through the mines. Jacob was intrigued with the culinary use of things growing in the wild and reported his adventures to his parents.

Another Polish family who lived nearby had a son who was the same age as Jacob. They were the Michalikis. Their son Albert spoke English as well as Polish, although his parents, Stanislaus and Francesca, spoke mostly their native language. Albert's mother and father cherished their perogies and sauerkraut, prepared as Mrs. Michaliki said in broken English, "chust like in Cracow." Stanislaus claimed that the immigrant officials had shortened his name from a longer form with "ski" at the end. Jacob was surprised to learn that names could be changed in that way.

One of Jacob's best friends during that summer of 1910 was Victor Degaugus who had been born nine years earlier in Belgium. He remembered how sick he felt when the sea was rough as they came from overseas. Their mutual friend, Henry LeMaillet, could carry on conversations with the Degaugus family in a language that Jacob didn't understand. Both families were surprised to learn when they arrived in Glace Bay that there was no baker in the area and that they had to make their own bread. The LeMaillets were starting to talk about making bread at home and asking the Rosses to offer it for sale at their store.

Herman Echo was a year older than Jacob and the other boys. He too claimed his name had been changed when they entered Canada. He had great stories about his grandmother back in Germany and the good pastry which she made. It was called "struedel" in German, but Herman didn't know what the English name was. His Dad, who had worked as a miner back in the old country was not well, so Herman knew that he would not be returning to school in September. He would be going to work underground to help support the family; "To keep bologna from your store on our table to feed the smaller children will be my job," Herman announced one day. He said this with some sadness for he too enjoyed searching out unexplored places and looking for buried treasure on the beach where local legends suggested chests had been buried long ago.

That summer, the Lee Family arrived in Glace Bay. Originally from China, they had lived in several other places in North America before they arrived in Cape Breton. Sung Lee, a year younger than Jacob, laughed at him when he tried to eat with chop sticks. "Such a mixture of pork and vegetables on my plate," Jacob reported to his parents after sitting down to dinner with the Lees.

The summer of 1910 passed as summers will. Jacob retained his great interest in all that he had discovered as he wandered with his friends. He delighted in the different foods he discovered were being prepared in small kitchens in his own neighbour-hood. Pulling his cart behind him as well, he continued to meet new people and to learn much about the cultures of other places. Jacob Ross would very soon be ten years old.

One day, just before school was about to resume, Jacob shared with his grandfather much that he seen and heard in the growing town of Glace Bay. Old Abraham Ross, who had arrived at the store with several recently butchered spring lambs and some recently dug blue potatoes to be put on sale, looked with much affection at his grandson who had so amused and delighted him since his earliest years. "You have a special gift, Jacob. You will go far from this store and this street in this mining town. Keep asking questions and looking deeply at all you see." Later in the day, Abraham said again to his son, John, "It may well be true what people sometimes say, 'the child is father of the man'," adding, "that boy will go far."

So it was with Jacob Ross that year of 1910 when he was nine years old, almost ten, in Glace Bay, Nova Scotia. Curiosity and exposure to many cultures in those early years of the 20th century provided him with a firm footing for later life in a wider and more cosmopolitan world – indeed, perhaps for what he would someday become.

At least one young person from Glace Bay went on to a career of managing a large hotel in Boston, Massachusetts, a business noted for its fine food and its hospitality: no doubt someone like Jacob Ross, their interest in fine food fostered in that multi-cultural environment of early 20th-century Glace Bay.

The Ethnic Connection

MENU

Borscht

Fish n' Brews

Corned Beef Hash

Irish Stew

Perogies

Cabbage Rolls

Sweet & Sour Pork

Miners' Favourite Cookies

Oatmeal Raisin Cookies

Hasty Raisin Pudding

Fritale

Jewish Knishes

Poppy Seed Cake

Borscht

2 quarts beef stock (2 L)
2 cups shredded beets (500 ml)
1 large onion diced (1)
1 rib celery chopped (1)
1 large carrot diced (1)

1 tbsp vinegar or lemon juice (15 ml)
1 tsp salt (5 ml)
½ tsp black pepper (2 ml)
1 cup sour cream (250 ml)

•   Heat beef stock. Add beets, onion, celery, carrot and vinegar. Bring to a boil. Reduce heat and simmer for approximately one (1) hour until vegetables are tender and flavourful. Season with salt and pepper.
•   Place sour cream in a small bowl. Slowly add one (1) cup (250 ml) of hot borscht a little at a time to sour cream, stirring constantly, until mixture is smooth. Return mixture to soup, stirring to combine well. Serves 6-8.

Fish n' Brews

1½ lb salt cod (700 g)
4 hard bread cakes (4)
½ lb salt pork cubed (225 g)

•   Soak salt cod in cold water overnight. (Cut in pieces if necessary.) If cod is very salty, change water once during soaking.
•   Soak hard bread in cold water separately overnight.
•   To cook fish, drain and return to saucepan, and cover with cold water. Bring to a boil and simmer for 15-20 minutes until tender. Drain.
•   In a skillet, fry cubed pork (called scrunchions) until golden and crisp.
•   Drain the hard bread. Place in a saucepan. Cover with water and bring to a boil to heat. Drain.
•   To serve, arrange bread on plate (it will be puffed and soggy). Place fish on top and spoon on the crisp scrunchions and melted fat.

Peter Rankin 2007

Corned Beef Hash

2 cups cold cooked corned beef (500 ml)

2 cups diced cooked potatoes (500 ml)   4 tbsp butter (60 ml)

1 large onion chopped (1)   Salt and pepper

1 clove garlic minced (1)   4 tbsp bread crumbs (60 ml)

- Trim fat from corned beef and chop or grind.
- Melt butter in skillet. Add garlic and onion. Cook until soft. Add corned beef and potatoes. Mix well to combine. Season with salt and pepper.
- Spoon into a buttered casserole. Sprinkle with bread crumbs. Bake in a 350^0 F (180^0 C) oven for 35-40 minutes.

> **NOTE**
> Corned Beef Hash was often served as a supper dish with poached eggs.

Irish Stew

4 lbs. boneless stewing lamb meat (1.8 kg)

6-8 medium potatoes peeled and quartered (6-8)

4 medium onions sliced (4)   1 tbsp salt (15 ml)

2 whole cloves garlic (2)   2 tsp pepper (10 ml)

1 bay leaf (1)   1 qt water (1 L)

- Cut lamb in 2-inch (5-cm) pieces. In a large casserole arrange meat and potatoes in layers starting and finishing with potatoes.
- Season well between each layer with salt and pepper, and onions. Add bay leaf and garlic. Pour water over all.
- Cover and cook in a 325^0 F (160^0 C) oven for 2-2½ hours or until meat is tender, and gravy is rich and thick.
- Avoid stirring, but shake the casserole from time to time to avoid sticking. Serves 6.

Perogies

<u>Basic Dough</u>
4 cups all-purpose flour (1 L)
2 eggs (2)
¼ cup vegetable oil (60 ml)
1¼ cups milk (310 ml)
½ tsp salt (2 ml)

<u>Filling</u>
6 large potatoes cooked and mashed (6)
½ lb old cheddar cheese grated (225 g)
2 tbsp butter (30 ml)
1 tsp pepper (5 ml)

- Mash potatoes and add cheese, butter and pepper. Mix well until smooth. Cool and use to fill perogies.

- In a bowl, place flour. In a separate bowl, whisk the eggs. Add oil, milk and salt. Pour into flour and mix well. Gather up into a ball. Place on floured surface. Cover with towel and let rest for 30 minutes.

- On floured surface, roll dough to ¼-inch thickness. Cut dough in circle about 3 inches (7.5 cm) in diameter with a cutter. Place approximately 1 tbsp (15 ml) of filling in centre of circle.

- Bring edges of dough together to form a half circle. Press edges together to secure. Place on baking sheet and cover with cloth until ready to cook.

- Fill a large pot with water. Bring to a boil. Add 2 tbsp (30 ml) salt and one (1) tbsp (15 ml) oil.

- Drop 12 perogies at a time in boiling water. Boil for approximately 5 minutes or until perogies rise to the top of the water.

- Remove from water using a slotted spoon. Arrange on a tray. Pour a little melted butter over perogies to avoid sticking.

- Serve perogies with sautéed onion and sour cream.

Cabbage Rolls
(holubtsi)

Buckwheat Filling

3 large potatoes peeled, cooked and mashed (3)

2 cups rinsed buckwheat (dried in oven) (500 ml)

1 tbsp salt (15 ml)

5 cups boiling water (1.25 L)

4 tbsp butter (60 ml)

¼ cup oil (60 ml)

2 large onion diced (2)

1 large green cabbage (1)

Topping

1 cup water (250 ml)

2 tbsp oil (30 ml)

½ tsp salt (2 ml)

½ tsp pepper (2 ml)

- To dry buckwheat, spread on a baking sheet and place in 200⁰ F (100⁰ C) oven for 15 minutes, stirring occasionally.
- Place buckwheat in a bowl. Add salt, boiling water and butter. Bring to a boil. Reduce heat, cover and simmer for 25 minutes. Remove from heat and set aside.
- Heat ¼ cup (60 ml) of oil in skillet. Sauté onion, and add to buckwheat with mashed potato. Mix well and set aside to cool.
- Remove core from cabbage. Place cabbage in a large pot of salted, boiling water. Bring to a boil and cook until leaves are soft. Cool.
- Separate cabbage leaves. Line a large casserole dish with a few leaves.
- Arrange remaining leaves on work surface. Place a heaping spoonful of filling on each leaf. Fold sides over and roll up securely.
- Place in casserole. Combine water, oil, salt and pepper. Pour over rolls. Cover and bake at 350⁰ F (180⁰ C) oven 1½ to 2 hours until tender. Serves 8.
- Serve accompanied with bread and dill pickles.

Sweet & Sour Pork

1 lb lean boneless pork cut in thin strips (450 g)
2 cups pineapple chunks with juice (500 ml)

1 tbsp oil (15 ml)   1 medium onion sliced (1)
½ tsp salt (2 ml)   ¼ cup vinegar (60 ml)
1 tsp pepper (5 ml)   2-3 tbsp soya sauce (30-45 ml)
½ cup cold water (125 ml)   2 tbsp cornstarch (30 ml)
4 tbsp granulated sugar (60 ml)   4 tbsp cold water (60 ml)
2 green pepper cut in strips (2)   2 medium tomatoes cut in wedges (2)

- Heat the oil in a large skillet. Add sliced pork and brown in batches until crisp.
- Return pork to skillet. Season with salt and pepper. Add water and simmer covered for 20-25 minutes until tender.
- Combine sugar, green pepper, onion, vinegar, pineapple and soy sauce. Add to pork and simmer for 5 minutes.
- Combine cornstarch and water. Add to ingredients in skillet. Bring to a boil and simmer until slightly thickened and sauce is clear. Add tomato wedges.
- Serve with rice or noodles. Serves 6.

Miners' Favourite Cookies

1 cup butter room temperature (250 ml)   2 cups all-purpose flour (500 ml)
1 cup granulated sugar (250 ml)   1 tsp baking soda (5 ml)
2 eggs beaten (2)   2 tsp cream of tartar (10 ml)
1 tsp vanilla (5 ml)   ½ tsp salt (2 ml)

- Cream butter and sugar until fluffy. Add beaten eggs and vanilla. Mix well.
- In a separate bowl, measure flour, baking soda, cream of tartar and salt. Add to creamed mixture and mix well.
- Form dough in one (1)-inch (2.5-cm) balls. Place on greased baking sheet. Flatten lightly with fork dipped in sugar.
- Bake in a 375⁰ F (190⁰ C) oven for 10-12 minutes until golden, approximately 2½ dozen.

Oatmeal Raisin Cookies

1 cup butter or shortening (250 ml)
1½ cups packed brown sugar (375 ml)
2 eggs beaten (2)
1 tsp vanilla (5 ml)
1 tbsp milk (15 ml)

1½ cups flour (375 ml)
2½ cups rolled oats (625 ml)
2 tsp baking soda (10 ml)
½ tsp salt (2 ml)
2 cups raisins (500 ml)

• In a bowl, cream butter or shortening with sugar until light and fluffy. Add eggs, vanilla, milk and mix well.
• In a separate bowl, measure flour, rolled oats, soda and salt.
• Add dry ingredients to creamed mixture, mixing well. Add raisins and mix to combine.
• Spoon large teaspoons of dough 2 inches (5 cm) apart on a greased baking sheet.
• Bake in a 350⁰ F (180⁰ C) oven for 10-12 minutes until slightly spread and golden. Makes approximately 3 dozen.

Hasty Raisin Pudding

4 tbsp butter (60 ml)
½ cup packed brown sugar (125 ml)
1 egg (1)
1 cup all-purpose flour (250 ml)
2 tsp baking powder (10 ml)
¼ tsp salt (1 ml)
½ cup milk (125 ml)
1 cup raisins (250 ml)

Topping
½ cup packed brown sugar (125 ml)
1 tbsp butter (15 ml)
2 cups boiling water (500 ml)
1 tsp vanilla (5 ml)

• In a bowl, cream butter and sugar until light. Add egg and beat.
• Combine flour, baking powder and salt. Add to creamed mixture with milk, beating to incorporate. Fold in the raisins.
• Pour batter into a well buttered 9 x 9 (23 x 23 cm) pan or casserole.
• Combine brown sugar, butter, boiling water and vanilla. Pour over batter.
• Bake in a 350⁰ F (180⁰ C) oven for 30-35 minutes until batter has risen and sauce in at the bottom. Serves 6.

NOTE
This hasty pudding was quick and delicious. Both cake and sauce are made together.

Fritale
(Deep Fried Italian Cookies)

2 eggs beaten (2)	2 tbsp milk (30 ml)
1 tsp vanilla (5 ml)	3 tsp baking powder (15 ml)
2 small oranges' rind and juice (2)	½ cup chopped raisins or apples (125 ml)
3 cups all-purpose flour (750 ml)	½ cup granulated sugar (125 ml)
1 tsp salt (5 ml)	1 tsp cinnamon (5 ml)

NOTE
The aroma of these small Italian cookies frying would have attracted Jacob to the Kitchen!

• In a medium bowl, beat eggs and sugar until light. Add vanilla, milk, juice and rind of oranges.

• Mix flour, salt and baking powder and add to egg mixture. Fold in raisins or apples. Mix well.

• Drop by small spoonfuls in deep hot fat 375⁰ F (190⁰ C). Fry until crisp. Remove from fat. Place on paper towels while still warm. Roll in cinnamon sugar mixture. Makes 4 dozen.

Jewish Knishes

	Cheese Filling
1 lb shortening (450 g)	2 cups dry cottage cheese (500 ml)
5 cups all-purpose flour (1.25 L)	1 egg (1)
1 tsp salt (5 ml)	1 tsp salt (5 ml)
2 cups sour cream (500 ml)	½ tsp black pepper (2 ml)
	1 tbsp butter (30 ml)

• In a medium bowl, combine flour and salt, cut shortening in cubes and work into flour using pastry blender or fingertips until crumbly.

• Add sour cream and combine well. Gather dough into a ball and divide into 4 pieces. Wrap each piece in plastic wrap and refrigerate for 30 minutes.

• In a bowl combine cottage cheese, egg, salt and pepper. Roll out each portion of dough into a 8 x 8 (20 x 20-cm) square. Spread a portion of filling over pastry and roll up like a jelly roll.

• Cut each roll into ¾-inch (2-cm) slices. Place on ungreased baking sheet and dot the top of each roll with a dab of butter. Bake in a 400⁰ F (200⁰ C) oven 20-25 minutes until golden. Makes approximately 3 dozen.

Poppy Seed Cake

½ cup poppy seeds (125 ml)
1 cup milk (250 ml)
1 tsp vanilla (5 ml)
¾ cup shortening (175 ml)
1½ cups granulated sugar (375 ml)

2 cups pastry flour sifted (500 ml)
2 tsp baking powder (10 ml)
½ tsp salt (2 ml)
4 egg whites (4)

- Soak poppy seeds in milk for 10 minutes. Add vanilla.
- In a bowl, cream shortening and sugar until fluffy. In a separate bowl, combine flour, baking powder and salt.
- Beat egg whites until stiff peaks form.
- Fold flour mixture into creamed mixture alternatively with milk and poppy seed mixture, combining well. Fold beaten egg whites into mixture, combining to form a light batter.
- Grease and dust with flour a 10-inch (25-cm) cake pan. Pour batter in pan. Bake in a 350⁰ F (180⁰ C) oven for 40-50 minutes until tester comes out clean. Remove from oven. Cool in pan for 10 minutes. Turn out on cooling rack and cool completely.
- This cake was often decorated with 7-minute boiled frosting. One (1) tablespoon (15 ml) of lemon zest may be added to cake batter.

Farewell St. Ann's

Peter Rankin 2007

*O*ne of the great planned migrations of the 19th Century – nearly a thousand men, women and children in six ships in eight years – left Cape Breton Island for new lives halfway around the world: final destination, the North Island of New Zealand. Why? The result of the vision and power of a charismatic religious and civic leader, the Rev. Norman MacLeod, a strongly dissident voice in the world of Presbyterians in both Scotland and Nova Scotia. An autocratic leader, MacLeod determined that the group of inhabitants around St. Ann's Bay on Cape Breton Island who worshipped together at the church controlled by MacLeod would be able to live as a group of like-minded people in better financial circumstances if they left St. Ann's and migrated to Australia. They later resettled in New Zealand. In 1851, after several years of preparation which included building a sailing vessel, the first group left on board the ship Margaret with MacLeod and his family among the passengers on board.

During the next eight years, five more ships followed the Margaret. Communications with those emigrants and their descendants have been maintained over the last century-and-a-half. A cultural institution, the Gaelic College, exists on the grounds where MacLeod once lived and is dedicated to him and to his group of congregants who were all Gaelic-speaking Scots. MacLeod was revered by many, feared by some and strongly disliked by others, but he was an influential man in his time. No diaries remain with details of preparations for the journeys or of the actual trips.

Through the fictional words of Hector Sutherland, who actually was a passenger on the Margaret, we meet a historical person who had doubts about the journey, and who remembered St. Ann's with fondness, but who nonetheless accomplished the task which MacLeod assigned him. The departure of these Gaels from Cape Breton had a detrimental effect on the development of Cape Breton and has been the subject of many books. But the arrival in New Zealand of these emigrants from Cape Breton had a major impact on the growth of the economy of that country.

Farewell St. Ann's

Hector Sutherland, once of St. Ann's Bay, reminisces at his home, in Waipu, New Zealand.

*N*ow, as an old man sitting in the sun on my veranda, looking out over the dry hillsides of New Zealand toward the waters of the Pacific Ocean, I find my mind going back to the green hillsides and the white-capped Bay of St. Ann's, Cape Breton. As Hector Sutherland, I am known here as a successful farmer with large flocks of sheep. In this year of 1881, I am one of the last surviving passengers of the ship *Margaret* which left our Cape Breton home thirty years ago. Even our noted leader, the Reverend Norman MacLeod, has passed from life after years of caring for us all.

Always, the Bay of St. Ann's is visible in my memory. I believe even my dreams are often located back in Nova Scotia. I see so clearly that splendid body of water: in the summer with the sheen of the sun reflecting from the surface; in the autumn, the hills colourful with the reds and yellows of the maples and birches mirrored all around the coves; in the winter, the blue-grey ice arranged in solid ripples under the full moon of February. From my childhood, when I arrived from Pictou, Nova Scotia, with my parents who were both natives of Scotland, I delighted in its beauty. As young people, my cousins and I swam in the summer and skated in the winter. We spent hours on its shores as we helped in the building of small boats and in the gathering of carrageen seaweed which was used to make a kind of pudding. As we grew older, we participated in harvesting of seafood from the water. Our fields with their flocks of sheep and the acres of grain turning yellow in the seasons extended from the top of the hillside to the edge of the rocky beaches. The bay was a constant presence in my life; I expected to raise my children along its shores and to be able to watch the changing patterns on its surface as I grew old. But that was not to be.

There came a day, in the spring of 1849, when Norman MacLeod brought forth a proposal which changed our lives. As was our custom on the Sabbath, as a family we came to the "Big Church" at Black Cove on the peninsula which jutted out into the bay. Our preacher and teacher, the Reverend MacLeod required that we all attend services, both in the morning and the afternoon. A powerful, energetic preacher in both Scottish Gaelic and English, he held the attention of all, even the smallest of children. The church building, with women seated on one side and men on the other, held nearly a thousand people and was filled every Sunday.

Even now, I can see the pulpit, made of local pine, high on a raised platform. Mr. MacLeod's voice was sonorous and resounded throughout the building as in no uncertain terms he reminded us of our sinfulness. The words of the preacher contained the powerful insistence that we should confess our evil ways to our Creator who was surely disappointed by our evil deeds and thoughts. As our minister and our Justice of the Peace and the leading school teacher, MacLeod was revered by the members of our community and almost never challenged in the power he held. He directed the lives of the people all around the bay and up into the glens of the hills above.

On that fateful warm spring day, the sun was coming through the clear glass panes which were carefully set in the arched windows. Although I was hearing the preacher's words, my eyes were attracted by the reflection of the sun off the water of the bay. I turned my head just a little, as I recall, so that I could look more directly out through the clear glass. Mr. MacLeod spoke my name in a loud rebuking voice as though I were a child, "Hector Sutherland, direct your whole mind towards the pulpit and hear the Word of God which will attempt to correct your errant ways." My young sons, seated by me, looked at me with astonishment. The view of my beloved bay was no longer in my eyes. Although a grown man, I felt once again the pain I had known as a young person when I was corrected again and again by our leader in the presence of others.

Silence was everywhere in the church. Nobody moved or even coughed. The people waited for our leader to continue his criticism of my disgraceful action and to remind me that the tortures of hell waited for such as me. My eyes fastened on his and I was held by his strong, demanding glare. He knew I was under his control. After some moments, he proceeded to speak, but in a different tone of voice and then came the announcement which we had reluctantly anticipated for some months. We all knew that Mr. MacLeod had corresponded recently with his son Donald who was living in Australia and working as a newspaper editor. From the pulpit, Norman MacLeod read the words of his son extolling the virtues of Australia. He was urging his father to leave St. Ann's Bay and to sail halfway around the world to a land where there was no frost and much opportunity.

My eyes were fixed on the Reverend Norman, but my mind was anticipating the words I knew were soon to come. And then he made the pronouncement... that we should plan to leave St. Ann's, all of us, the whole congregation. It was very evident that our leader, after months of thought and prayer, was now convinced that we should prepare to sail twelve thousand miles to an unfamiliar place. I was not surprised that my immediate reaction was that I would resist leaving St. Ann's Bay. I was reluctant even to consider the possibility that I would leave behind all that we had laboured so hard to create as a community. "After all," I said to myself, "this is my home, and this is where my parents lie in their final resting places." Silently, I began to list all the reasons we should not go and to name all the complexities of the possible journey.

Although nobody spoke, there was some shuffling of feet and some shifting around in the pews as people tried to take in what was being required of us. I learned later that some of the congregation thought the minister had taken leave of his senses, but many were nodding their heads in tacit agreement with MacLeod's announcement that the time had come to leave this place. We all heard him repeat the words he had written in a letter of reply to his son Donald, "I humbly trust in submission to the will of Heaven." It seemed a certainty that a ship would be built, provisions gathered, properties sold and emigration undertaken. Led by Rev. Norman MacLeod, we were to sail out of St. Ann's Bay, never to return.

Even now, more than thirty years after that spring morning in the church by the edge of Black Cove, I can see the faces of those around me and recall the thoughts which coursed through my mind. Dear St. Ann's Bay – how could I leave it behind? How could we sail from this beloved harbour with the awareness that we were undertaking a journey of much potential danger? How could I put my family at risk? Could I possibly disagree with MacLeod, our temporal and spiritual leader?

Then, with a concluding prayer and the singing of Psalm 121 in Gaelic, the minister brought the service to the end with the reminder that we would assemble again in the afternoon for instruction and worship. With a heart full of conflicting emotions, I left the church so dear to me and which I had helped to build years earlier.

During the next week, for several hours a day, I walked along the shore of the bay in an attempt to sort out my conflicting thoughts. In our daily family worship time, I prayed for guidance for me, my wife and children. I considered going to MacLeod's house, just up the hill from the church, to tell him of my uncertainty. But his words telling us to submit to the will of God resounded again and again in my ears. One night, I woke before dawn as I heard a rising wind coming from the north. I rose and went to the barn to be certain the doors were fastened tightly and the animals all safe. As I stood in the dooryard and looked out over the darkness that was the surface of the bay, I saw the moon shining on the waters at the far end where the waves of the harbour mingled with those of the sea. Immediately, a great weight was lifted from my heart and I knew that one day I would follow the waters of the bay out to the great ocean beyond.

Within a week or so of Mr. MacLeod's announcement, I sensed that enthusiasm for the proposed venture was rising throughout our settlement around St. Ann's Bay and beyond, in Middle River and Baddeck, where we all had friends and relatives. After several years of great anxiety about the future, people seemed to be emboldened by the idea of a new start. During the last two years, a blight on the potatoes had occasioned a near famine in our community and around the Island of Cape Breton. Although my own crop was not much damaged, several of my near neighbours watched as their potatoes rotted in the fields. There was considerable fear in the community that God was punishing us for our lack of faith and good works. Potatoes were a major portion of our sustenance, particularly during the winter. People even fed them to cattle when the harvested hay of the previous summer was running short.

In addition, we were shipping less lumber each year to Britain and to the West Indies for reasons we did not fully understand; the business just seemed not to be there. Many of our young people were growing restless. Some had already left for Upper Canada or parts of the United States. So, Australia seemed to promise a new beginning for us in a land where there was no frost, no potato blight and a much more moderate climate, at least according to Donald MacLeod's letters. Were we being encouraged by God to undertake the move as Reverend MacLeod stated? Many thought so.

One morning, a week or so after the announcement, MacLeod arrived at my house early in the morning. It was a beautiful day. The ice was all gone from the bay and fishing was about to begin. He greeted me in as friendly a manner as ever he could muster and spoke calmly to my wife and my children. My minister came, I quickly became aware, not to reprimand me but to request my services in planning the nature and the amount of provisions which would be required for our journey to sustain about one hundred and fifty men, women and children on board a sailing ship for six months. Others of the congregation would see to the cutting of the required trees and the framing of the vessel which would be built in Black Cove, just below the Big Church. My task, he said, if I would undertake it, was to ensure that adequate provisions were on board when the ship set sail – maybe in a little more than a year. I was to provide a carefully prepared list of what was needed, how it was to be stored on the ship and how much each family would provide.

So it seemed that a decision had been made for me. MacLeod was convinced that God was urging me to take this responsibility. Remembering my vision of the moon on the water and my awareness that I would be leaving St. Ann's Bay, I agreed to do as he requested. As we began to speak of the preparations required for the journey, we noted that food and water and clothing and bedding were necessities. Each family would need to be responsible for some portion of its own needs. I would make certain that some enclosed cooking ovens would be fashioned by the blacksmiths and that sufficient material for repairs to sails and rigging would be in the hold. My first task would be to prepare lists of all the provisions which we could prepare ahead of time.

As we spoke, we realized that ship captains who sailed into St. Ann's Bay from time to time or into nearby Baddeck could help with suggestions as to what was needed and in what quantity. Recent immigrants, as well, could tell us what kind of food might be found at ports of call during our journey. It was evident, however, that money was going to be short since the building of the vessel required much capital. Until families sold their properties, they would have but small resources to purchase provisions. We would need to rely on the willingness of the merchants in Baddeck to allow us to buy on credit. During our conversation, I came to be aware as never before of the vitality of Norman MacLeod and of his ability to bring a vision to reality. I was ready to follow him halfway around the world, despite my earlier doubts.

After we finished our meeting, I watched him walk back down the road with his top hat firmly fixed on his head as usual. Beyond him, I could see the whitecaps on the blue waters of the bay as a strong westerly wind raced across the surface. My heart was sad as I recorded the view in my memory, but my mind was firm now that I would assist in this undertaking to the very best of my ability. Plans had to be developed and shared with all the congregants, those who were going on the first ship and those who would follow afterwards in other ships.

On the next Sunday, with much fervour and a sense of urgency, the minister addressed the congregation. Although he berated us for our shortcomings, as was his custom, he soon began to speak about the coming journey. After informing us that the MacGregor brothers, noted local shipwrights, were prepared to oversee the construction of the vessel, he told us that the keel would be put in place within six weeks. Help, therefore, would be needed from all the men and boys in supplying the necessary timbers. People would have to go first into the woods this spring before going out on to the bay to fish or to the fields to complete the yearly ploughing. As an afterthought, he stated that the ship would be named *Margaret*, for his youngest daughter, since he was putting much of his own money into the construction of the ship. Black Cove was to be turned into a shipyard.

Addressing us from that high pulpit, so much a feature of the Big Church, he noted that several other vessels would be constructed as well in the coming years so that those who would follow the first contingent would have transportation. The pattern established for this first journey would be followed by later emigrants, even after his departure on the first boat. He also challenged those who would later follow to remain strong in their faith and to proceed as though he were still in their midst and to not be misled by ministers of other churches – "false prophets," he called them.

With a strongly worded sermon concerning the courage of the Biblical Sarah as she prepared to leave with Abraham in search of the promised land, he reminded the women of the strength and courage of their own mothers and grandmothers and of their ancestors in the faith. I could not help but think of my mother who had followed MacLeod from Scotland to Pictou, Nova Scotia, and then here to St. Ann's Bay, confident that he spoke the true words of God. And now, we were trusting him to lead us to a new promised land. As I look back, I can easily recall how stirred we all were that Sunday.

His closing words that day ensured the congregation that God would be with us and was expecting them to undertake those preparations and the forthcoming journeys so that our community could be established anew in a place where they would be free from all the temptations of the society which was encroaching on them in Cape Breton. He reminded them that increasingly other preachers were permitting the members of their congregations to relax in their disciplining of the young and were allowing women to wear fancy clothing and to place ribbons on their bonnets, entirely contrary to the teachings of the Bible. Clergy of other congregations were even writing letters to be published in newspapers in which they condemned him for his methods in directing the affairs of the community of St. Ann's Bay. They criticized his refusal to meet with other ministers as members of the governing board of the Presbyterian Church of Cape Breton. Thus, his vision was that their future location would be one where their children and their grandchildren would be safe and healthy and where they could live as a settlement apart from the sinfulness of the world.

And then, holding up his huge, gnarled hands in supplication and with his eyes lifted to the heavens, he pronounced a benediction full of Biblical references and with requests that the presence of God would be with the people as they left the House of God. He then asked the women to meet with me on one part of the hillside after we partook of our cold lunches and prior to our return for the afternoon service. MacLeod then added that "Hector Sutherland will have suggestions about the kinds of provisions we will take on board. I am requesting him to provide a detailed listing of what is required of each family." In answer to a question, he responded that there would be no room on the *Margaret* for household furniture, just bedding and pallets to sleep on. Each family could take one spinning wheel. There would be room for only the very best of the weaving looms.

As we sat on the ground outside the strong walls of the church with Black Cove below us, we were happy with the spring warmth in the air and well aware of the sunshine as it reflected off the surface of the bay. It seemed to be dancing on the top of the waves, even though our minister would not approve of such actions among his parishioners. As was our custom of many years, we ate together in family groups, but with much sharing among our relatives and friends.

Then, as older children looked after those who were younger, the men began a conversation about the cutting of timber and I met with the women on the other side of the hill to begin to make our plans. I well remember our discussion about how to prepare potatoes for the journey by shredding them and then exposing them to the air or to the heat of an oven in order to dry them, before wrapping them in birchbark. Each family would prepare some for their own use and some for the community. Although that activity would be some months ahead, it seemed well for us all to try to perfect the process.

Cod and other fish could be dried, salted, wrapped in bark and stowed in barrels a process that could begin soon. Each household would also provide pickled meat. I shared with them a procedure for evaporating milk sweetened with maple sugar so that it would last for some weeks. Unleavened bread could be prepared well beforehand. Sufficient oatmeal for the entire group would be stored in tightly sealed bins. Suitable amounts would be distributed each day as families in turn prepared a supply of cooked oatmeal in small metal stoves which would be on the open deck.

To all it was evident that we would have time to learn how best to prepare the appropriate foods. People would practise to be sure they had the proper techniques. Each family would provide some maple sugar tightly packed in jars. Homemade cheese, packed in salt in firkins, would be welcome.

Before we returned to the church, I went to some of the men and reminded them that we would need to keep out some of the best seeds from our fields of oats and wheat and barley so that we would be able to plant crops as soon as possible when we reached our new homes. It seemed well for each family to take at least one hoe and a digging fork, and we would take one plough which could be shared around the community. With some certainty, we were realizing the enormity of the task of planning for six months at sea and for some months after we arrived. Before long we returned to the church to hear more words of truth from Norman MacLeod.

As the warm days of summer arrived in Cape Breton, we were all pleased with the progress being made in the building of the *Margaret*. She was going to be a three-masted barque (or clipper ship, as some called the style). It was quite a sight to see her rising from the edge of the bay on a fine day with the bluest of skies overhead and white puffy clouds floating across the heavens. Standing on the hillside above the cove, I could see all the way to the narrow channel at the far end of St. Ann's Bay where the ocean spread out in the distance. I was already lonesome for the view.

Little by little, we learned how best to prepare the foodstuffs that we would require. People were starting to set aside casks for the packing of salt fish and preserved meats. Some families had already made arrangements with distant kin who lived in the glens back in the hills to buy their properties around the bay. The energy in the community was evident as preparations accelerated.

But, as the autumn rains descended on our fields, we were saddened to see some of the potato crop turn black once again with blight. Money was scarce in the settlement. Even the minister began to look concerned. As yet, he had no sale for his own fine property. Prayer meetings began that week, during which the minister led us in supplication to the Creator to assist us with our plans for departure. Although the hills around the bay were splendid with the colours of the autumn foliage, our hearts were despondent, our fears increased.

For another year, we waited for money from some source so that the rigging of the vessel might be completed. She was tied tightly to the trees on the shore as the winter winds battered her masts, but all remained in good condition. At times, I wondered if we were engaged in a foolish activity with our hopes turning as cold as the ice on the bay.

Finally, after eighteen months, Norman MacLeod announced that a buyer had been found for his property and the money gained would be sufficient to finish the ship and to purchase canvas for sails. As the seasons had come and gone with their great variety of weather, we learned much about the preparation of food. By the end of the summer of 1851, several hundred casks were lined up near the shore. They were to be filled with fresh water and salted meat and fish and quantities of dried potatoes and other foodstuffs. As the autumn came once again, our last on the shores of St. Ann's Bay, I watched with much satisfaction as the casks and wooden crates and bundles of bedding were loaded onto the vessel. Dismantled looms and spinning wheels were tightly packed in the hold of the ship.

And so it was that after thirty-one years in Cape Breton, we faithful, who were called "Normanites" by some, gathered on the hillside beside the Big Church. Some of us had come with the Reverend Norman MacLeod from Scotland, but most were born in Nova Scotia, many in log houses on farmsteads around this bay. The time for the final worship service had come. Although it could hold nearly a thousand, the Big Church was too small to hold the many people who had arrived to hear one more time the words of their revered and feared preacher. His white hair, blowing in the wind, was in contrast to the blackness of his ecclesiastical gown. Even his usual sturdy voice broke with emotion as he bid his followers "*beannachd leibh*" ("God bless you," in Gaelic).

Those of us who were going on the *Margaret* gave our final farewells to our neighbours and cousins who were remaining behind. The autumn leaves from the nearby trees were underfoot as we made our way to the beach to board the vessel which would carry us so far away. Some of those remaining in St. Ann's would later come on vessels now being planned – one already on the shipway. Little ripples of the salt water of the bay rolled to the shore as we climbed into the small boats which would carry us to the ship at anchor just off shore. Our journey, indeed our pilgrimage, was beginning: like Abraham and Sarah, we were setting out to find our promised land.

As we cast off the lines and raised anchor, our minister raised his eyes to heaven and prayed aloud for the safety of those of us onboard and for the firm faith of those left near the dear church which had been so much a part of his life. A good breeze carried us toward the opening which led to the sea and, for the last time, I read through my long list of provisions and equipment required for our journey. With a thankful heart, I noted that everything planned had been accomplished.

It was a sad day, that 28th of October in 1851, as we looked to each of the hills we had known so well and pointed out where our friends and relatives had made their homes. The water of St. Ann's Bay was bright with the reflected colour of the leaves and gleaming in the autumn sun. With his ever-present top hat in his left hand and his large Gaelic Bible held firmly to his chest with his right arm, MacLeod looked to the open sea and to the future.

Now, in memory, I see the waters and the land we left behind. Tears were in our eyes the day we said farewell to St. Ann's Bay. Our journey went well. Our provisions were sufficient and were supplemented when we called at the Cape Verde Islands and at Cape Town, South Africa. There, we bought fruit and vegetables and fresh water for the final leg of our journey. Although we looked ahead with hope, and some apprehension as well, our conversation was often about what we had left behind. But Reverend Norman constantly reminded us to keep our eyes looking ahead to the promised land, as Sarah and Abraham had done.

After a time in Australia, we found our permanent home here in New Zealand. Our community prospered and expanded as five more ships arrived with our neighbours and cousins from Cape Breton. The vision of the Reverend Norman MacLeod has come to reality and is now more fully appreciated. In sadness and disquiet, we heard his final words for us, spoken from his deathbed urging us "to look to yourselves, my children, the world is mad." But life has been good for most of us here.

As the small number of us who still survive from the journey of 1851 meet from time to time, we share our many memories, but particularly we give thanks that our planning ahead ensured that we had sufficient provisions for the long journey from Cape Breton. Most of all, for some of us, our recollections of the beauties of our old home in St. Ann's are uppermost in our conversation. We know we will never return, except in our dreams and memories.

These are the thoughts of Hector Sutherland, once of St. Ann's but now of North Island, New Zealand.

Hector Sutherland's
List of Staples for the Journey
– Destination Australia –

Barrels of Salt Meat
Dried Salt Cakes
Crocks of Pickled Salmon
Preserved Head Cheese
Blood Pudding
Marag
Dried Potato Chips
Barrels of Cranberries Stored in Water
Sacks of Potatoes
Sacks of Turnip
Kale
Oatmeal - Cornmeal
Whole Grain Flour
Salt - Vinegar
Maple Syrup - Molasses

Destination Australia

Voyage Menu

Head Cheese
Blood Pudding
Curd Cheese

Boiled Codfish
Pickled Salmon
Dried Potato Chips

Cranberry Chutney
Spiced Apples

1800 Griddle Cakes
Ash Cake Bread
Scottish Oatcakes
Scottish Shortbread

Blackberry & Apple Preserves

Orange Marmalade

Vinegar Candy

Head Cheese

4 lbs pork shoulder (bone in) (2 kg)   2 tsp salt (10 ml)

1 lb pork fat (450 g)   5 whole cloves (5)

4 large onions peeled and chopped (4)   6 whole allspice (6)

1 tsp black pepper (5 ml)   6 cups cold water (1.5 L)

• Cut pork shoulder and pork fat in large pieces. Place in a large pot. Add onion, salt, pepper, water and spice bag.

• Bring pot to a boil. Reduce heat and simmer for approximately 1½ hours or until meat falls from the bone.

• Discard bones and continue cooking until mixture is thick and water has partially evaporated, stirring occasionally.

• Remove from heat. Cool slightly and mix well, removing any fat pieces. Taste and adjust seasoning if necessary.

• Spoon mixture into buttered moulds, packing down well. Pour melted lard or butter over mixture. Makes 2-lb mould.

• Store in refrigerator or freezer.

> NOTE: Originally, head cheese was made utilizing the pig's head. This was a long and tedious process, which I observed my mother doing on several occasions. I have worked out a simpler version which is delicious. Head cheese was stored for the winter in crocks in the cellar. YL

Curd Cheese

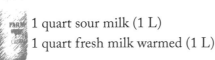

1 quart sour milk (1 L)

1 quart fresh milk warmed (1 L)

> NOTE
> Curds can be made creamier by adding ½ cup whipping cream and mixing to combine.

• Heat sour milk until lukewarm. Add fresh warmed milk. Set aside.

• Line a large strainer or colander with a double layer of cheesecloth. Place strainer over a bowl.

• Pour milk into strainer and gather cheesecloth to form a bag and secure milk.

• As milks sour they will coagulate and form curds. The strainer should be above the bowl so whey can drip in the bowl. (This can take several hours.)

• Discard the whey and transfer curds to a bowl. If desired, break up curds.

Blood Pudding

4 cups pig's blood (1 L)

1 tbsp vinegar (15 ml)

4 large onion chopped (4)

½ cup lard (melted)

2 lbs fresh pork fat (diced) (1 kg)

1 tbsp salt (15 ml)

2 tsp black pepper (10 ml)

1 tsp ground allspice (5 ml)

¾ cup white wine or wine vinegar (175 ml)

¾ cup whipping cream (175 ml)

- In an earthenware bowl, combine blood and vinegar to prevent coagulation. Set aside.
- Heat melted lard in a large skillet and cook onions until soft.
- Dice fresh pork and soften in a skillet without browning until cubes of pork become translucent.
- Add onion mixture to pork and cook for 20 minutes over medium heat. Add salt, pepper, allspice and wine or vinegar.
- Remove from the heat and, stirring constantly, add the blood. Add cream and combine well.

To assemble blood puddings: (Use plastic casings purchased from supplier.) Tie a secure string on bottom before filling.

- Insert a large open funnel in casing opening and fill casing with blood mixture, packing filling firmly using a plunger.
- Tie filled casing securely with string. Pierce casing all over with pin.
- Place pudding in large roaster of rapidly boiling water. Reduce heat and poach for approximately 20 minutes. As puddings rise to the surface, prick them with a pin to release the air.
- Remove from the water. Drain well and leave to cool under a cloth.

To serve blood pudding: Slice in 1-inch thick portions and fry in butter until heated through. Serve with potatoes, eggs or fried apple slices.

Boiled Codfish

1 large dried cod fish (500 g)
¼ cup melted butter (60 ml)

- Cut codfish in pieces. Place in a large saucepan. Cover with cold water and soak for several hours or overnight, draining and adding fresh water to cover during that time.
- Drain fish and cover completely with cold water. Bring to a boil. Reduce heat and simmer for 20-25 minutes or until fish flakes.
- Drain. Transfer fish to a bowl and serve with melted butter.

Pickled Salmon

3-4 lbs salmon, cleaned (1.4-2 kg)

Pickle
2 cups vinegar (500 ml)
3 cups cold water (750 ml)

2 onions sliced (2)
6 whole cloves (6)
4 whole allspice (4)

- Place whole salmon in a large oval roaster. Cover salmon with cold water and sprinkle with 1 tsp (5 ml) salt. Bring to a boil uncovered. Reduce heat and simmer for 30 minutes.
- Remove from heat and allow salmon to cool in roaster.
- In a saucepan, bring vinegar, water, onion, cloves and allspice to a boil. Reduce heat and simmer for 30 minutes.
- Remove salmon from roaster and place in a large crock. Pour spiced pickle over salmon, making sure salmon is completely covered.
- Place a weight on salmon to keep it immersed in liquid. Cover and store in a cool place.
- Serve salmon with egg slices and greens.

NOTE
For MacLeod's journey, salmon would have been served as a celebration treat.

Peter Rankin 2007

Dried Potato Chips

6 large potatoes (6)

- Wash potatoes. Place in a large saucepan and cover well with cold water. Bring to a boil and cook until potatoes are barely tender (testing with the point of a sharp knife).
- Remove potatoes from heat. Drain well and cool completely.
- When potatoes are cold, peel and slice ¼-inch (5-mm) thick. Arrange slices on baking sheets and place in a 200⁰ F (100⁰ C) oven until crisp, turning every 20 minutes.

> NOTE
> Potatoes could also be dried by placing outdoors in the hot sun for several days.

Cranberries

Cranberries were one of the easiest of fruit to keep for long periods of time. They could be stored in a cool place, spread out on a cloth or placed in a barrel and covered with water. Cranberries must be completely immersed in water.

Cranberry Chutney

1½ cups water (375 ml)
1½ cups cider vinegar (375 ml)
2½ cups packed brown sugar (625 ml)
6 whole cloves (6)
1 stick cinnamon (1)
½ tsp ground ginger (2 ml)

4 tart apples peeled, coarsely chopped (4)
1 cup raisins (250 ml)
½ cup currants (125 ml)
¼ cup mixed lemon peel (60 ml)
8 cups fresh cranberries (2 L)

> NOTE
> Cranberry Chutney is a wonderful way of keeping cranberries, and recipes for chutney are very old. Chutney would have been stored in crocks.

- In a large saucepan, bring water, vinegar, sugar, cloves, cinnamon, ginger to a boil, stirring until sugar is dissolved.
- Add apples, raisins, currants and mixed peel to liquid and simmer for 15 min.
- Add the cranberries. Mix well and continue cooking for 30 minutes until cranberries have popped and are tender, and mixture has thickened.
- Spoon into sterilized jars. Seal and store in a cool dry place.

Spiced Apples

8 lbs apples peeled and sliced (4 kg)
4 lbs sugar (2 kg)
1 quart water (1 L)

1 quart vinegar (1 L)
1 cinnamon stick (1)
4 cloves (4)

> **NOTE**
> Wax seal is made by melting paraffin wax and pouring over hot spiced apples.

- In a large saucepan, place water, vinegar, sugar and spices. Bring to a boil. Add apples, reduce heat and simmer until apples are barely tender.
- Remove from heat and strain, reserving the syrup. Place apples in a sterilized crock or jars.
- Return syrup to saucepan and boil for 10 minutes. Pour hot syrup over apples. Cool slightly and cover with wax seal.
- Store in a dry cool place.

1800 Griddle Cakes

2 cups cornmeal (500 ml)
1 cup flour (250 ml)
1 tsp salt (5 ml)
1 tsp baking soda (5 ml)

4 eggs lightly beaten (4)
4 cups milk (1 L)
2 tbsp melted butter or lard (30 ml)

> **NOTE**
> At that time, griddle cakes would have been cooked on a griddle hanging from the hearth.

- Measure cornmeal, flour, salt and baking soda in a bowl. Add beaten eggs, milk and melted butter or lard.
- Beat until well combined and mixture is light.
- Drop by large spoonful on a heated griddle (batter will spread). When bubbles form, turn over once and cook until crisp and golden.
- Serve with butter and maple syrup.

Ash Cake Bread

2 cups whole wheat flour (500 ml)   4 tbsp melted butter (60 ml)
1 quart cornmeal (1 L)   2 tsp salt (10 ml)
4 tbsp melted lard (60 ml)   3 cups milk (750 ml)

- Combine flour, cornmeal and salt. Add melted lard and butter and just enough milk to make dough pliable. Gather dough in a ball.
- Knead the dough well, sprinkling flour if needed. Make it into two (2) round flat cakes.
- Sweep a clean place in the hottest part of the hearth. Place cakes on hearth and cover with hot wood ashes. Cook until firm.
- Remove from hearth. Brush away ashes and wash away any residue before eating.

NOTE: This bread, dense, coarse and heavy, was a keeper. For today's cook, sprinkle bread generously with flour. Bake bread in a 350^0 F (180^0 C) oven until firm and crisp, approximately one (1) hour.

Scottish Oatcakes

2 cups ground oatmeal (500 ml)   ½ tsp baking soda (2 ml)
2 cups whole wheat flour (500 ml) ¾ cup lard (175 ml)
4 tbsp brown sugar (60 ml)   ½ cup cold water (125 ml)
½ tsp salt (2 ml)

- In a bowl combine oatmeal, flour, sugar, salt and baking soda.
- Work lard into oat mixture, using fingertips, until all is crumbly.
- Add water a little at a time, tossing with fork to combine. Gather dough in a ball.
- Knead lightly on floured surface and roll out. Cut into circles or squares. Arrange on lightly greased baking sheet.
- Bake in a 375^0 F (190^0 C) oven for 15-18 minutes until golden and crisp. Makes 4 dozen.

NOTE
The use of ground oatmeal gives the oatcakes a very crisp texture.

Scottish Shortbread

1 cup brown sugar (250 ml)
2 cups butter (cold) (500 ml)
4 cups all-purpose flour (1 L)

- In a bowl measure sugar and flour. Cut butter in cubes and, using fingertips, work butter into flour mixture until rich and crumbly.
- Form dough into a ball and knead lightly on floured surface until smooth.
- Divide dough in two (2) pieces. Pat or roll each piece into ¾-inch (2-cm) thick rounds.
- Transfer rounds to ungreased baking sheet. Prick all over with fork and crimp the edges. Score top to indicate wedges.
- Bake in a 275⁰ F (140⁰ C) oven for 45-50 minutes or until lightly golden and crisp.
- Remove from oven. Cool for 10 minutes and cut into wedges.

Blackberry & Apple Preserves

4 cups blackberries (1 L)
3 cups apples peeled and diced (750 ml)
¾ cup water (175 ml)
5 cups granulated sugar (1.25 L)

NOTE
To test if preserve is cooked, drop a teaspoon on a chilled saucer. Return saucer to freezer until preserve is of a jelled consistency.

- In a large saucepan, combine apples, berries and water. Bring to a boil. Simmer covered for 35 minutes or until fruit is soft.
- With fruit simmering, add sugar slowly, stirring continuously until sugar is dissolved.
- Bring to a boil. Boil uncovered without stirring for approximately 20-25 minutes or until jam jells when tested.
- Remove from heat. Stir for 3 minutes. Pour into hot sterilized jars. Seal when cold. Makes 8 cups.

Orange Marmalade

5 large oranges (5)

5 cups water (1.25 L)

5 cups granulated sugar (1.25 L)

3 tbsp lemon juice (45 ml)

- Cut oranges into quarters using a sharp knife. Remove pits and rind from each quarter.
- Cut orange flesh into thin slices. Place in a bowl. Discard seeds.
- Cut rind into very thin strips. Place in bowl with orange flesh. Cover with half the water and let stand overnight.
- Place orange mixture in a large saucepan. Add remaining water and lemon juice. Bring to a boil. Simmer, covered, for 40 minutes or until rind is soft.
- Add sugar. Stir over low heat, without boiling, until sugar is dissolved.
- Bring to a boil. Boil uncovered without stirring for about 20-25 minutes or until marmalade jells when tested. Pour into hot sterilized jars. Seal. Makes 7 cups.

Vinegar Candy

2 tbsp butter (30 ml)

2 cups sugar (500 ml)

½ cup vinegar (125 ml)

- Melt butter in a heavy pan. Add sugar and vinegar. Stir until sugar dissolves. Wash down sides of pan with brush dipped in cold water to clear any sugar.
- Boil to brittle stage, 256^0 F (122^0 C).
- Turn into buttered shallow pan. As mixture cools around sides, fold toward centre.
- When cool enough to handle, gather up and pull until porous, light-coloured and firm.
- Cut into pieces with shears or sharp knife, and arrange on slightly buttered plates to cool.

> NOTE
> Vinegar Candy is very old and would have been a "surprise treat" for children on the voyage.

Peter Rankin 2007

Rebecca's Fireplace: March 30, 1789

Peter Rankin 2007

*O*n the western shore of Cape Breton Island, Port Hood was the location of a pioneer settlement of people of European background in the late 1700s. To the fine harbour formed by a sandbar extending to a small island offshore came United Empire Loyalists from the newly formed United States after the American Revolution. They were joined by settlers from the southwestern corner of Ireland and people from England and a large contingent of Gaelic-speaking Scots. Among the very first were the members of the Smith family from Cape Cod, Massachusetts. They established their home on Port Hood Island where they fished and farmed and hunted for seals in the winter.

In the third year of their being there, Captain David Smith lost his life while out on the ice with two of his sons. His story has often been told. His widow, Rebecca Smith, bravely remained in the developing community and raised their family, including a child born five months after Capt. David was lost. Her story deserves a hearing too, for it was her strength and courage that enabled these children to grow into adulthood and contribute much to the growth of the area. We can imagine her busy at her huge fireplace in their first house, a log building, more than two hundred years ago. Today the structure is gone, as is the sandbar, but the island remains, as do memories of Rebecca Smith.

Rebecca's Fireplace: March 30, 1789

*C*ome with us, just before dawn as the sky brightens. Imagine yourself able to partake of a bird's eye view of a sandy shoreline on the western coast of Cape Breton. See how the beach grows into a sandbar which in 1789 reaches out into the bay and attaches to a mile-long island. In the middle of the peninsula, and surrounded by several acres of land cleared of bushes and trees, is a fine-looking log house, ten metres by seven. An impressive chimney constructed of cut stone rises above the roof line. From it comes a narrow line of smoke going straight up into the misty air. Except for a small log barn and a couple of sheds, this is the only structure on this tranquil-looking place, known as the inner island of Port Hood, even though it is connected to the mainland. Just beyond its farthest tip, across a narrow channel is another island, but one without inhabitants.

Look to the other side of the well-protected harbour and across the sweep of the landscape where low hills surround an extended piece of level ground along the sandy shore. Just above the beach, a nearly straight track goes from house to house, all of them log. Perhaps there are five or six, all built with notched timbers at the corners, some as large as the dwelling on the island and some a bit smaller. They are each on a separate tract of land, and a few hundred metres from one another. No church building or school house or government office can be seen in this newly established community. Above the high-water line rest half-a-dozen sailing vessels, some just large enough for inshore fishing, but one or two of sufficient size to sail across the Gulf of St. Lawrence to mainland Nova Scotia or to Prince Edward Island. At this time of the day, only a dog or two can be seen in motion. Otherwise all is quiet. Streams of gray smoke show that fires were kept burning on hearths all night long, for it is only the end of March and nights are still cold. This morning, a light frost covers the ground. From our vantage site, there is no evidence of the grief and the uncertainty which hold this new community in a tight grip.

Come with us now to the log house on the island. As we step inside, we see the dining table and benches in the centre. Along the walls are various chests and baskets and piles of dry firewood and small tables covered with dishes and containers. Garments hang from wooden pegs driven into the logs. In one corner is a large bed with a cradle to the side. Against the wall opposite the door is a strongly made ladder leading to the sleeping loft overhead. But the dominant feature of this one room cabin is the large stone fireplace with its chimney. Above the opening, which is more than a metre high, two wide and one deep, is a carefully carved mantelpiece. On it are several candlesticks, a seal oil lamp, a primitive barometer and a looking glass. Within the large hearth are two large maple logs burning slowly. A crane, five feet in length, is fastened to one of the walls of the fireplace. Suspended from it are a half dozen iron pots attached by "s" hooks. Several kettles rest on the stones set in the floor in front. A large spinning wheel sits to one side and six ladder-back chairs form a semicircle around the opening; wool in a large wicker basket on one of them waits to be spun. It is evident that this fireplace is the center of activity in the home of widow Rebecca Smith. Although nobody is moving about in the room in the early dawn we can sense an atmosphere of grief in this dwelling, in its quiet location on a sandy peninsula of a newly settled land.

The Day Begins

Quietly, two teen-age boys, Lewis, age 18, and young Davey, age 14, climb down the ladder from the loft above. With a quick look to the bed in the corner where their mother, Rebecca, and two year-old sister, Becky, seem still to be asleep, they move across the room to the pile of kindling. As quietly as they can, the boys bring the fire to a blaze with the help of small branches and pieces of birch bark. They ladle water from a crock into one of the kettles and move the crane over the fire so that the liquid will come quickly to a boil. It will be ready for their mother when she starts to make the breakfast porridge. After eating a slice or two of their mother's homemade bread spread with butter, they put on their warm caps and jackets and silently leave the house to go to the barn to milk the cows. The day is starting in the house built by Rebecca's late husband, Captain David Smith, to house his family in the autumn after their arrival in 1786, as United Empire Loyalists from the newly formed United States.

The forty-two-year-old widow begins to raise herself from her feather bed after putting aside the quilts and woollen blankets that covered her and her young daughter. From the side of the bed, she can see across the room to the huge stone fireplace. With pride, she has watched her two young boys taking on responsibilities for the well-being of their younger brothers, Isaac, Parker and Harding and little sister, Becky.

Grief Remembered

Born Rebecca Lombard on Cape Cod, Massachusetts, she is facing another day of realization that her husband will not return from his venture out onto the ice in search of seals just six weeks ago. The coldness of that realization is born anew this day as she rises to the tasks ahead of her. Her night's rest has been fitful – she awoke several times in the half-awake hope that somehow David has come back. As well, she had needed to comfort her young daughter, little Becky, who slept in a cradle next to her bed. Before dawn she had taken the young girl into bed with her.

Rebecca is increasingly aware of the new child growing in her womb. Her walking is a little slower and a bit more awkward than usual. Conceived in the autumn, the new life will come into the world in the middle of the coming summer, but without a father to welcome it. As she comes to be fully awake, Rebecca for a moment holds the sleeping Becky to her breast, covers her and rises to face a new day with its sadnesses and joys.

After dressing quickly, Rebecca stands by the window where the light of dawn is visible across the ice-covered harbour and behind the distant hills. There, on the other side of the frozen expanse is the recently constructed dwelling of her neighbours and good friends, Edward and Phoebe Hayes, immigrants like herself, but from Wexford, Ireland. The smoke rising from their stone chimney is going straight up. According to the old weather signs, that thin line of smoke predicts a change in the weather, perhaps before dark. Could there be another snowstorm? Or perhaps an early spring rain? The needs of her family call her from the window to the hearth, the centre of this house. The chill of the early morning and the chill in her heart are not quickly warmed by the strong blaze in front of her, but she commences the preparation of the morning oatmeal porridge.

Six weeks have passed since that terrible day in February, when her husband and the two boys left this very room early on a frosty morning to go out on the ice pack surrounding the island. She remembers how they looked as they went out with clubs, a gun and a length of rope and accompanied by their young dog. David and Lewis and young Davey left the warmth of this hearth and the comfort of their morning porridge to go in search of seals whose pelts would provide material for coats and boots and whose fat could be burned in small lamps.

Although nearly grown men, she knows that the boys are still awaking every morning with a recurring nightmare as they continue to relive the horror of that day. A sudden squall of snow came from the north and the ice cake on which they were standing broke in two with a loud crack. The split separated them and their dog from their father, the experienced Captain David. They can still hear the shouts of their father as he disappeared into the blackness of the snow. Although they threw the rope in his direction, again and again, there was no tug on the other end to signal he had caught and would soon join them. There was no answer to their voices shouting to him. "Father, father, where are you?"

Rebecca shudders as she thinks again and again of the long walk the boys had along the shore after they came to the beach near Mabou Harbour. She can still see the anguish in their eyes as they told her what had happened. And now, six weeks have passed. The ice cakes, or clampers as some call them, hold the land tightly in their grip. On bright days, miles and miles of the frozen surface of the sea could be seen as far as one could look. As the wind changed or the tide rose and fell, the sound of cake grinding against cake could be heard even in their warm cottage. Only now, as April approaches, the ice is disappearing and open water can be seen here and there in the harbour.

For these six weeks, people have walked the shore from the small settlement of Judique, ten kilometres up the coast, to the mouth of the Mabou River, eleven to the north, in the hope of finding the body of Rebecca's husband. They looked in piles of rocks in small harbours and underneath ice cakes washed up on the beaches. Every day the half dozen families, all recent immigrants, have tried as well to comfort Rebecca; they bring food to her children and speak encouraging words to the boys who had gone out with their father, but came back without him. Recently arrived from Ireland or Cape Cod or New Jersey or Connecticut, these caring people have had to take the place of any officials who might have been consulted in older or larger settlements. Here there is no minister, no priest, no teacher, no public official who could have read words of comfort or perhaps organized a search effort.

Now, just two-and-a-half years after she and David invited all their neighbours to a Thanksgiving feast served in front of their newly constructed fireplace, Rebecca is starting another new day without her husband. As the porridge cooks slowly, she sits by the fire for a few moments and reads a selection from the Book of Psalms as a way of trying to find words of comfort for herself and her children. As she pauses in the reading after the words, "The Lord is my shepherd, I shall not want, He leadeth me … ," she feels the motion of the new child within her body. "Oh, how am I going to provide for another mouth? Surely God will somehow bring David back," she thinks as though in prayer. After finishing the passage, she proceeds to stir the porridge and adds some of the water the boys had put on to boil. From the foot of the ladder, she calls to the three younger boys who are still asleep in the loft overhead. After a few moments, down the ladder they come, one after the other – Isaac, Parker and Harding – slowly awakening to the new day.

New Morning, New Insights

After Davey and Lewis return from the barn with a wooden bucket nearly full of warm milk, she strains the milk into large crockery bowls and pours some into a small pewter pitcher that her grandmother back in Massachusetts gave her for a wedding gift. Some maple sugar is broken into lumps and placed on the table. With little Isaac's help, she spoons the morning porridge into the wooden bowls. Together the mother and her children, five young boys and a little girl, give thanks for their food. An empty chair to the side was that in which David once sat at the head of the table. Slowly, as Rebecca brings the pewter spoon with its helping of warm porridge sweetened with maple sugar to her lips, she feels a cold shudder across her shoulders and deep into her heart.

To herself, she says, "David has really died out on that frozen surface, far away from this hearth of which he was so proud; never again will he know the simple goodness of morning porridge or of beef stew slowly simmered at the back of the fireplace." In her heart, she ponders the implications of her new understanding: "How can I go on? Should we go back to Cape Cod and live with my parents and my brothers? How can I help my children and myself move beyond our sadness? How can I come to be both father and mother to these children and begin to direct the activities of this whole family by myself?" As her children chatter among themselves, she hears these words within her head.

After they finish their meal, the two older boys set forth again to the barn to look to the livestock and then to bring up fresh water from the spring on the hillside below the house. As Rebecca rises to clear the dishes from the large dining table brought from Cape Cod and used on board their sailing ship before David and the boys finished the house, the morning sun begins to shine through the east window and bring warmth and a promise of spring. With a thought to the noon meal, she puts beef and sliced onion and several potatoes into the pot hanging from the middle of the fireplace crane. It is now time to see to the morning needs of little Becky, a patient child who is just starting to move across the floor on her own and now enjoys a taste of porridge and says some babbling words.

Visitors

But before she can finish changing Becky's clothes and washing her wriggling little body, through the door come her neighbours from the other side of the sandbar, Phoebe and Edward Hayes. Their voices are artificially cheerful as they comment on the growing warmth of the sun and on the good aroma coming from the stew in the kettle. Both born in Wexford, Ireland, their accents always made David laugh, for their voices were so much more rhythmical than the flatter Yankee twang of the Smiths. David and Edward had developed a strong trust in each other although they were of such different origins. David was going to help him build a small structure near the shore in front of his house where he planned to open a small store, the first along this coast.

In addition to a johnnycake and some fish chowder in small crocks, Phoebe has put cookies in her large wicker basket and as well a small container of dried mint leaves. With a glint of fun in her bright blue eyes, Phoebe says, "Good for a lady with a baby in her belly; keeps them both jolly when put in a cup of tea." Although this is the first time, she has mentioned Rebecca's pregnancy, she has noticed for a week now that her friend, still in such deep grief, has been starting to move more slowly and to show her swelling belly. With the easy humour of Phoebe Hayes and the mention of mint leaves, Rebecca knows that she is now sharing her news with others and she will soon have to tell her boys.

With quick words exchanged among them all and special greetings to the boys and some special attention to little Becky, Phoebe and Edward warm themselves by the fire. They are chilled after their mile walk across the sand bar and along the path to the middle of the island. Edward has brought a small bottle of brandy and several newly cleaned rabbits caught in a snare behind his house. They are ready for cooking. Rebecca appreciates how helpful her neighbours, good friends indeed, are being as the family struggles to find their way in new circumstances. While Phoebe removes her cap and mittens and heavy cape, Edward says he will go to the barn to see what he can do to help Lewis and Davey.

Although the boys have been doing their best to keep things going as they take care of the two cows and the small flock of sheep and the chicken, and make certain there is water for the house and for the barn and ample firewood in the house, Rebecca knows that they have needed the encouragement of an older man now that their father has gone. In the last several days, she has noted they have regained some of their energy and seem to be recovering from their hours out on the ice that day, as they floated along until they finally reached the beach and then walked the many miles to home. She knows they still have bad dreams and will wonder again and again what they could have done to save their father. Surely, they are aware as well that they too might have died out on the ice.

As she marvels at their growth and courage, Rebecca is aware that the boys are uncertain as to how to proceed once spring arrives. Will they go fishing in their father's boat? Will they be able to put in a garden of root vegetables? How will they get along with Edward Hayes now that he is starting a small store near his house, when it comes time to barter for goods the family will need? She is starting to realize that they will be strong young men and gain new courage as they consult with other older men in the area such as Benjamin Worth and Matthew Hawley. And then the thought passes across her mind, Maybe it would be well to remain right here, in the house their father built as shelter for us all. Maybe, there is a continuing warmth in this home after all.

As they sit together in front of the hearth, speaking about food and spinning and children, the two women keep an eye on the three young boys who were amusing their little sister by creating small boats out of little pieces of wood. As well, they maintain the fire and keep watch over the stew and the johnnycake which Rebecca has placed in the small metal oven at the edge of the hearth. Warm coals from the back of the hearth will keep it warm. When Phoebe asks if she and Edward might take Becky and little Isaac back to their house for a day or two as company for their own young child, Mary, Rebecca agrees with some reluctance. "A day or two will be all right." She insists, however, that they all gather for a noon meal before Phoebe and Edward and her two youngest children set forth back across the sandbar. With a bright tone to her voice, the widow Smith says to her friend Phoebe, "It will be well for them to be with you off and on, so that when the new little one comes, they will be accustomed to being away from home for a few days. You are a good friend and I trust you with my children. I hope we will have many years together in this place." As she speaks these words, she realizes she is coming to understand that it would be well for them all to remain here on this island.

Outside, Edward Hayes sets forth down the hill to the shore with Lewis and Davey to see how their father's boat has survived the winter and to make plans for some repairs to the sail. Within the increasingly warm house, Phoebe and Rebecca work side-by-side preparing the noon meal. They place wooden bowls for stew and spoons on the table. Then, they put out baked apples, fresh bread and johnnycake with butter from their own cows on the table. As Edward and the boys come back from the shore, full of conversation about things to be done, the two woman serve the stew from the kettle. With little Becky asleep in her cradle placed near the table, Rebecca and her five boys, and Phoebe and Edward Hayes sit down together. Grace is spoken by little Davey with a special added prayer in Irish Gaelic by Phoebe. As a treat, Edward prepares a hot toddy from the brandy sweetened with maple sugar – a small mug for each person – even the children have a weaker version, the brandy more diluted than that served to the adults.

New Resolve

As Rebecca rises to bring cups to the table for the tea she is brewing in the fine china teapot her parents had given her back in Cape Cod, she looks back across the table at her children and her good neighbours all carrying on conversations. The chill has gone from her body. The warmth is returning to her bones and to her house, and not just from the logs burning on the andirons. She is experiencing new comfort from the awareness of the unborn child within her. She turns and looks to the large hearth with its mantelpiece so carefully carved by her husband. Here, she realizes, is her home; here is the place she needs to be; here by her fireplace so well built for the future; here she will stay and prosper and one day build a frame house with the stone chimney and hearth in the center, as she and David had planned. In several months, the baby will come into the world and she will welcome this new life and surround this last of David's children with love.

As she stands there, between the liveliness of the talk around the table and the warmth of the blazing fire, she sees in a quickening of her memory all the fireplaces of her childhood back in Cape Cod in both her parents' home and that of David's father and mother, and even in that immense one in the home of her grandfather, a minister. She knows that she and David have brought a good heritage with them to this new place. The warmth and the nourishment which she feels now will continue for many years. "Rebecca's fireplace," she thought, "my place, no matter what storms may come in the future." And then to her children and to her friends, she states in a clear, hopeful voice, "I am staying here by my hearth, David's gift to me and his children. I am now aware he will not return, but we will go on. Now, have some tea and more johnnycake."

Soon Phoebe, with young Isaac by the hand and Edward carrying a carefully bundled up little Becky, set forth back across the peninsula and the sandbar to their own home. When they are halfway there, Edward stops for a moment and turns to look back. He sees that the an ample plume of smoke is still rising straight up from Rebecca's fireplace chimney. The weather will perhaps hold and soon fair days will come. The ice will soon all have disappeared and with it some of the harshness of the memories of the last six weeks.

Making their way back to the other side of the Harbour, Edward and Phoebe Hayes agree that regardless of what may come, Rebecca Smith, widow of Captain David, is going to be all right. They admire her courage and determination, as have generations of people since those days of 1789.

So now we leave Rebecca Lombard Smith, busy at the work around her ample hearth and well aware of the words of the Psalm: "I shall not want." Some day, come and stand where she lived and ponder all that she endured and accomplished.

The Kitchen, Fields & Garden
of Rebecca Lombard Smith

❧ MENU ❧

Fish Chowder
Clam Chowder
Scalloped Mussels
Fried Smelts

Rabbit Stew
New England Boiled Dinner
Codfish Cakes
Baked Beans
Mutton or Lamb Stew with Dumplings

Fiddleheads with Butter

Steamed Cranberry Pudding
Brown Sugar Sauce
Pound Cake
Banbury Tarts

Corn Bread
Steamed Brown Bread

Rhubarb Relish

Blackberry Jam

Fish Chowder

2 lbs cod or haddock fillets (900 g)
½ lb salt pork diced (225 g)
1 large onion thinly sliced (1)
3 cups boiling water (750 ml)
4 cups potatoes peeled and diced (1 L)

2 tsp salt (10 ml)
1 tsp black pepper (5 ml)
2 cups milk (500 ml)
½ cup cream (125 ml)

> **NOTE**
> If preferred, butter can be used to replace salt pork. However, the pork imparts a unique flavour.

- Cut fillets in 2-inch (5-cm) pieces. Set aside.
- In a soup pot, sauté pork until cubes are crisp. Add onion and cook until soft.
- Add boiling water, potatoes, salt and pepper. Bring to a boil. Reduce heat and simmer until tender.
- Add fish and continue simmering until fish is tender and flakes.
- In a separate saucepan, heat milk and cream. Pour into fish mixture, stirring gently.
- Taste and adjust seasoning. Serves 6.

Scalloped Mussels

1½ lbs mussels (700 g)
½ cup cold water (125 ml)
1 bay leaf (1)
½ tsp pepper (2 ml)
1½ cups fine breadcrumbs (375 ml)
½ tsp salt (2 ml)

½ tsp black pepper (2 ml)
½ cup melted butter (125 ml)
1 tbsp chopped parsley (15 ml)
½ cup whipping cream (125 ml)
½ cup mussel stock (125 ml)

- Scrub mussels and place in a large saucepan. Add water, bay leaf and pepper. Cover saucepan and bring to a boil. Reduce heat and simmer for approximately 5-7 minutes until mussel shells have popped open. Remove mussels from liquid. Reserve the liquid. (Discard any closed shells.) Remove remaining mussels from shells.
- Butter a 1.5 quart (1.5 litre) baking dish. Arrange mussels in bottom of dish.
- Combine whipping cream with milk and strained mussel liquid. Pour over mussels.
- Mix butter, bread crumbs, salt, pepper and parsley. Sprinkle over mussels.
- Bake in a 350⁰ F (180⁰ C) oven for 20-25 minutes until golden and tender. Serves 4.

Clam Chowder

6 cups shucked clams (1.5 L)
¼ lb salt pork cubed (115 g)
2 onions finely diced (2)
8 medium sized potatoes diced (8)
1 tsp salt (5 ml)

½ tsp pepper (2 ml)
4 cups milk (1 L)
1 cup cream (250 ml)
4 tbsp butter (60 ml)

- Rinse clams in clam liquid (clam liquid comes from clams when shucked) and chop coarsely. Remove black cap or beard. Strain, reserving ¾ cup (175 ml) of liquid. Set aside.
- In a medium pot, fry salt pork until brown and crisp. Drain on paper towel, reserving fat.
- Sauté onion and diced potatoes in fat. Sprinkle with salt and pepper and sauté for 5 minutes.
- Add chopped clams and ½ cup (125 ml) cup of reserved clam liquid to sautéed vegetables. Cover and simmer for 20 minutes until potatoes are tender. Add fried pork.
- In a medium saucepan, heat milk, cream and butter. Add to clam and potato mixture, combining well. Taste and adjust seasoning. Serves 8-10

> NOTE
> Clams were plentiful along the shore. "Digging for clams" was child's play.

Fried Smelts

24 smelts cleaned (24)
2 eggs lightly beaten (2)
¾ cup yellow cornmeal (175 ml)

½ tsp salt (2 ml)
½ tsp black pepper (2 ml)
Oil for frying

- Combine cornmeal, salt and pepper. Whisk eggs in a medium bowl.
- Dip smelts lightly in beaten egg. Dredge in cornmeal mixture to coat completely.
- Heat oil in large skillet. Arrange smelts in skillet. Fry until golden brown, turning once.
- Remove from skillet. Drain on paper towels. Serve 4-6.

> NOTE
> "Ice Fishing" was and still is a delightful way to enjoy fresh fish in winter.

Peter Rankin 2007

Rabbit Stew

½ lb salt pork cubed (225 g)

2 medium rabbit cut in pieces (2)

4 tbsp dry mustard (60 ml)

½ cup all-purpose flour (125 ml)

2 large onion sliced (2)

6 large carrots sliced (6)

6 medium potatoes quartered (6)

1 small turnip sliced (1)

2 tsp salt (10 ml)

2 tsp black pepper (10 ml)

2 bay leaves (2)

4 cups water (1 L)

- Soak rabbit in cold water with 2 tbsp (30 ml) vinegar for several hours. Sponge dry. Rub with dry mustard and cut in pieces.
- Dredge rabbit pieces in flour and set aside.
- In a large skillet over high heat, melt salt pork until brown and crisp. Remove crisp pieces to cooking pot, leaving fat in the skillet.
- Put pieces of dredged rabbit in hot fat, turning to brown on both sides.
- Remove browned rabbit to cooking pot and toss with crisp pork. Add sliced onion, salt, pepper, bay leaves and water, just enough to barely cover meat. Place lid on pot. Bring to a boil. Reduce heat and simmer for approximately 1½ hours or until meat is partially cooked.
- Add vegetables and continue cooking until meat and vegetables are tender, adding more water if necessary. Serves 6-8.
- Thicken stewing broth by combining 2 tbsp (30 ml) of flour with ½ cup (125 ml) water. Add to cooking pot and simmer several minutes until broth is thickened.

> **NOTE**
> To provide additional meat, snaring rabbits was a winter sport. This succulent meat could be prepared in many ways.

Fiddleheads with Butter

1 lb fiddleheads (450 g)

2 tbsp melted butter (30 ml)

1 tbsp lemon juice (15 ml)

½ tsp salt (2 ml)

¼ tsp black pepper (1 ml)

- Wash the fiddleheads carefully in cold water so as not to break them.
- Bring water to a boil. Add salt and washed fiddleheads. Boil 4-6 minutes or until tender. Drain well.
- Return fiddleheads to saucepan. Pour melted butter over fiddleheads and sprinkle with pepper. Toss lightly.
- Place in a serving dish and serve immediately. Serves 4.

> **NOTE**
> Fiddleheads, the unopened fronds of fiddlehead ferns, are a welcoming addition to spring. Foraging for fiddleheads was a way to add greens to the diet.

New England Boiled Dinner

5-6 lbs corned beef (2.25-2.7 kg)
8 large carrots peeled and thickly sliced (8)
1 large turnip peeled and cut in wedges (1)
1 medium cabbage cut in large wedges (1)
8 medium potatoes peeled and cut in half (8)
4 large onions quartered (4)

- Drain and rinse corned beef with cold water. Place meat in a large pot and cover with cold water. Bring to a boil.
- Reduce heat and simmer meat for 3-4 hours. (Skim off any accumulated fat.) Meat should be almost tender.
- Add carrots, onion and turnip. Cover and cook for 30 minutes. Add potatoes and cabbage, and continue cooking until vegetables are tender.
- Remove meat from pot and place on a large platter, served with vegetables. Serve with melted butter to pour over vegetables. Serves 8.

Codfish Cakes

2 cups cooked and shredded salt cod (500 ml)

4 cups mashed potatoes (1 L)	1 tsp summer savory (5 ml)
2 tbsp melted butter (30 ml)	Salt as needed
1 medium onion chopped fine (1)	2 eggs lightly beaten (2)
½ cup dried breadcrumbs (125 ml)	(Flour for coating)
1 tsp black pepper (5 ml)	(Oil for frying)

- In a bowl combine cod and mashed potato. Set aside.
- In a small skillet, melt butter and sauté onion until soft. Cool.
- Combine sautéed onion with cod and potato. Add bread crumbs, pepper, summer savory and salt in needed. Fold in beaten eggs and mix until well incorporated.
- Form mixture into 3-inch (7.5-cm) patties. Dredge in flour. Panfry in oil for 2 minutes, turning once, until golden and crisp. Makes 12 cod cakes.

Baked Beans

> **NOTE**
> Chili sauce was made and used to enhance many foods.

2 lbs yellow-eyed beans (900 g)
¼ lb salt pork diced (115 g)
1 small onion chopped (1)
2 tsp salt (10 ml)
1 tbsp dried mustard (15 ml)

1 tsp black pepper (5 ml)
½ cup brown sugar packed (125 ml)
½ cup molasses (125 ml)
4 tbsp chili sauce (60 ml)

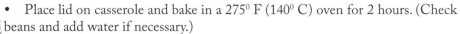

- Rinse and sort beans. Place in a large pot. Cover with cold water and allow to soak overnight.
- Drain soaked beans. Return to pot. Cover with cold water and bring to a boil; cook for 5-8 minutes until skins split.
- Drain beans and reserve liquid. Place beans in a bean crock or large casserole. Add salt pork, onion, salt, dried mustard and pepper, and enough reserved liquid to completely cover the beans.
- Place lid on casserole and bake in a 275⁰ F (140⁰ C) oven for 2 hours. (Check beans and add water if necessary.)
- Combine molasses, brown sugar and chili sauce. Carefully fold mixture into beans. Cover and bake for an additional 45 minutes at 350⁰ F (180⁰ C) temperature until beans are tender. Serves 10-12.

Corn Bread

1 cup cornmeal (250 ml)
1 cup all-purpose flour (250 ml)
4 tsp baking powder (20 ml)
½ tsp salt (2 ml)

½ cup granulated sugar (125 ml)
2 eggs lightly beaten (2)
4 tbsp melted butter (60 ml)
1 cup milk (250 ml)

- In a medium bowl, combine cornmeal, flour, baking powder, salt and sugar.
- In a separate bowl, whisk together eggs, butter and milk.
- Add to dry ingredients and mix to combine.
- Pour into a greased 8 x 8 (20 x 20 cm) pan. Bake in a 350⁰ F (180⁰ C) oven for 30 minutes or until golden brown. Cut in squares and serve.

Lamb Stew with Dumplings

3 lbs lamb stewing meat, cubed (1.3 kg)
2 large onion sliced (2)
4 tbsp melted fat or oil (60 ml)
1½ quarts stock or water (1.5L)
1 tbsp dried mustard (15 ml)
2 tbsp flour (30 ml) ⎫ (Combine for
4 tbsp cold water (60 ml) ⎬ thickening)

2 bay leaves (2)
6-8 potatoes quartered (6-8)
6 medium carrots thickly sliced (6)
1 small turnip sliced (1)
2 tsp salt (10 ml)
2 tsp black pepper (10 ml)

Dumplings
1 cup flour (250 ml)
1 tbsp butter (15 ml)
2 tsp baking powder (10 ml)

½ tsp salt (2 ml)
½ tsp pepper (2 ml)
½ cup milk (125 ml)

• In a large pot, heat fat or oil. Sauté onion until soft. Remove and set aside. Add cubed meat to hot oil and brown, turning several times. Return onion to mixture. Add stock or water, dried mustard and bay leaves. Bring to a boil. Reduce heat. Cover pot and simmer until meat is almost tender.

• Add potatoes, carrots and turnip to meat. Season with salt and pepper, and continue cooking until vegetables and meat are tender.

• Combine flour and water, and add to meat mixture, stirring constantly until thickened.

• Dumplings: In a small bowl, measure flour, baking powder, salt and pepper. Cut butter into flour mixture. Moisten with milk. (Mixture will be thick.)

• Drop dumplings from spoon on meat. Cover and cook until dumplings are light and fluffy, approximately 10-12 minutes. Serves 6-8.

Steamed Cranberry Pudding

½ cup butter, room temperature (125 ml)
1 cup granulated sugar (250 ml)
2 eggs (2)
2¼ cups all-purpose flour (560 ml)

2½ tsp baking powder (12 ml)
½ tsp salt (2 ml)
½ cup milk (125 ml)
2 cups cranberries (500 ml)

- In a large mixing bowl, cream butter and sugar. Add eggs one at a time, beating well after each addition.
- Measure flour, baking powder and salt, and add to creamed mixture alternately with milk.
- Stir in cranberries.
- Grease a mould or pudding dish and pour in mixture. Cover with plastic wrap and secure with foil wrap.
- Place in a large saucepan or steamer on a rack. Half fill saucepan with hot water. Bring to a boil. Cover saucepan and steam for 2 hours. (Check to maintain water level.)
- Remove mould from water and allow to sit for 10 minutes. Turn upside down and unmould pudding. Serve warm with sauce. Serves 6-8

Brown Sugar Sauce

½ cup butter (125 ml)
2 cups brown sugar (500 ml)
4 tbsp flour (60 ml)

2 cups boiling water (500 ml)
1 cup cream (250 ml)
1 tsp vanilla (5 ml)

NOTE
Brandy enhances the flavour of this sauce. Add 2 tbsp (30 ml) of brandy and omit vanilla.

- In a medium saucepan, melt butter. Combine brown sugar and flour, and add to melted butter, stirring over a medium heat until sugar is caramelized.
- Remove from heat and slowly add the boiling water, stirring continuously. Return to heat and bring to a boil. Stir until thickened, approximately 4-5 minutes.
- Add cream and combine well. Add vanilla. Makes 3 cups (750 ml).
- Serve sauce with steamed pudding.

Pound Cake

2 cups butter, room temperature (500 ml)

2 cups granulated sugar (500 ml)   2 tsp almond flavouring (10 ml)

1 tbsp lemon zest (15 ml)   1 tsp baking powder (5 ml)

1 tbsp lemon juice (15 ml)   ½ tsp salt (2 ml)

8 eggs (8)   3 cups all-purpose flour (750 ml)

- Grease and flour a 10-inch (25-cm) tube pan or springform pan. Set aside.
- In a bowl, cream butter until soft. Add sugar and continue creaming until light and fluffy, 4-5 minutes. Add lemon zest and juice.
- Add eggs one at a time, beating after each addition. Add almond flavouring.
- Combine baking powder, salt and flour. Add to creamed mixture in three (3) additions, beating well after each addition. (Batter will be thick.)
- Spoon into prepared pan, spreading batter evenly. Bake in a 300⁰ F (150⁰ C) oven for 1½ hours or until tester comes out clean.
- Remove from oven. Cool in pan for 20 minutes. Turn out on cooling rack.
- When cold, wrap securely and allow to mellow for a day before serving.

NOTE
Pound Cake was special occasion cake, first made by the Loyalists. It consisted of a pound of each ingredient.

Steamed Brown Bread

1 cup cornmeal (250 ml)   ¼ cup brown sugar (60 ml)

1 cup all-purpose flour (250 ml)   1½ cups raisins (375 ml)

1 cup whole wheat flour (250 ml)   ¾ cup molasses (175 ml)

2½ tsp baking soda (12 ml)   2 cups buttermilk (500 ml)

1 tsp salt (5 ml)

- Grease and flour steaming moulds or tins. (See Note.) Set aside.
- In a large bowl, measure cornmeal, white and whole wheat flour, baking soda, salt, brown sugar and raisins. Combine well.
- In a separate bowl, mix molasses and milk, and add to dry ingredients. Beat to combine and turn into prepared moulds, filling each mould about 2/3 full.
- Cover with plastic wrap and foil. Secure with string.
- Place moulds in a hot water bath and steam for 2½ -3 hours.
- Remove from steam bath. Discard covering and place in a 250⁰ F (120⁰ C) oven for 20 minutes to dry top.

NOTE
Steaming moulds or empty 19-oz (525-ml) tins can be used. Grease and coat inside with flour.

Banbury Tarts

<u>Pastry</u>
2½ cups all-purpose flour (625 ml)
1 cup lard or shortening (250 ml)
1 tsp salt (5 ml)
5-6 tbsp cold water (75-90 ml)

<u>Filling</u>
1 cup raisins chopped (250 ml)
¼ cup mixed peel (60 ml)
¼ cup nuts (60 ml)
1 apple peeled grated (1)
½ cup brown sugar (125 ml)
1 tsp cinnamon (5 ml)
½ tsp cloves (5 ml)
¼ tsp nutmeg (1 ml)
3 tbsp melted butter (45 ml)

> NOTE
> Banbury Tarts are an adaptation of the Banbury cake introduced by the Loyalists. The original was an oval cake made of pastry and filled with dried mixed fruit.

- Pastry: Place flour and salt in medium sized bowl. Using a pastry blender or fingertips, work lard or shortening into flour until crumbly. Sprinkle with water as needed.
- Gather dough into a ball and flatten into a disk. Wrap and chill.
- In a medium bowl, combine raisins, peel, nuts, apple, sugar, spices and butter. Stir to combine and set aside.
- Roll pastry into a 12 x 15 (30 x 38 cm) rectangle. Cut into 4-inch (10-cm) squares.
- Place 1 tbsp (15 ml) of filling on square. Fold over like a triangle. Press edges together and prick with a fork.
- Place on lightly greased baking sheet. Brush with milk. Bake in a pre-heated oven at 400⁰ F (200⁰ C) for 12-15 minutes until golden. Makes approximately 12 tarts.

Peter Rankin 2007

Blackberry Jam

6 cups blackberries (1.5L)
3 apples peeled, cored and chopped (3)
¾ cup water (175 ml)
4 cups granulated sugar (1 L)
Juice of one lemon

- Select firm fruit. Pick over berries. Combine with chopped apples. Add water and cook covered until fruit are soft.
- Remove cover from saucepan. Add sugar, stirring until sugar is dissolved. Add lemon juice. Simmer fruit until thickened, 25-30 minutes. (To test, place a spoonful of fruit mixture on a saucer and chill. If mixture is ready, chilled fruit will have jelled.)
- Ladle fruit into sterilized jars and cover with secure lids. Place jars in a pot of boiling water and boil for 5 minutes. Remove from water. Cool jars and store in a cool place.

Rhubarb Relish

4 cups diced rhubarb (1 L)   2 cups cider vinegar (500 ml)
1 tbsp dried mustard (15 ml)   2½ cups brown sugar (625 ml)
4 large onions thinly sliced (4)   1 tsp salt (5 ml)

2 tsp whole allspice (10 ml)   ⎰ Tied in
1 tsp whole cloves (5 ml)   ⎱ cheesecloth

- In a medium saucepan, combine rhubarb, mustard, onion and vinegar. Bring to a boil. Reduce heat and cook for 20-25 minutes until onion and rhubarb are soft.
- Add sugar, salt and spice bag. Simmer for an additional 30 minutes, stirring occasionally until thickened.
- Ladle in sterilized jars. Seal and store in cool place. Makes approximately 6-8 cups of relish.
- Serve to accompany cold meats such as pork, beef, chicken.

A Parade Without a Piper

Peter Rankin 2007

Welcome to the Orangedale Station, 1886.

A number of Intercolonial Railway stations were constructed in the 1880s and 1890s, during the time that the railway line was being completed from the Strait of Canso to Sydney, Cape Breton. The second floor of these new structures was designed and built as living quarters for the Station Agent and family. Thus, the agent was available at all hours and the children had the amusement of watching the trains and passengers coming and going. One such station was at Orangedale, Inverness County, which came to be a major transportation centre for people in central and western Inverness County and in many parts of Victoria County. To this station came visitors and summer residents such as members of the Alexander Graham Bell Family of Baddeck, Cape Breton, and Washington, DC.

At the time the station was ready for occupancy in 1886, James Edward MacFarlane, the first Station Agent, or Master, and his wife Margaret (Cameron) MacFarlane arrived with their family of four young children to live upstairs.

The other buildings on the property of the railway station included a freight shed and outdoor toilets and a small barn for the cow and other livestock of the station agent's family. The station came to be the centre of the community as people came and went. In addition, telegrams could be sent through the services of the Intercolonial Railway. Both MacFarlane and his wife were capable telegraphers and could send and receive in both English and Gaelic.

The MacFarlanes lived at the station for three generations. The first station master, James MacFarlane, is that of the song by Jimmy Rankin, "The Orangedale Whistle." Rankin is a great-great-grandnephew of this station master. Through the efforts of a volunteer group, the Orangedale Station is preserved and maintained as a railway museum open to the public.

The journey to the station from their former home in Mabou was remembered for many years by the children, who regaled friends and relatives with an account of the moving day adventure. Their recollections are the source for this story. Five other children were born in the station after the family came there to live, but they were not yet in the world when "the Parade" took place.

A Parade Without a Piper

"Why do I have to leave Grampa's farm to go to live in a railway station." "Can I take my kitten?" "Can we ride on the train every day?" "How long will we stay at the Station?" "Can we sleep in our own beds tonight?" "Will we go to school there or come back to Mabou?"

With questions such as these on their minds, the four children of James (more generally known as Jim) and Maggie MacFarlane revealed that they were not very enthusiastic about leaving Mabou to go to live in the newly-constructed railway station in Orangedale. MacFarlane had recently been appointed to be the first Station Agent at the important stop on the Intercolonial Line, as it was built across country and along the shores of the Bras d'Or Lake from the Strait of Canso to Sydney. It was considered a very good job for MacFarlane who had previously run a store and livery stable for several years. As both Jim MacFarlane and his wife Maggie were competent telegraphers, they would be busy sending and receiving messages for business interests and for local people who had relatives living a distance away.

The children – Hugh, age 9, Peter Edward, age 7, Catherine Jane "Kate" age 5, and Bessie, age 4 – were active young people who had been spending a lot of time at the farm of one of their grandfathers and at the hotel and store operated by their other grandfather. As the oldest grandchildren of each set of grandparents, they were great favourites and would be much missed by their relatives in Mabou, both adults and children. Although Hugh was much interested in going to live at the station, for he had been there several times with his father while it was under construction, his younger siblings were unhappy about the move.

Notwithstanding of the objections of the children, the MacFarlanes were going to take up new residence in the upstairs of the newly completed station. The time for the journey was set for a day in August, 1886. Life was going to change for the whole family, but not without a bit of adventure along the way. Goodbyes would have to be exchanged, but the trunks and boxes had been packed and all was ready for departure.

In order to placate his oldest grandson, Hugh, Grampa MacFarlane gave the young lad a splendid young calf which the boy had been tending while he was staying at the farm. The heifer had the name "Star" for a mark on its forehead. Young Peter Edward received from his grandfather Cameron a fine young puppy, just four months old and full of life. "Buster" was to be its name. A quiet and thoughtful child, Kate was very fond of young lambs and had helped to feed one of the young woolly creatures whose mother had died. So she had insisted that she take her lamb with her. Its name was declared to be "Muffin" since it once ate one of the confections, so called – a blueberry one at that. Little Bessie had decided she was going to take a kitten to her new home – and selected one with red and white markings from the litter in Grandpa's barn. She was calling it "Fluffy" for its thick fur.

So, in addition to furniture and clothing, the MacFarlanes now had four animals of various sizes and needs which were going to accompany them. But everyone agreed that the difficulties of taking the animals with them would all work out somehow. Fortunately, the day had dawned with a clear sky and there was light, warm breeze from the southwest, so it looked as though no rain would come during the day.

With their household goods, beds, chairs, tables and trunks full of clothes loaded into a truck wagon to be driven by Jim MacFarlane and with a double-seated buggy to be driven by Maggie's brother, Ewan, and with Jim's brother, Dan, going along on horseback, the family was prepared to leave Mabou early in the morning. They had a large hamper full of food, jars of tea and milk, and packets of homemade cookies. Grandfather Cameron had provided a sack full of apples from the counter in his store for their lunch along the way. Grandmother Cameron gave each child a festive sunhat and a small coin in a little purse. In the back of the buggy, hay was stowed for the calf and the lamb. With loud goodbyes, a few tears and some loud instructions to the horses, the procession set forth. "Giddy up, we're off to Orangedale," said Jim MacFarlane.

Up the main road in Mabou, they went: two wagons and a rider on horseback leading a calf; a lamb bedded down in a box in the back of the buggy; a puppy in one child's lap and a kitten in another's.

"It's like a parade," said young Hugh, "just like Queen Victoria has."

"I saw the picture in the paper at Grandpa's store," added Peter Edward, not to be outdone by his older brother.

"But where is the piper?" asked little Kate. "The Queen always has a piper."

Uncle Dan replied, "Ewan and I will be the pipers," and promptly he started to make a groan like a bagpipe warming up. He was soon joined by Ewan who added a sound like a "skirrrrrrrl."

"Hurrah," shouted Hugh and he was joined by his brother and sisters who began to imitate their uncles with "toot, toot, toot" and "skirrrl, skirrrl, skirrrl."

All the noise from the uncles and the children and the general clatter brought the village dogs out to the road. They all began to bark at once as the parade went past their lanes. All of this noise was too much for the calf which stopped short and refused to budge and then began to bawl for its mother. The little lamb, Muffin, was not to be outdone and from its cage came "baaaa... baaa." With a little urging from Uncle Dan and the offer of some fresh hay, the calf began to follow along, although still calling for its mother.

Then, the horse pulling the buggy and the team drawing the truck wagon, thinking that they were being urged to go faster, picked up speed just as the entourage was starting to go down a steep hill. Chairs began to bounce up and down and a table nearly came off the back of the wagon. The drivers were calling "whoa, whoa" to the rapidly moving animals. Clapping their hands with glee at the speed, the two little girls were very surprised when their sun hats flew off their heads and landed at the side of the road. But gradually, the horses slowed their steps and all was well.

The parade stopped at the foot of the hill so that Uncle Dan could get off his horse and walk back for the hats. Meanwhile, the calf he was leading somehow or other got loose from the rope that was attached to the saddle of the horse and it headed for the nearest water, a river with a deep channel. Into the stream went Star, the calf, only to discover that it was too deep for it to get good footing. It began to struggle to keep its head above water. Down from his wagon jumped Uncle Ewan, while Maggie, the children's mother, held the reins. He jumped into the stream with all his clothes on. A good swimmer and an able young man, he brought the calf back to the bank of the river. Jim MacFarlane put the rope around its neck and brought it back to the roadway. The children then clapped and applauded and Uncle Ewan, although quite thoroughly wet, proceeded to bow to all present. Peter Edward pronounced that their uncle deserved a life-saving medal. And all cheered while their uncle shook the water out of his boots.

"He looks like a wet frog, not a piper," said Hugh. His uncle grinned in reply.

Although they gone only five of the thirty-kilometre journey, it seemed a good time to stop for a lunch as the children were asking for cookies and Uncle Ewan needed to dry out a bit. Maggie drew out a long towel from one of the trunks and threw it to her brother who began to do a dance with it as though he was doing the sword dance. So, once again, Uncle Dan imitated the sound of the bagpipes, "toot... toot," drawing laughter once again.

"I never saw a wet frog dancing before," was Hugh's observation. And more laughter ensued. At this time, a serious elderly man driving in his buggy on his way to Mabou came along the road. Stopping his horse and looking astonished at what was going on, he looked over the rims of his glasses, accusing them all "of drinking in the morning and in the presence of children at that." That made the adults and the children laugh all the more as the man drove off in a huff, shaking his head in disbelief.

Thick slices of homemade bread with slices of cold pork and cheese in between and tea with milk from the jars were brought forth and passed around. The ripe and juicy apples were welcome. And then, there were cookies for all, since the children's need of goodies had not been forgotten. When all seemed to be satisfied, Maggie firmly placed the hats on the heads of the girls and they prepared to resume.

But Star and Muffin, apparently having seen the humans being nourished, decided they wanted hay and began to make strong objections identifying their wants. So the parade paused for a few more minutes while Star chomped a handful of fresh hay and Muffin gulped down her portion. Then puppy needed to take a walk ... on the end of a long tightly-held leash. Suddenly, Peter Edward thought he had been stung by a bee and ran crying back to his mother leaving Buster behind with nobody holding onto the rope. Hugh had to run ahead and try to catch the puppy now delighting in being free to run. Thinking it was all a game, he growled as Hugh caught him and led him back to the wagon.

"Time for the parade to begin again," said Jim MacFarlane. "We'll never get there by dark at this rate."

So off they went along the road, past farms with dogs barking, along the edges of fields with horses neighing and meeting young boys on their way to fishing spots, who delighted at the unusual sight. The procession left quite a cloud of dust behind as the horses moved along at a good clip, much of it settling on the travellers and their possessions.

Not far from the place known as Brook Village, where two brooks met and several stores had been built, the uncles began again with their bagpipes "toot... skirrrl... toot... skirrrl." Little Bessie, napping with her head on her mother's lap suddenly awakened to the noise and began to cry. And then she let out a wail. "Where is Fluffy?" Her kitten was not to be seen – it had climbed out of its small box which Bessie had in her lap. The little girl was disconsolate.

The two buggies came to a quick stop in front of Jamieson's store as Bessie insisted her father find her kitten – which he did; Fluffy was quite quietly curled up on a cap which was under the buggy seat. Jamieson, the storekeeper came out to see what the noise was all about. Seeing all the children, the animals, the chairs and the beds all covered with road dust, he offered Jim and Maggie an opportunity to wash off the dust. To each of the children, he gave a small brown sack filled with peppermints from the counter in his store.

After washing their hands and faces, and thanking the merchant for the candy, James MacFarlane got everyone organized and announced that the parade should begin again. But just before he called to his team of horses to start up, Maggie went back to the truck wagon and found some wooden spoons and a couple of metal pots. "For keeping time to the pipers," she said with a look of mirth in her eyes, giving a spoon and pot to each child.

So the procession wound along the road, past tall elm trees shading the highway, and fields where people piling hay into stacks paused to wave at the passersby. The children kept time – well almost – with the wooden spoons hitting the pots, as the uncles imitated bagpipes. In his jacket pocket, Hugh found a tin whistle and with great glee began to accompany the pipers and the drummers. "Tweet... tweet" went the whistle. "Bang... bang" sounded the spoons, "Skirrrl... skirrrl... toot... toot..." went the uncles. Now and again, the dog let out a "woof... woof." Even the horses seemed to step more lively to the sounds. The little calf just plodded obediently along behind the horse.

Soon, noontime was near and a place was needed where they could water the horses and give them an opportunity to rest. In addition, everybody was starting to feel hungry. As good luck would have it, they were almost at James MacFarlane's grandmother's house, the great-grandmother of the children and a favourite of all, young and old. Although nearly ninety, she was still an agile dancer who loved to tell stories about the old days when she came to the area as a young woman. She had grown up as a minister's daughter in a town and had never lived on a farm. She had had a lot to learn and often told, with great mirth, of her difficulties in learning to milk a cow. Her husband, now long gone, had a large stock of animals and he bought and sold horses, so his wife soon learned how to take care of the livestock and to cook for their growing family. She loved children and singing and delighted in visitors. She now lived with two of her sons who worked during the day in the woods.

Her house was near the road and so Jim and Ewan guided the horses into the farmyard. Close by was a rapidly flowing brook which provided ample water for the horses, the lamb and the calf. As soon as she saw who was in her yard, great-grandmother Jane came out to greet them and in the spirit of the day, did a little jig step right in front of them as Hugh continued to play his tin whistle and the children pounded on the pans and the uncles imitated the pipers. She took both little girls by the hands and danced a bit with them and all laughed and clapped. As luck would have it, they had the treat of hot fresh biscuits from great-grandmother's oven and cool buttermilk from her milk house and all sat under trees, dining on the ample food from the hampers. Then hot tea for all was served – even for little Bessie who tried to give some to her kitten, Fluffy, who sputtered and sputtered and looked quite wide-eyed at all that was around her.

Nobody really wanted to leave, for great-grandmother was starting to tell stories, but parade leader Jim soon insisted they get ready to set forth again. After trips to the outdoor toilet and the wash basin in the kitchen of the old farmhouse, all took their places in the procession. Then, great-grandmother asked them to wait a minute. Off she went to the barn and quickly came back with four laying hens in a small wooden crate.

"You'll need these when you go looking for eggs for breakfast," she said, "and perhaps they can cackle to the pipers as you go along the road."

Maggie and Jim wanted to say, "No thank you; not just now." But Kate, whose middle name was Jane for her great-grandmother, insisted: "I'll take care of them and see that they are fed." So the crate with the surprised-looking hens was put on the top of the load in the truck wagon. Off they all went shouting goodbye to great-grandmother in Gaelic and resuming their musical accompaniment. Watching them go, the old lady clapped her hands in rhythm – a look of great happiness in her eyes.

As the afternoon sun began to cross the sky, the parade turned into the Orangedale Road and all knew the end of the trip was near. But there in front of them on the road was a large flock of sheep. The fleecy animals had found a break in the fence and looked as though they were going to Orangedale, too. But when they heard the noise behind them, they began to scatter, left and right, adding their confused bleating to the sounds of the uncles and the children. Slowly, the parade moved past the woolly animals and turned a corner, the horses' hooves clattering on the planks of a newly built bridge and then they came into the settlement of Orangedale, its fine new station all freshly painted reddish-purple, a mark of the Intercolonial Railway.

Past the new shop built for a tailor and a new schoolhouse went the wagons and the children and the adults and the animals – the calf mooing, the lamb baaing, the puppy barking, the hens cackling – and maybe the kitten purring quietly in Bess's lap. The uncles once again began their "toot... skirrrl... toot... skirrrl." Hugh put his tin whistle to his mouth and started to blow into it so that "tweet... tweet... tweet..." was added to the sounds once again. And Peter Edward and Kate and even little Bessie banged on pots with the wooden spoons.

James and Maggie waved and laughed as the people living near the station lined the road to see the procession, clapping their hands. A cheerful greeting was exchanged among all. Who would have expected the Station Agent and his family to arrive with a parade, but everybody enjoyed their coming.

A journey was over. They were at their new home. The children would sleep in their own beds that night and would have many more adventures at the station. For many years they all talked about the trip to Orangedale and how they really did have a parade – with pipers, of a sort. Maybe even Queen Victoria would have approved.

The MacFarlane Parade

❦ MENU ❦

All Season Vegetable Soup

Creamy Fish Chowder

Beef Stew with Dumplings

Baked Stuffed Cod

Roast Chicken with Grandma's Bread Stuffing and Gravy

Buttered Kale

Scalloped Potatoes

Cottage Pudding with Butterscotch Sauce

Date Sandwich Bars

Raisin Drop Cookies

Potato Scones

Buttermilk Tea Biscuits

All-Season Vegetable Soup

4 tbsp butter (60 ml)
1 large onion chopped (1)
3 medium carrots peeled and diced (3)
½ medium turnip peeled and diced (½)
3 medium potatoes peeled and diced (3)
¼ cup pearl barley rinsed in cold water (60 ml)

3 quarts rich stock (2 L)
1 tsp salt (5 ml)
1 tsp black pepper (5 ml)
1 bay leaf (1)
1 tsp dried thyme (5 ml)

• Prepare vegetables and melt butter in a large pot. Sauté vegetables in butter for 5 minutes. Add drained barley and stock. Bring to a boil. Add salt, pepper and bay leaf.

• Reduce the heat and simmer for 40 minutes until vegetables and barley are tender. Add thyme and simmer for an additional 10 minutes. Serves 6.

Creamy Fish Chowder

3 tbsp butter (45 ml)
1 large onion chopped (1)
2 ribs celery chopped (2)
6 large potatoes peeled and diced (6)
3 cups water (750 ml)

1½ lbs cod fillets cut in pieces (675 g)
1 cup milk (250 ml)
1 cup cream (250 ml)
Salt and pepper

• In a large heavy saucepan, melt butter. Cook onion and celery until soft. Add potatoes and toss to coat potatoes. Add water, bring to a boil, reduce heat. Cover and simmer for 12-15 minutes until potatoes are tender.

• Place cut-up fish in saucepan with vegetables and simmer for 5-8 minutes until fish flakes.

• Combine milk and cream. Slowly add to fish mixture, stirring gently. Heat until piping hot (do not boil.)

• Season with salt and pepper.

• Serve in warm bowls. Serves 6.

Beef Stew with Dumplings

2½ lbs stew meat (1.25 kg) cut in one-inch (2.5-cm) cubes
3 tbsp oil or melted fat (45 ml)
¼ cup all-purpose flour (60 ml)
1 tsp salt (5 ml)
½ tsp pepper (2 ml)
1 large onion sliced (1)
4 cups stock or water (1 L)
2 large carrots peeled and sliced (2)
2 cups diced turnip (500 ml)
6 potatoes cut in half or quartered (6)

<u>Dumplings</u>
1½ cups all-purpose flour (375 ml)
4 tsp baking powder (20 ml)
1 tsp salt (5 ml)
2 tbsp butter (30 ml)
¼ tsp pepper (1 ml)
1 cup milk (250 ml)

- Mix flour, salt and pepper in a bowl. Dredge cubed meat in flour to coat, shaking off excess flour.
- In a large skillet heat oil or melted fat from meat.
- Place the cubed meat in skillet a few at a time, browning cubes on all sides. Transfer meat to large saucepan.
- Sauté the onion and add to meat. Add stock or water to barely cover the meat. Bring to a boil. Cover the saucepan and transfer saucepan to a 350⁰ F (180⁰ C) oven.
- Cook stew in oven for 1½ hours, Add the carrots and turnip. Cook for an additional 40-50 minutes, and add potatoes. When meat and vegetables are tender, add dumplings.
- To prepare dumplings: In a bowl, measure flour, baking powder, salt and pepper. Cut in fat. Add milk and stir to combine.
- Remove stew from the oven. Increase temperature to 400⁰ F (200⁰ C). Drop spoonfuls of dumpling batter on top of stew. Cover tightly. Return to oven and cook for 12-15 minutes. (Do not uncover until they have steamed 12 minutes.)
- Spoon into bowls, ladling sauce from meat over dumplings.

NOTE
Beef Stew was a favourite meal, as it could be cooked in one pot. Reheated, it was also a treat.

Baked Stuffed Cod

4 lbs whole fresh cod (2 kg)

3 cups bread cut in cubes (750 ml)

1 large onion chopped (1)

2 ribs celery diced (2)

1 tsp dried summer savory (5 ml)

½ tsp salt (2 ml)

1 tsp black pepper (5 ml)

¼ cup melted butter (60 ml)

1 tbsp milk (15 ml)

- Clean fish. Wash and sponge dry.
- In a bowl, combine cubed bread, onion, celery, herbs, salt and pepper. Add melted butter and milk. Mix well.
- Stuff fish cavity with dressing. Fasten the opening securely with wooden picks.
- Place fish in a buttered baking pan. Brush with additional melted butter. Bake in a 425⁰ F (220⁰ C) oven for 25-30 minutes, or until fish flakes with a fork. Remove from oven. Serves 6-8.

> NOTE
> If the thought of facing a whole cod seems challenging, purchase 4 medium cod fillets, place two fillets in buttered pan. Spoon dressing on fillets and top with remaining fillets. Follow steps in recipe.

Buttered Kale

1 large head of kale (1)

2 tbsp butter (30 ml)

1 tsp salt (5 ml)

1 tsp pepper (5 ml)

4 tbsp heavy cream (60 ml)

- Wash kale. Discard roots and remove centre rib from leaves. Place leaves in a saucepan of simmering salted water. Simmer covered for 25-30 minutes until tender.
- Drain and coarsely chop. Add butter and cream. Season to taste. Serves 4-6.

Peter Rankin 2007

Roast Chicken
with Grandma's Bread Stuffing and Gravy

4-5 lb roasting chicken (2-2.25 kg)
rinsed and sponged dry (reserve neck and gizzard)

Grandma's Bread Stuffing
6 cups bread cut in cubes (1.5 L)
1 large onion finely chopped (1)
½ cup butter (125 ml)
¼ cup warm chicken stock or water (60 ml)

2 tsp salt (10 ml)
1 tsp pepper (5 ml)
1 tsp ground sage (5 ml)

• In a large bowl, combine bread cubes, salt, pepper, sage and onion. Toss in butter and stock and mix. Stuffing should be soft but have a firm texture.
• Fill cavity of chicken with stuffing. Cross the drumsticks and tie together with string.
• Place chicken in large roaster with neck and gizzard. Brush with melted butter and season with salt and pepper.
• Roast in a 400⁰ F (200⁰ C) pre-heated oven for 20 minutes. Reduce heat to 325⁰ F (160⁰ C) and continue roasting, allowing 20 minutes per pound, basting during the last 30 minutes.
• Remove roaster from oven. Transfer chicken to heated platter.

Grandma's Chicken Gravy

3 cups stock made from drippings (750 ml)
1 small onion finely chopped (1)
Salt and pepper

3 tbsp butter (45 ml)
3 tbsp flour (45 ml)

• To juices in roaster, add 3 cups (750 ml) of water or stock. Bring to a boil. Reduce heat and simmer for 20 minutes. Set aside.
• In a medium saucepan, melt butter and add onion. Sauté until onion is soft. Sprinkle in flour and cook for one (1) minute, whisking continuously.
• Slowly add stock from roaster to sautéed mixture. Bring to a boil. Reduce heat and simmer, whisking continuously until thickened. Season and strain.
• Serve gravy to accompany roast chicken.

Scalloped Potatoes

6 large potatoes peeled and sliced thinly (6)

1 large onion sliced thinly (1)

1 tsp salt (5 ml)

2 tbsp butter (30 ml)

1 tsp pepper (5 ml)

3 tbsp all-purpose flour (45 ml)

2½ cups milk heated (625 ml)

• In a buttered casserole dish, arrange a layer of sliced potatoes topped by some sliced onion. Dab with half the butter, sprinkle half the flour, salt and pepper. Repeat layers twice.

• Pour enough hot milk over top of potatoes to just be able to see through the top layer.

• Bake covered in a 350⁰ F (180⁰ C) oven for 50 minutes. Uncover casserole and bake an additional 30 minutes until potatoes are tender.

> **NOTE**
> Scalloped Potatoes was an easy dish, as once assembled it was placed in the oven and did not require constant attention.

Date Sandwich Bars

2 cups all-purpose flour (500 ml)

<u>Filling</u>

2 cups rolled oats (500 ml)

3 cups pitted dates chopped (750 ml)

1½ cups brown sugar (375 ml)

1 cup brown sugar (250 ml)

1 tsp baking soda (5 ml)

1¼ cups boiling water (310 ml)

½ tsp salt (2 ml)

1 tsp vanilla (5 ml)

1 cup butter room temperature (250 ml)

1 tbsp lemon juice (15 ml)

1 tbsp butter (15 ml)

• Place dates in a medium saucepan. Add sugar and water. Cook over a medium heat, stirring often until dates are very soft and almost smooth, 15-18 minutes. Add vanilla, lemon juice and butter, and cool completely.

• In a large bowl, combine flour, rolled oats, sugar, soda and salt. Blend in butter until mixture is crumbly.

• Pat half the crumble in a buttered 9 x 13 (23 x 33 cm) pan. Spread filling evenly over crumble. Sprinkle with remaining crumble, patting gently.

• Bake in a 350⁰ F (180⁰ C) oven for 30-35 minutes until brown. Cool and cut in bars or slices. Makes 48.

> **NOTE**
> Whatever we choose to call them, and across the country they went by different names, date bars were a favourite for their flavour and keeping quality.

Cottage Pudding with Butterscotch Sauce

½ cup butter (125 ml)
1 cup granulated sugar (250 ml)
2 large eggs (2)
2 cups all-purpose flour (500 ml)
2½ tsp baking powder (12 ml)
½ tsp salt (2 ml)
1 tsp vanilla (5 ml)
¾ cup milk (175 ml)

Sauce
½ cup butter (125 ml)
2 cups brown sugar (500 ml)
2 tbsp all-purpose flour (30 ml)
2 tbsp corn syrup (30 ml)
2 cups boiling water (500 ml)
1 tsp vanilla (5 ml)

NOTE
Cottage pudding was a popular dessert. Its origin is unknown but its taste is remembered by all!

- Pudding Batter: In a bowl cream butter and sugar until light. Add the eggs one at a time, beating well after each addition. Beat in vanilla.
- In a separate bowl, combine flour, baking powder and salt.
- Add flour to creamed mixture alternatively with milk, beating well after each addition. Butter and flour a 9 x 13 (23 x 33 cm) pan. Spread batter in pan. Bake in a 350 F (180⁰ C) oven for 35-40 minutes or until tester comes out clean.
- Remove from oven. Cool for 10 minutes and turn out on cooling rack. Serves 8.

- To Make Sauce: Combine brown sugar and flour.
- Melt butter in medium saucepan. Add sugar mixture and stir continuously over low-medium heat until sugar is melted and caramelized. Add corn syrup and stir.
- Remove saucepan from heat and slowly add boiling water, whisking continuously. Return to stove, bring to a boil and simmer while whisking until sauce is transparent. Add vanilla.
- Serve sauce warm or at room temperature with cottage pudding.

Raisin Drop Cookies

2 cups raisins (500 ml)
1 cup hot water (250 ml)
1 cup butter or shortening (250 ml)
1 cup granulated sugar (250 ml)
1 cup brown sugar (250 ml)
3 eggs (3)
1 tsp vanilla (5 ml)

4 cups all-purpose flour (1 L)
1 tsp baking powder (5 ml)
1 tsp baking soda (5 ml)
1 tsp salt (5 ml)
2 tsp cinnamon (10 ml)
½ tsp allspice (2 ml)
¼ tsp nutmeg (1 ml)

- In a medium saucepan combine raisins and water. Bring to a boil and simmer for 7-8 minutes until raisins are plump. Remove from heat and cool.
- Strain raisins and reserve ¼ cup (60 ml) of liquid.
- In a bowl cream butter or shortening with sugar until light and fluffy. Beat in eggs one at a time, beating after each addition. Add vanilla.
- Stir together flour, baking powder, soda, salt and spices. Add to creamed mixture with raisins and liquid. Stir to combine ingredients.
- Drop teaspoonfuls onto greased baking sheets, allowing space for spreading. Bake in a 375⁰ F (190⁰ C) oven for 12-15 minutes or until set and golden brown.
- Transfer to cooling rack. Makes 5 dozen.

NOTE
These cookies became popular in very early 1900 and have travelled in lunch pails and been enjoyed from the cookie jar for generations.

Buttermilk Tea Biscuits

2 cups all-purpose flour (500 ml)
1 cup whole wheat flour (250 ml)
2 tsp baking powder (10 ml)
1 tsp baking soda (5 ml)

1 tsp salt (5 ml)
2 tbsp granulated sugar (30 ml)
¾ cup lard or butter (175 ml)
1¼ cups buttermilk (310 ml)

NOTE
Buttermilk biscuits can also be rolled and cut in circles.

- Measure dry ingredients in a medium bowl. Work fat into flour until crumbly. Stir in the buttermilk until just blended.
- Drop batter by spoonfuls on a greased baking sheet.
- Bake in a 415⁰ F (210⁰ C) oven for 12-15 minutes until golden brown. Makes 16.

Potato Scones

½ cup oatmeal (125 ml)
1½ cups all-purpose flour (375 ml)
¼ cup granulated sugar (60 ml)
4 tsp baking powder (20 ml)
1 tsp salt (5 ml)

¼ cup butter or shortening (60 ml)
½ cup currants or raisins (125 ml)
2 eggs (2)
½ cup cream or milk (125 ml)
1 cup mashed potatoes (250 ml)

- In large bowl, combine oatmeal, flour, sugar, baking powder and salt. Work butter or shortening into flour mixture until crumbly.
- Add currants or raisins. Whisk eggs and cream or milk. Add to dry ingredients with mashed potatoes. Mix with a fork until well moistened.
- Turn out dough on lightly floured surface and knead about 12 times.
- Shape and pat dough into a circle about ½ inch (1 cm) thick. Place on an ungreased baking sheet. Cut into 16 wedges, separating slightly.
- Brush with cream or milk and sprinkle with granulated sugar.
- Bake in a 400^0 F (200^9 C) oven for 12-15 minutes or until lightly brown. Makes 16 scones.

Peter Rankin 2007

About the Authors

YVONNE C. LEVERT is retired from a teaching career at Cape Breton University (hospitality administration). In retirement she operates *La Cuisine des Gourmets*, a licensed catering business, from her home. She consults to the hospitality industry and has a food commentary on CBC Cape Breton *Information Morning* called "Taste Sensations."

Yvonne pursued studies in home economics in Montreal, majoring in foods. She was employed for nine years with the Nova Scotia Department of Agriculture. She hosted her own food program called *Cooking with Yvonne* on CJCB television, Sydney; later she obtained her teacher certification and taught in a secondary public school culinary program. While teaching she decided to fulfill a long-time dream, by attending l'Académie du Cordon Bleu in Paris, France, where she obtained the coveted "Grand Diplôme." In addition to teaching, Yvonne operated *La Cuisine des Gourmets*, a cooking school from her home, and taught French culinary techniques for ten years.

Yvonne has had numerous recipes published in cookbooks. To name a few: *Healthy Pleasures* (The Canadian Diabetic Association with the Canadian Culinary Association); *Out of Nova Scotia Gardens* (Marie Nightingale). With master photographer Warren Gordon, she edited the *Cape Breton Pictorial Cookbook*, which features Cape Breton's cultural and ethnic cuisine.

She holds memberships in the Canadian Federation of Chefs, la Confrérie de la Chaîne des Rôtisseurs, the Canadian Opimian Society, Cuisine Canada (founding member), Sydney and Area Chamber of Commerce, Destination Cape Breton and Old Sydney Society. Yvonne has the best of both worlds: cooking and food research are her profession and hobby.

PETER RANKIN is Cape Breton born and bred and specializes in illustrating the traditional way of life. A fisherman as well as an artist, his illustrations in *Making Room* by Joanne Taylor won the 2004 Lillian Shepherd Memorial Award for Excellence in Illustration. Peter is also illustrator of Alistair MacLeod's *To Every Thing There is a Season*.

JIM ST.CLAIR has, for two decades, been the voice on the CBC Cape Breton's *Information Morning*'s "Up and Down the Island," sharing with listeners his enthusiasm for Cape Breton people and places. A graduate of Harvard College and Harvard Graduate School of Education, he has taught at both the secondary and college levels. A writer of three columns on local history and genealogy, he is co-author with Dr. Mary K. MacLeod of two books on Cape Breton architecture. The writer of a children's book *MacCallum House*, he also did the genealogical research of sixty early families of Inverness County published in *Mabou Pioneer - Book 2*.

A resident of Mull River, Inverness County, he lives on family property which includes a large old-growth forest under permanent ecological protection: The MacFarlane Woods.

A recipient of an honorary doctorate from Cape Breton University, he has been an active community worker in heritage organizations, the Nova Scotia Highland Village and community development agencies.

Sources (Stories by James St.Clair)

Published

Dunn, Charles. *Highland Settler: A Portrait of the Scottish Gael in Nova Scotia.* Toronto: University of Toronto Press, 1953.

MacDougall, John L. *History of Inverness County.* Belleville, ON: Mika Publishing Co., 1976.

MacKinnon, Rev. A. D. *A History of the Presbyterian Church in Cape Breton.* Antigonish, NS: Formac Ltd., 1975.

MacNeil, S. R. *All Call Iona Home.* Antigonish, NS: Formac Publishing Co., 1979.

MacPhail, Margaret. *Loch Bras D'Or.* Windsor, NS: Lancelot Press, 1970.

McPherson, Flora. *Watchman Against the World: The Remarkable Journey of Norman McLeod and His People from Scotland to Cape Breton Island to New Zealand.* Wreck Cove, NS: Breton Books, 1993.

Murray, Rev. John. *History of Presbyterian Church in Cape Breton.* Truro, NS: News Publishing Co., 1921.

Patterson, *History of Victoria County* with related papers compiled and edited by W. James MacDonald. Sydney, NS: University College of Cape Breton Press, 1978.

Robinson, Neil. *Lion of Scotland.* London, U. K.: Hodder and Stoughton,1952.

Stanley-Blackwell, Laurie. *Tokens of Grace, Cape Breton's Open-Air Communion Tradition.* Sydney, NS: Cape Breton University Press, 2006.

Stanley, Laurie. *The Well-Watered Garden, The Presbyterian Church in Canada.* Sydney, NS: University College of Cape Breton Press, 1983.

Stone, Arthur J. *Journey Through a Cape Breton County, Pioneer Roads in Richmond County.* Sydney, NS: University College of Cape Breton Press, n.d.

Turk, Marion. T*he Quiet Adventurers in Canada.* Detroit, MI: Harlo Press, 1979.

Unpublished

Chiasson, Les. *History of the Chiasson Family of Margaree Forks, Cape Breton.*

St.Clair, James O. Stories and accounts relating to the Campbell Family of Isle of Skye and Cape Breton .

St. Clair, James O. Stories and genealogical account of MacFarlane Family of Mull River and Orangedale, Cape Breton.

Archives Consulted

Beaton Institute, Cape Breton University, Sydney, NS.

Gut of Canso Museum and Archives, (Port Hastings Museum), Port Hastings, NS.

Miners Museum, Glace Bay, NS.

Mi'kmaq Resource Centre, Cape Breton University, Sydney, NS.

Nova Scotia Highland Village Library and Archival Holdings, Iona, NS.

Public Archives of Nova Scotia, Halifax, NS.

Census Records of Dominion of Canada as transferred to microfilm.

Newspapers

Cape Bretonia, 1834

Nova Scotian, 1840

Sources (Recipes by Yvonne LeVert)

Anderson, Carol and Katharine Mallinson. *Lunch With Lady Eaton*. ECW Press, 2004.

Charsley, Simon R. *Wedding Cakes & Cultural History*. Routledge, Chapman and Hill, 1992.

Cormier, Marielle and Melvin Gallant. *A Taste of Acadie. Fredericton*, NB: Gooselane Editions, 1978.

Coutrine, Robert J. *Larousse Gastronomique*. 1964.

The Diamond Cookbook. Cream of Wheat Company. Minneapolis, MN: 1910.

Duncan, Dorothy. *The Canadian Table*. Toronto: Dundurn Press, 2006.

Duncan, Dorothy. *Nothing More Comforting*. Canada's Heritage Foods. Oxford: Dundurn Group Toronto, 2003.

Dunton, Hope. *From The Hearth*. Cape Breton University Press, 1986.

Farmer, Fannie Merritt. *The Boston Cooking-School Cook Book*. Little, Brown and Company, 1896, 1913, 1921.

Ferguson, Carol and Margaret Fraser. *A Centenary of Canadian Home Cooking*. Prentice-Hall Canada, 1992.

Fitzgibbon, Theodora. *A Taste of London*. 1978.

Five Roses Cookbook. Lake of Woods Milling Co. Ltd., 1915.

Geddes, Olive M. *The Baird's Kitchen*. The National Library of Scotland, 1994.

Gordon, Warren and Yvonne LeVert. *Cape Breton Pictorial Cookbook*. Sydney, NS: Steel City Publishing, 1993.

Heirloom Recipes. Compiled by Florence M. Hilchey. Halifax, NS: Nova Scotia Department of Agriculture, 1967.

Heritage Recipes, Maritimes and Newfoundland. Halifax: Formac Publishing 1988.

Howard, Maria Willett. *Lowney's Cookbook*. Boston: The Walter M. Lowney Co., 1907.

Lucas, Fiona. *Hearth and Home*. Toronto: James Lormier and Company Ltd., 2006.

MacDonald, Helen & Eleanor Anderson, eds. *Treasured Memories and Recipes from Coal Mining Town Glace Bay.* Glace Bay: Northside Printers, 1982.

McCann, Edna. *The Canadian Heritage Cook Book.* Prentice-Hall Canada, 1996.

The Modern Cook for Nova Scotia and Prince Edward Island.

A Modern Kitchen Guide. Farmers Advocate. Canadian Countryman's Farmers Magazine. London, Canada. n.d.

Nightengale, Marie. *Out of Old Nova Scotia Kitchens.* Pagurian Press, 1971.

Ogle, Jennifer and Gregory Kennedy. *The Canadian Cookbook.* Edmonton: Lone Pine Publishing, 2006.

Pattinson, Nellie Lyle. *Canadian Cook Book.* Toronto: The Ryerson Press, 1923.

The Purity Cookbook. Western Canada Flour Mills Co. Ltd. Toronto: Hendrick-Jewell, 1932.

Recipe Book. Louisbourg Chapter I.O.D.E., 1946, 1942.

Settlement Cook Book. Settlement Cook Book Company. New York: Simon & Schuster, 1915.

Spencer, Evelyn, et al. *Fish Cookery.* Little, Brown and Company, 1922.

Tasty Meals for Every Day. Maple Leaf Products. Canada Packers Ltd., 1933.

Taylor, Demetria M. *Complete Book of Home Canning.* Ziff-Davis Publishing Company, 1943.

Tea with Mrs. Beeton. Text and Illustrations Ward Lock Ltd. London: Villiers House, 1990.

Toussait-Samat, Magulonne. *History of Food.* Translated by Anthea Bell. Maple-Vail Manufacturing Group, 1992.

Tyree, Marion Cabell. *Housekeeping in Old Virginia.* John P. Morton and Company, 1879.

Recipe Index